EATING FOR A LIVING

Notes from a Professional Diner

CYNTHIA WINE

VIKING

Viking
Published by the Penguin Group
Penguin Books Canada Ltd, 10 Alcorn Avenue, Toronto,
Ontario, Canada M4V 3B2
Penguin Books Ltd, 27 Wrights Lane, London W8 5TZ,
England
Viking Penguin, a division of Penguin Books USA Inc., 375
Hudson Street, New York, New York 10014, U.S.A.
Penguin Books Australia Ltd, Ringwood, Victoria, Australia
Penguin Books (NZ) Ltd, 182-190 Wairau Road, Auckland 10,
New Zealand

Penguin Books Ltd, Registered Offices: Harmondsworth,
Middlesex, England

First published 1993
10 9 8 7 6 5 4 3 2 1
Copyright © Cynthia Wine, 1993

Printed and bound in Canada on acid free paper ∞

Canadian Cataloguing in Publication Data
Wine, Cynthia
        Eating for a living
ISBN 0-670-83833-0

1. Restaurants, lunch rooms, etc. - Anecdotes.
2. Dinners and dining - Anecdotes. I. Title.

TX945.W55 1993   642'.5   C93-093829-1

"The Haitian Peasant Declares His Love" from Dudley Fitts:
Anthology of Contemporary Latin-American Poetry, copyright
© 1942, 1947 by Dudley Fitts. Reprinted by permission of
New Directions Publishing Corp.

To the memory of my father,
Martin Berney,
and to my mother,
Ada Berney,
who fed him, familied him
and made him happy.

Acknowledgments

This project began as a scattering of bits of paper and notes on conversations. It has become a book through the generosity and patience of friends, especially:

Sheila Kieran whose unstinting support—technical and otherwise—kept the lights on, Mary Adachi whose talent has kept thoughts clear and concise and whose commitment to making it right extended well beyond professional obligations, and Ford Clements who gave titles and counsel.

A number who were generous with their knowledge are mentioned in the text; others are listed here alphabetically because it seems safely democratic, though as a "W" I know the inequality of the alphabet. I am especially grateful to: Andrew Bertram, Dr Howard Book, Brian Cooper, Angus Duff, Alison Fryer, Dr Sol Goldstein, Catherine Jordan, Dr David Kenny, Don Kugler, Marilyn Linton, Carolyn Meehan, Dr David Mock, Glenn Pushelberg, Denise Schon, Rosie Schwartz, Gail Singer, Philip Slayton, Bonnie Stern, Brian Trottier, Lucy Waverman and George Yabu. They gave their time generously. Ian Urquhart, in granting me a leave from my job, gave me my time. Penguin Publishers, through Meg Masters, guided the project to completion, coaxing the critical path into a straight line.

And finally, but always first, I thank Hayley, Josh, Damon and Ryan who provide the real nourishment.

Contents

Eating for a Living

Introduction

Rattling The Food Chain

This is a book of dispatches from the front lines of the food revolution. Since 1972 I have been part of the hungry hordes who describe what's in, what's out, the latest book, the newest chef and the hot restaurant that just turned tepid.

Since the early seventies, against a backdrop of deprivation in the rest of the world, privileged people in privileged countries became obsessed with the variety, healthiness and fashion-worthiness of our abundant food. (People only try new things when they can afford to reject them.) People suddenly began running their gastronomic lives as if there were exams at the end, collecting food experiences as if they were Ralph Lauren Polo shirts. Food became, not the stuff of sustenance, but of status.

News about food, once marginalized in the "women's" sections routinely turned up on the front pages of the newspapers: the appearance of the McLean Burger was treated like the discovery of a new galaxy; restaurant closings showed up on local television, chefs appeared on the cover of *People* and *Time* magazines. As I write, the American-based Television Food Network is beginning eight hours a day of food-related programming. If this reminds you of hockey coverage, it should. Eating has become a competitive sport.

Food is political, lifestyles expressed in foodstyles. The title of a best-seller, *Real Men Don't Eat Quiche*, has become part of the idiom. I knew a woman who wouldn't eat sweet cream because it was bourgeois, but did eat sour cream because it was a peasant food. Robert Bly coaxes new age maleness at a seminar in San Francisco, sneering: "What's the matter? Too much yogurt?"

Even the British royals, not commonly known for their attention to palate, are in on it. Prince Charles, in the spring of 1992, publicly demanded that the European Community not interfere in the production of French cheese. This is thought to be the only time since Henry VIII tossed meat bones on the floor that a member of the Royal Family has made a public pronouncement on gastronomy.

Attendance in restaurants began its ascent in the early seventies. In the preceding decade the percentage of the food dollar spent outside the home was 18 per cent. It is now 37 per cent. Restaurants might have started out as places to eat (the word actually comes from the French to restore and was coined in the eighteenth century), but they have evolved into places to talk and to meet. In big cities, they are centres, a neutral place that's not your place nor mine, but ours.

Eating for entertainment is a relatively new concept. When I was a child, going out to a restaurant happened a few times a year—and always on labelled occasions like anniversaries or graduations. For our children, eating food prepared outside the home is common—hamburgers and pizza are part of everyday life. Though there was always a segment of the population for whom eating out was routine—mostly in sophisticated cities like Paris, New York and Rome—recreational eating spread into the general population and through the socio-economic layers.

People who think they never eat out ought to count up how often they pick up a slice of pizza, grab a McMuffin, or order in. If we have less money to eat out, we change the places we eat in, not the practice. During the recession businessmen didn't start brown-bagging it again—they just downscaled to a low-priced place. And if we don't have enough even to downscale, we worry about it over a cup of cappuccino at the local espresso bar or at the neighbourhood doughnut shop.

Fast food is often blamed for the disappearance of the family dinner, with much whining about how family members don't eat together any more. But we remember those meals through rose-coloured glasses. The family table was where everyone was meant to catch up, share stories, and maybe that even happened—at the Waltons'. But more than a few people have told me their own memories of the family dinner as the scene of squabbles and quiet seething, the venue of the flung-down fork, the shouted hurt, the tearful flight upstairs. Maybe the family table needed changing. Maybe fast food is not at fault.

The thing that sticks in my craw about fast food is not that food is made fast. It is that it's eaten fast and in dehumanizing interiors: denatured meals are unwrapped from plastic and eaten in an overlit room at tables that have chairs attached to them, instead of tables where the chairs move to accommodate conversation.

It is no wonder that people overeat in these places. They are futilely looking for some satisfaction in

flavour and texture and warm human nourishment.
They are left not so much hungry, as dissatisfied,
which feels about the same. It suggests that eating is
an activity best dispensed with as quickly as possible.
As if there were something better to do than eating.
Better than eating?!

Both the meal and the platter has evolved to meet
the changes in the way we run our lives. Three
squares have become nibbles—and the term
grazing—meaning food eaten on the hoof—became
part of the language. The three-course square meal—
soup or salad, meat and potatoes, and dessert—
has gone the way of the dodo. The plate that once
held meat and potatoes now holds rice and octopus
tentacles. Not much food for people who grew up
eating meat at most meals. Maybe we eat constantly
because we can't get a square meal.

There have been many earnest explanations for
the shifts. Observers cite: the convenience required
since Mom no longer dedicates her life to making
dinner; television and travel making the foods of
foreign places accessible and familiar; immigrants,
especially from cultures which emphasize eating,
introducing us to strong flavours and titillating
variety.

Every observer has a take on why the food
revolution happened. In an article for *Vanity Fair*
on food critic Mimi Sheraton, writer Arthur Lublow
explains it this way:

"To understand the boom in American restaurants
that began in the late seventies is to see it as a post-
Vietnam assertion of American pride played out in a
frivolous arena."

The *Sunday Times* of London quoted writer
Egon Ronay explaining the change in British food:
"I am firmly convinced that the turning point came
in the 1960s when non-public schoolboys started to
hold positions which gave them ample disposable
incomes. Until then, only the upper classes had
money to spend on dining—and their needs were
catered to by the grand hotels. But in the 60s,
hairdressers, photographers, advertising and PR
people—and, of course, the Michael Caines of this
world—started to spend, and they did not hesitate
to voice their opinions. Having not been brought up
in boarding schools and stately homes, they had no
taste for badly cooked nursery food, and the industry
reacted accordingly."

Where once I watched with amusement, I now
regard with horror. When the food silliness began, it
may have been superficial and frivolous. What is now
happening is sombre and scary.

To our obsession with food, we have added another
about eating. Or more particularly, about not eating.
We are fascinated less now with adorable vegetables
than with who eats what. We are preoccupied with
what we put into our mouths and what others put
into theirs. We grant status according to body size—
the smaller the better—we are haunted by fat grams,
pursued by vitamins and oppressed by nutritional
correctness. "The body never lies," scolded dancer
Martha Graham, and a generation of people
rushed to chisel their bodies to fit the fashion of the
times. Concerns about personal well-being have
traditionally been private, but now we feel qualified
to assess other people's. "My God, he's not going to
eat again," said the woman at the next table when

she spotted a fat man levering himself into a restaurant chair.

We are actually afraid to eat. Ironically, one of the world's first generations of people with the luxury of having all the food we want voluntarily decided, en masse, to make ourselves hungry. At its sombre worst, the food revolution has been a revolution in which eating and food lost their original meaning as nourishment for the body, a symbol of hospitality and a catalyst for conversation, and became talked about more in political, psychological and scientific terms. The epidemic of anorexia—defined as a fear of eating—may be a metaphor for our times.

There are echoes here of the Puritan attitude to sex (and look where that got us). Food is grudgingly taken for the sake of nutrition, as sex was once tolerated for the purpose of procreation.

At the same time we were professing liberal notions about the rules about sexual abstention, we were replacing them with a Puritan code about food and eating. Drop a knob of sweet butter on a guest's baked potato and you'll get a reaction as if you'd tried to French kiss a member of the Victorian clergy— the guest will stiffen, pursing lips to remind you that that sort of thing isn't done.

Eating has become more moral than oral. Amazingly, we have come to regard our natural appetites as a curse to be controlled.

Self-denial is regarded as a virtue. American essayist Barbara Ehrenreich has argued that the increase in dessert sales results not from people losing control but out of an effort to prove that they have it. A businessman tells me that he likes to order his meal and leave it virtually untouched in front of him, because it shows his strength and unnerves everyone around him.

I was a member of a group visiting one-hundred-year-old artist Beatrice Wood in her hilltop house in California, which was full of her fabulous ceramics and paintings. But instead of admiring her work, we were riveted by her companion's description of how little she eats: an eighth of an apple for breakfast, about the same for lunch and dinner. Maybe a tablespoon of rice. But she has a chocolate with each meal, preferably milk chocolate. We marvelled at her self-control and wondered if that was the basis of her health and longevity.

Our attitudes towards the other deadly sins pale beside our contempt for the overweight. Prime-time talk shows discuss grotesque sexual deviations. Trusted politicians are cited for usury, the deeds of the religious drip with evil. But we save our repulsion for lush hips and soft bellies. "Gluttony is the sin you can see," explains Janet Polivy of the University of Toronto.

I am in no way devaluing the importance of taking care of ourselves or the valid observations that have been made about the importance of healthy eating. The population swell of baby boomers has now reached the age when health is earned, not granted.

But there are echoes of prohibitionist notions. In the United States, a strong temperance movement aims to force governments to clamp down on wine drinking. The walls in restaurants are covered with warnings about wine consumption and about the health risks involved in other behaviour associated with dining: there are quick guides to Heimlich manoeuvres and prohibitions about smoking tobacco.

You'd think people had made their dinner reservations in a nuclear substation. Watch for a label on crème caramel warning of the dangers of sidestream fat.

During the years that I have been writing, guilt and food terrorism have escalated. The proponents are not the nutritionists—many of whom are not only blameless but are fighting for some balance—but are the promoters of odd diets or of purges that "cleanse the body of toxins"—and us who believe them.

When you see the good that breaking bread together has done, the pleasures of shared tables, the magic that happens when a group of disparate people begin to relax with food and drink as a catalyst, you get real mad about the facile rules about how we eat, what we eat and when we eat.

It's heartbreaking to see the harm to our joy in pleasure that has made today's table a battlefield of repression, a sterile laboratory—where we measure every mouthful and condemn our natural appetites. The tight-lipped censors that complain that families don't eat the way they did when we all lived down on the farm ought to cool their jets; the scolding nannies ought to chill out, and the prissy puritans who holler rape when someone offers them a chocolate oughta put a sock in it.

We have learned little of the joy of eating from our leaders. Prince Charles's action may help redress the balance of the shoddy examples the Windsors have been: Princess Di, barfing into the Royal Toilet; the once full and lush Sarah Ferguson, now fashionably skinny and deprived-looking. What a sell-out: I loved her sensuous laugh, the rounded body which showed an appetite. Now she's a wasted skinny like the rest of them, pale, zipped up, restrained. What these two might have done for humankind by allowing some softness to settle on their hips after their second children.

Let us look now to the new world: Ever since Bill Clinton was elected president of the United States, I have been feeling cheered about the future of food. Unlike his pinched and scrawny predecessor, Clinton is an eater. From a president whose strongest statements on the pleasures of the palate were made when he threw up on the Japanese prime minister and when he announced that as president he didn't have to eat broccoli, the Americans have lucked into an administration with appetite. We already know of Clinton's love for barbecue and fast food; we can look forward to at least four more years of pork chops and French fries. We have hopes of glory. This may mark the end of the cold war on food and the demise of puritanical eating as we know it.

Perhaps Canada might share the pleasure, since the examples from our leaders have been so mingy. We knew little about Brian Mulroney's table and less about his successor. For all his style, Pierre Trudeau was notorious only for his parsimony with food. When he was prime minister, he hosted "Wonderful Wednesdays" when he would invite a few MPs for lunch and conversation. Said one of them: "If you were a hungry man, you came to those lunches hungry and you left hungry."

This book is a collection of observations and experiences. It is also full of stories told to me by people who, relaxed over a good meal, have talked about food phobias, sex in restaurants and sometimes just about food. They are really all stories of how we meet across tables and how much fun it is to eat.

The *ßlini* **Boondoggle** and **Other** **Crimes** of **Fashion**

When the food revolution began, spices were subversive and red wine was still the dubious drink of bohemians and Italian immigrants. A rare night out in a restaurant started with a boat of celery sticks and olives and ended with crème de menthe parfait. Ethnic variety was Chinese and that meant deep-fried foods with a plastic sheen and red dye #2. Vegetables were a garnish, unless they were served by people in saffron robes in earnest, calm places. (You'd go home and listen to Pete Seeger after.) Starch was a filler, not a saviour.

Now there are more regions of Chinese food than there are people in China, and you can't find anyone to join you for a battered pork ball because they'd rather eat hot-and-sour soup. Everyone knows about what they should eat, because for twenty years we have debated balsamic, pondered polenta, and argued whether pure spring water should be served with lemon, lime or quince.

We got from there to here trend by trend with seasonally adjusted food fashions.

So, here is the good news: we have access to better food than we did twenty years ago, especially in restaurants. The food explosion of the eighties led us to expect fresh vegetables, decent fish and meat, and a respectable standard of preparation. Our choices are wider, our awareness better, and much of the food tastes better.

But the food explosion also brought a pandering to trends, which, though entertaining at first, fast became excessive and obnoxious. Although the recession brought some relief—the same social and economic forces that moved our lives from the fast lane into a parking lot cleaned up our platters and brought us back to our senses (what a relief)—the need to know what's new and to eat what's different became entrenched.

So blame the press. Each year food writers, anticipating a year's worth of space to fill, get together over Perrier and Pop Tarts to predict what the best-fed folk will be wearing on their plates this year and to denounce what was on them last year. In 1982, the out-list of a national magazine denounced green peppercorns in favour of pink; wine and cheese parties, unless the wine was from California and the cheese was from goats. That year an American food editor told me that anyone seen sipping a mixed drink or smoking a cigarette was sure to be over the age of fifty. The in-list included little salads of squid tentacles or any raw fish. Said food author Roy Andries de Groot: "If you want to be really different come hell or high water, you serve raw fish."

Food writers said things like that, but I don't know why anyone listened. We hardly ever got it right. In fact, food writers, like other soothsayers, are spectacularly bad at spotting trends.

In 1989, for example, we figured that all the talk of glasnost would make readers goofy for things Russian. Fashion editors promised racks of Russian greatcoats; interior decorators insisted samovars were the thing; food editors touted blinis and borscht. We combed the regions of Russia, found the grilled chicken of Georgia, the peroshki of Moscow and began to produce articles about Russian regional cooking.

Irresponsibly unaware that I was leading the avant-garde, I had been eating perogies and borscht for years. My mother's family was from Russia and I was delighted to have a leg up on the trend.

To get the scoop on Russian food, I called my Uncle Benny. He had spent the first fifteen years of his life in Russia, before poverty and persecution forced him to flee to a place where he could catch the latest trend in food at that time—a square meal.

"Uncle Benny, I'm writing an article on the latest fashion, Russian food."

"You mean like in that movie where they ate blinis with lots of vodka?"

"No, I mean the kind of food you ate when you lived in Russia."

He seemed baffled. "Who had food? That's why we had to come to Canada."

My Uncle Benny had hit on one of the greatest challenges facing food writers today. At our annual foodgabs, there is always some spoilsport who insists that the new trend has to be "honest." The actual phrase that they use is "the honest food of the people."

This is a problem because, as Uncle Benny pointed out, the food of the people is often too meagre to make good copy. For example, when the trend was Asian food, we really had to scramble to avoid telling readers that the food of the people is rice. Period.

The Russian trend didn't catch on because readers noticed that the food of the people in Russia was cabbage—if they were lucky.

We tried to make childhood food the "in" eating. A few years ago we reported that mashed potatoes would be the metaphor for the warmth and comfort that had gone from our lives. We argued that the recession made us want to be reminded of our mothers, of the safety we felt when she was around. So we touted meatloaf. And mashed potatoes.

Looking back, I realize that I wrote more about how we would be eating mashed potatoes than I ate. I think this trend lost to another trend. At the time, recovery groups were telling us that we were wrong in the first place to think we had been safe with our mothers: their food, cooked fearlessly with butter and fat, clearly exhibited a latent hostility towards us.

The flavours of nouvelle nursery put us into further conflict with our phobia about fat on our plates and on our bodies. Diners never did see the heaps of carbohydrate and the cauldrons of comfort meals that we food writers had promised. Instead, we got a hybrid of scaled-down comfort food: sort of nouvelle Mom. As the recession wore on, the excess of mashed potatoes promised over mashed potatoes actually eaten would fill a fondue fork factory.

Ironically, for the forests of print and all of the hype that the food revolution has created, the newest cuisine is the same in all major cities. We are eating

4

arugula in Amsterdam and Acapulco, blinis in Boston and Birmingham, and pizza everywhere, because chefs everywhere work with the same materials, creating dishes which are driven by the current fashion. We have traded salads made from iceberg lettuce for mixed greens with funny names. We eat them at underdecorated restaurants in Saskatoon and London. If you shut your eyes, nothing in the meal would tell you where you were. Or what season it was.

Blame technology. Once, food was available when nature gave it to us in its season. Now the availability of produce from every corner of our tortured earth at almost any time has produced a city cuisine full of ingredients that are as foreign to us as kiwi was to our parents. Restaurant fruitplates in countries that have only a few months' growing season are made from produce that originates in countries that enjoy it all year long: tomatillo, coral, papaya, Trinidadian gooseberry.

Bananas were once new and exotic but mass marketing is the enemy of chic. Chilies became fashionable and pretty soon we were measuring status by who knew the difference between an ancho and a chipotle. Vegetables were miniaturized—baby carrots, infant potatoes, foetal zucchini pods—but after a few tastings, they ceased to be exotic.

Technology is also to blame for grazing: the word that describes how cattle eat was adapted to describe how humans are eating on the hoof—a bun and coffee at eight, pizza slice at twelve, cappuccino at two, a sandwich at five and a bite of sushi at ten. Machines have made it possible. People didn't graze cookies and milk when folks had to grind wheat for flour and milk

5

the cow for something to drink.

Odd fruits and coffees have always been available, but they were bought only by the rich or eccentric who traditionally dabbled in exotica. What changed is that working, mortgage-paying persons began suddenly, and in droves, to lay out hard cash for them. Blame status-seeking. In the last twenty years, people have traded food experiences the way we once impressed each other with new shag rugs. Judy Schulz, food editor of the *Edmonton Journal* says, "It got to be that people were afraid to be seen eating the wrong thing."

Brillat-Savarin may have said, "Show me what you eat and I'll show you who you are," but today he might say, "Show me where you eat..." People become as embarrassed by not knowing about the latest restaurant as they once were at not knowing the latest best-seller.

We have calmed down a bit—in a poorer world, being too much in tune is déclassé—but in the frenzied eighties we were so keen to be in the know that we ran promiscuously from one restaurant to the other. Places considered to be at the acme of the apex of the zenith of the happening for several months would be shunted aside, nowheresville, when a new one opened. Celebrity restaurants, which were once the territory of Hollywood, New York and Rome, joined the race: the search for the fabulous was everywhere.

Before the revolution, most fancy restaurants served either French or continental cuisine. The latter took its name from the varied offerings of Europe—mostly from France, Italy and Eastern Europe.

As I write this, the vogue is for earthy, peasant foods. Everyone serves beans, breads, pastas and salads. (Continental food is now so unfashionable, so weak and feeble that it should be called incontinental.) You have only to look at the name of a restaurant for a chronology of fashion since the revolution: steakhouses ("House of Beef") defined the sixties; granola ("Alice's Groovy Goodies") the seventies; and chef-driven urban cuisine ("Tyrone") marked the eighties.

Bistro has remained very big. "Café," a romantic name evoking streetside brasseries in Paris, has been taken over by all sorts of places, among them the second-floor cafeteria in Winnipeg's largest hospital complex. "Bar & Grill," seen less in the sixties and seventies than the fifties, is enjoying a revival. The mainstreaming of Italian food will soon mean that trattoria and ristorante will become synonymous with restaurant. Yesterday's omelette is tomorrow's frittata.

Ethnic food has been mass marketed and has become de-ethnicized. Don't be surprised to find souvlaki in Wong's Trattoria Bar and Grill. Or sushi in a coffee shop. No matter what your ethnic origin, it is unfashionable to serve the food of your childhood at dinner parties. No one who is Greek would be caught serving dolmades, and no one who is Jewish serves matzoh balls. Pizza is no longer exotic, it's just what we eat. Middle Eastern food has danced from sheik to chic. Falafel sandwiches are commonly eaten by teenagers, harbingers of adventuresome eating. Watch for a chain called Hoummous R Us.

More than countries, we have been fascinated by regions—especially American regions. Cajun style had us blackening every food (one observer wondered when we would see blackened salad), southwestern had us eating so much coarse cornmeal that it looked like we were rolling our lunch in gravel. In Canada, the national quest for an identity insinuated itself into our stomachs. We had gone along, irresponsibly eating the foods that satisfied us. Then along came Expo '67, the festivities in Montreal that celebrated the country's centennial, and food patriots were embarrassed to realize that our larders contained little of what might be identifiably Canadian. Chefs scrambled to devise menus that included foods urban Canadians hadn't had to eat since the last century, when they were sitting around campfires, or in cabins or taverns.

Food writers declared a Canadian cuisine and chefs foraged field and stream to find it. Salmon was twisted into every configuration, including many in which the fish was so thoroughly disguised it might as well have been Captain High Liner. Since then, we have eaten variations on tree bark and forest moss. At the now-defunct Nekah restaurant in Toronto (Nekah means wild goose) a consommé of pine began the one-hundred-dollar fixed-price meal.

You might well wonder how far we've come, paying high prices for poor people's food—olive oil, homemade bread, barnyard chickens, natural produce—which were once staples of the farms of other countries. Foods our grandparents escaped from.

We have the last decade to blame for the feeling that we must continue to search for, and keep up with, trends. When it came to food in the eighties, nothing exceeded like excess. For those years, restaurant menus were exhaustingly and constantly creative.

There were too many flavours, too many ingredients: dishes used every ingredient known to urban humans. You might expect this sort of frantic novelty from tourist-drawing downtown places, but the trends seeped even into our safer suburbs. Beef tenderloin strudel with a pesto and goat cheese sauce was served in the suburbs. The same place served smoked salmon wrapped around bok choy. They called it sushi. I called it strange.

In the eighties, some dishes were concocted just for shock value: different flavours that had nothing to do with each other seemed outrageous and chic together, like chiffon and denim. I had a bass wrapped in lettuce, the lump of flesh and leaf baked in red wine sauce. It was revolting. But go figure. At La Cachette in Vancouver I once ordered a dish consisting of a fresh fig wrapped in smoked salmon and drizzled with vinaigrette, only because it sounded so silly it might make a few lines of copy. It was fabulous.

One thing food writers do know is when a trend has died. Quiche, like Black Forest cake, was hot in the early seventies; you could serve either at dinner parties and call yourself a pacesetter. But the day they appeared in department store cafeterias, anyone who cared a whit for style knew it was time to move on.

These days, the menu in a department store dining room is a real indicator that times have changed. In a dining room where, once, I could count on being soothed by motherly chicken à la king and tinned peas, chicken Alfredo may dally with snow peas and pine nuts or teriyaki chicken with mandarin cashew compote. All around me, Lunching Ladies with Hats who would have been perfectly happy with asparagus rolls and cottage cheese fruit plates are now nibbling the likes of lamb sausage with chèvre and duck fritters with two sauces.

Still, there are a few enduring legacies of the era of frenzied fashion.

The make-up of the plate has changed. Now it is not what you eat, but what you eat with what you eat that counts. In the fifties, meat was central, with starch for bulk and vegetables for garnish. Now the starch and vegetables fill the plate; the meats are in a little blob and you no longer concern yourself only with them. Instead, you must consider the beef in play with the shiitake mushrooms and the zucchini blossoms.

Dressing your dinner looks like it's here to stay. It is an art, something like dressing a person: the suit may anchor the outfit, but the shoes, tie and shirt give it style and make it satisfying. With nouvelle cuisine, food became more visual, when plates were accessorized like your best frock as chefs tried to convince you that there was more on the dish than a few sprouts. But soon the excesses of that cookery were regarded as a gastronomic joke, even by industry insiders. ("Three pea pods put on a plate with tweezers. You call that cuisine?" snorted Franco Prevedello, an Italian restaurant magnate.)

Today in ritzy restaurants, vegetables lie under colourful purées and plate rims are dusted with finely chopped herbs. Fresh flowers and pieces of fresh herbs the size of tree trunks routinely show up on the plates in aspiring restaurants. The idea is that the whole platter should become a sense bath for the eyes, nose and palate.

The fashion for fitness has modified our eating for keeps. Pasta was anointed as a healthy starch (the food of athletes) and olive oil, the golden girl of fats, since it is unsaturated. The grainy textured foods of the southwest and the earthy peasant foods are revered because they make physiological sense: we believe they will do for us what Roto-Rooter does for pipes. Beans are welcomed for their high fibre and though they may result in a kind of gastronomic distress which will hardly make one welcome in a stylish salon, the resourceful British have made a virtue of the trend, calling it Fart Food Chic.

Szechuan food introduced many of us to spice, but Szechuan food is no longer chic, even though our tolerance for spicy foods has been increasing. Foods from countries where the flavouring is spicy tend to use less meat, more vegetables and lots of grains. Chilies are hotly in fashion, their popularity perhaps boosted by reports that spicy foods increase the metabolism and help burn fat.

Many North Americans endure their spice as it is smeared on chicken wings, the once-wasted part of the bird which has been brilliantly salvaged and marketed. Until American writer Calvin Trillin paid tribute to the wings at Buffalo's Anchor Bar in a *New Yorker* article, no one except chickens noticed that they were there.

Now the limb is celebrated and routinely served in restaurants that have Tiffany lamps, frantically friendly atmospheres and names that include the word "emporium." Furthermore, restaurateurs compete to come up with increasingly inflammatory adjectives: "suicide" or "yeow" to describe their incendiary wing sauces. When I coaxed a teenager to try one, he said the spice made him feel "like my brain is being dragged out through my nose."

Chicken and other fowl are seen as fair in these nutritious times and trendfollowers favour it over beef. Chicken has received the benediction of the fat police who have pronounced it low in fat relative to the amount of protein it delivers.

It appears that quail will maintain its status as the chicken of the chic, although its popularity presents one of the strongest challenges to eating etiquette that nouveau eaters have yet encountered. A book by Rochelle Udell, a former art director for *House & Garden* magazine, was some comfort: in *How To Eat an Artichoke and Other Trying, Troublesome, Hard-To-Get-At Foods*, she advises that "It is permissible to pick up quail legs with the hands, but never, ever pick up the body."

I haven't picked up a quail by hand or by fork since the time I helped a chef by peeling piles of quail eggs, a challenge of decidedly gargantuan proportions. The minuscule bits of shell often gouged holes in the white of the egg, leaving small craters in what should have been a flawless oval.

They were being used to garnish a dish in which the bird was prepared in parts: the tiny tits were sautéed and laid on a bed of warm shredded greens. Next came the little legs, fast roasted, left pink at the bone, and placed at right angles to one another. The eggs were sliced thinly and laid like tiny coins for garnish. The plate looked like a Lilliputian lunch. (It was, of course, the era of nouvelle cuisine.)

Still, better that than the quail served whole. My lunch partner ordered one in a fancy hotel restaurant once. The waiter lifted the silver dome to reveal a platter holding two wee birds, their tiny feet in the air. They looked stunned and rigid in their casket of rice—like sparrows after they hit a plate-glass window.

It has become fashionable to serve fowl rare, as revolting a fashion as we have embraced. It began sensibly, I suppose, in the sixties, when fabulous chef James Beard suggested that roast turkey should be pink at the bone so that the meat was left moist—and that duck breasts should be slightly red, mostly because they are as dense and rich as beef.

But rawness has become the rage. Carpaccio is on every Italian menu; raw fish has migrated from sushi bars to mainstream restaurants—salmon tartare, tuna carpaccio. I was served swordfish carpaccio, with a warm sauce—the warmth made the fish seem so alive, I could almost feel the pulse.

Maybe the fashion for rawness is penance for the years we overcooked everything. Rare beef and lamb are a blessing after the carpeting we ate before we figured out how to do it right. The same is true of fish: a tuna steak rare in the middle is a relief after years of fish cooked until it fell into shards at the touch of a fork. Even people who don't like fish seem to like tuna steak. The man at the market calls swordfish and tuna Chicken Fish. He means that they don't have the qualities people hate about fish, namely that it smells, has bones, and tastes like fish.

Although North Americans have oceans of saltwater fish and lakes of freshwater fish and farms to supply more fish at cheaper prices, fashion still dictates that we eat Mahi Mahi from Hawaii or orange roughy from Australia.

Red meat will never die. It is interesting that even though red meat in general, and beef in particular has been strongly denounced, it still remains popular.

13

In the last months before this book went to print, the sales of beef were rising and a trend to Big Food, which meant extra large hamburgers, was in full tilt. Some see it as a backlash to prissy, lean food—the gastronomic equivalent of thumbing the nose.

I think the fact that there are still lots of steak houses around speaks volumes for the strength of resistance to change. Steak houses have lasted because contemporary restaurants change their menus all the time. Steak houses never do. In modern establishments, you just get your mouth up for the baked potato and some chef in the throes of creative passion has made it look like a persimmon and taste like pike.

Even so, a lot of people react to my invitation to a steak house as if I'd poured PCBs into their Perrier. Maybe that's because they remember the way we used to eat in steak houses before it became trendy to undereat. We would start with the basket of garlic bread. (I once got a recipe for garlic toast from a steak house and you might be surprised to know that a basket of it carries your weight in butter.) The onion soup that followed had cheese crusted over the top and down the sides so you could chisel it off with the little fork used to spear the flaccid shrimp in the shrimp cocktail.

Then came Caesar salad made with baco-bits and powdered Parmesan and lots of garlic, followed by a perfect steak with a baked stuffed potato. Note the use of garlic. In those days, garlic was about the only thrill you could get outside of an onion sandwich.

There was no garlic in the cheesecake—which, aside from the parfaits, was, and often still is, the only dessert in steak houses. It had canned cherries or blueberries in a pile so shiny the fruit looked as if it had been dipped in acrylic. The difference between the blueberry or cherry toppings was not in the taste but in the colour. Cherry topping tasted more red. We never drank wine with these dinners in case it filled us up.

The slap-em-silly slabs of red meat are always in portions large enough to seem like a gimmick. Sometimes, if you finish one of these portions, you get the meal free. This triumph will be less valuable to you than the last rites you will really need.

A lot of beef and sausages are still eaten on the Prairies, but then there's lots of spreading room out there.

Even now, steak houses can be found in those sections of the city near coliseums where blood sports— hockey, boxing or rock concerts—are held. They usually have bars where a man is happy to be known by the Scotch he drinks.

But drinking fashions have changed as well. People under the age of fifty hardly ever drink hard liquor in restaurants. We have become demanding about wines and beers. We drink lots of bottled water—despite reports that tap water in many cities is as good, if not better. Maybe we compromise by putting tap water ice cubes in our bottled mineral water.

Much of our obsession with food fashions has been expressed through our new attachment to greens. Canadians who live in a climate that is cold much of the year dress our outsides in wool and our insides in chilled vegetables. We eat summer food all year round.

Rebels have found ways to have their salad and call it cake. Watch them at a salad bar, where they dump globs of blue cheese dressing over the lettuce, leaving the poor little leaves cowering and gasping for air. At a local restaurant I once piled high the radicchio and loaded up with pancetta and dressing that gave it about the same caloric content as a Big Mac.

I wonder if the most enduring legacy of the food revolution may not be the word "lite" and the resulting flurry of product names with odd spellings and feeble flavour.

Which brings us to the latest trend in eating. Not eating. The pursuit of lightness shows that it's not chic to eat at all. Today's slender beauties cannot reasonably take in anything but Perrier and air, no matter how keen their talk about the latest restaurant. They have merely become adept at hiding the food on the plate, burying the petit pois under the pommes and slipping the sushi to the Samoyed.

Tasting may be toney, and sipping is stylish, but can you imagine Madonna with a mouthful?

Are the Stars Out Tonight?

I 've always been a sucker for places owned by famous people. I've even gone to sports bars headed up by guys whose games I wouldn't watch on a bet. In the last few years, I've been hard pressed to keep up with the new galaxies of star restaurants.

Sylvester Stallone, Dudley Moore, Mikhail Baryshnikov, for heaven's sake—they all put some of their dough into food. Some did it more than once. Michael Caine's outrageously famous Langan's Brasserie in London got a sibling when Caine added The Canteen in Chelsea Harbour. Planet Hollywood, a buzzing hub in New York owned by a stream of stars, has also added a London location. There, the Brits have extended their royal watching to American celebrities.

I don't think stars open restaurants because they are hungry. I do think their accountants have cooked up a way to dispose of all of that indisposable income from megabuck pictures. That makes sense, of course. People who once thought they were in the restaurant business to sell food and drink know that nothing draws the crowds like a celebrity clientele, and it didn't take movie stars long to cash in on the money other folks were making off their fame. British writer and politician Sir Clement Freud opened an espresso bar with actor Robert Morley in 1957. Freud writes: "I did the work; he came in from time to time and sat at the window table so people passing saw him, and the place flourished."

It also makes sense that the celebrities would put their names on the door, to make hay while their stars shine—as in Samantha Fox's London eatery, Sam's, and Wayne Gretzky's new place in Toronto. But, perversely, some stars like Dudley Moore, Ringo Starr and Mariel Hemingway choose chic, up-to-the-minute monikers instead of their own. Moore's L.A. places are called 72 Market Street and Maple Drive; Mariel Hemingway's New York hot spots are called Sam.

When places are coy about their celebrated owners, you have to know what's what and who's who to get to where's where. Maybe that's the appeal. I've gone to a gazillion famous-star restaurants, always hoping for a glimpse of famous flesh. But the stars are never there.

Years ago, I tried to get a reservation at Michael Caine's restaurant in Mayfair, but that proved tougher than a security check. On the phone, Langan's receptionist was clipped and frosty: "There is no table tonight, tomorrow and certainly not for Saturday, madam." I even tried asking for a table on the second floor—where the tourists are hidden.

I achieved the impossible with the help of the well-spoken young woman behind the front desk at my hotel, who got a table first try for that night "on the main floor where you can see the stars, not upstairs where they put the tourists." The problem, she explained, was my accent.

I felt the difficulties were an omen that the Man Himself would be there. I arrived even before the 11:30 p.m. reservation, but was kept cooling my heels out of sightlines in a bar at the back for forever—half an hour. (Though by that time, restaurants in North America have long since rolled up their sidewalks, in London the witching hour after the theatre is prime time.)

Finally, I was led to the hard-won table in the middle of the floor at the back of the cavernous, noisy room. I watched for Michael Caine until 1:00 a.m. through some pretty good bangers and mash with onion sauce and a plateful of ho-hum fish and chips (at an astonishing equivalent of twenty dollars). For those prices, Caine should have been there offering a quick smile beside the bangers or a Caine-ish blessing o'er the cockles. But he never came.

I once went to Tribeca in Manhattan, the coffee-bean plant turned eatery owned by a whole menu of stars including Baryshnikov, Sean Penn, Bill Murray, Barbra Streisand and Robert de Niro. I wanted de Niro, but I would have been happy with anyone. Alas, there was no Baryshnikov by the barre, no de Niro decanting, no Streisand sipping a spritzer. There was no one famous, only people like me hoping to see people like them.

I am beginning to wonder if Sylvester Stallone ever flashes his biceps over the bivalves at Planet Hollywood in Manhattan or its siblings in London or L.A. Or if Roy Rogers ever branded a burger at the eatery named after him. Maybe these stars don't like the food. Maybe they would rather be home with a salami sandwich. Perhaps they're shy.

I have rubbernecked along with the bleached and blazered at Chuck and Harold's in Palm Beach, where it is reputed that Tom Selleck and Zsa Zsa Gabor pop in regularly. But I have never seen them. And I have never seen a Kennedy at Au Bar just down the road, although the newspapers keep telling us that's where they hang out—there or at Tabu on the ritzy Worth Avenue, where simply everyone knows the rich and famished hang out. Am I going at the wrong time?

Even when I was in Winnipeg, that could be a problem. In the sixties, there was a coffee shop said to be a favourite hangout for hippies and beatniks. But when I went there, all I ever saw were two people with long hair and forty others staring at them, waiting for them to say something in hippie.

I hear that the reason Schatzi, Arnold Schwarzenegger's Los Angeles restaurant, is so popular is that the star himself is always there. That makes sense. I wouldn't cross the street to see an Arnold Schwarzenegger film, but I'd walk a mile to eat bratwurst and noodles at Schatzi if I knew for sure he'd be there. Maybe there'd be someone famous sitting with him. I heard Bette Midler had lunch with him there one day. You might think that he would just wave the bill away, being an owner and all—but he didn't. He handed it to his agent to pay. Arnold believes that time is valuable too. You can learn a foreign language while you pass a few moments in Schatzi's washrooms—it sure beats Muzak.

In New York it's considered cool to be oblivious to celebrities. Real New Yorkers think that fawning is for the fatuous dweebs who live in California. It's a bit like that in Toronto, where I live. We see stars all the time, especially during the annual fall film festival or when any of the many movies shot here every year are in production. Everyone knocks themselves out pretending not to notice the stars going about their business.

When Midler sat over a plate of fresh fruit at Toronto's Pronto Ristorante (their dessert fruit plates are very theatrical), just like a regular person, no one in the restaurant—with the exception of the people at my table who couldn't keep their eyes off her—appeared to notice. At Cibo, another Toronto restaurant, everyone was trying not to look at Jane Fonda nibbling at a Spartan plate of pasta. (I wonder if these stars eat correct food when they're in public and Kraft Dinner when they're at home. Not Jane Fonda, I guess.)

Restaurateurs like to brag when a star has eaten there, just like those U.S. inns that used to boast that "George Washington slept here." When I phoned the owner of a Spanish restaurant in Toronto to ask him about his menu, he told me, "Goldie Hawn ate here. With her kids." Restaurateurs always try to make it sound as if the stars travelled all the way from L.A. just to eat in their restaurant, when the probable reason is that the place is near their hotel, and they eat there for the same reason you and I do when we're out of town—because we can't face another silver dome from the dining room.

Sometimes the restaurant is the celebrity. In the last ten years, L.A.'s hottest eateries have been those owned by chef Wolfgang Puck and his publicity-conscious wife, Barbara Lazaroff. They opened Chinois

21

on Main, and Spago, reputed and disputed birthplace of the designer pizza and the open-to-view kitchen. For a while, Spago was about the hardest restaurant in the world to get into and just getting a reservation got to be a sort of game, the West Coast equivalent of the tourists in Rome trying to get an audience with the Pope.

Spago is austere, right-on hip, situated in a home-ly part of west Hollywood, a stark white room with a low ceiling. When it was hot, Maryln Schwartz, *Dallas Morning News* food writer, couldn't get a reservation any night for three months. Puck told her that he saves tables every night between 7:30 and 9:30 p.m. for his regulars (most of whom are movie stars).

As long as it was the hottest place to be turned away from, people who wanted to feel superior refused to go there. I apparently got to Los Angeles during the refusal but after the fad—just missing things again. When I tried to talk a foodie friend into going with me to Puck's, she balked, "I'll have to get all dressed up to be insulted and get a bad table."

Now, Spago has gone from noun to verb. To Spago means to treat someone like a tourist and take them to a restaurant where they think they'll see celebri-ties. "Spago is where we take people from Missouri," an insider confided. How fleeting is fame. Yesterday's hot spot is today's sneer. Within a year, locals shifted affections to the Puck/Lazaroff sibling, the Granita restaurant in Malibu. Its interior is flashy: marble, aquaria full of psychedelic fish, and spherical lights atop tall columns.

A friend treated as a tourist at Spago's shifted her affections to the Trinity restaurant, run by nightclub people from New York and known for the company it keeps. "The first five times I went there, I saw Francis Ford Coppola, Christian Slater, Kiefer Sutherland and Cher. Now that's a hangout!" If I decided to go to Trinity, it would be the night they were all home washing their hair.

One Los Angeles restaurant is famous only among the famous. You have to be famous to recognize the movers and shakers that inhabit the tables at Morton's, owned by Peter Morton, who used to own the Hard Rock Cafe in New York. Those in the know know to go Monday nights, when the powerful and the private infrastructure of Hollywood dines. On that night, everyone is a someone, a someone's close friend or someone to whom a someone owes a favour. I was there on a Wednesday.

Morton always sits at Table 2 at the front. That kind of hierarchy of tables is crucial to a celebrity restaurant: there must be places of privilege for the haughty, purgatory slots for the tourists, and in-between yearning seats for the wannabees.

At Morton's, all the best tables are at the front, near the entrance, with a view into the cozy room divided by huge potted plants and unseen rules. The chosen can be seen from the tables near the entrance and—equally important—they can see the whole room, especially the entrance. We were seated in Siberia, at 7-B, nowhere: not near the front, not beside the windows that bank one wall, not near the bar with its comings and goings—on a busy aisle, with another table fitted in tightly beside us.

The one-page, Spartan menu said coolly "Things To Eat." They included foodstuffs on beds of shredded greens. The greens were piled high like haystacks:

wild mushrooms on shredded lettuce and Hawaiian grilled shrimp on shredded cabbage. The bill, comparatively cheap for the hype and the crowd—less than one hundred dollars for two with wine—surprised me. Although that's a lot of lettuce for lettuce.

Most of the thirty tables were filled with men, nearly all of them in dark business suits, although the temperature had hovered near ninety that day. The few women there were were blonde, young, and with older men. The man behind us was very solicitous of his curvaceous young partner and as they stood up, he announced to the surrounding tables that she was pregnant. Not that anyone could tell. There wasn't room in that dress for a raisin.

The cars in the lot were all ritzy and one Porsche was parked near the door. There were as many car jockeys as waiters, it seemed to me, and as much attention being paid to jockeying for car positions as for the clientele.

I wonder how many waiters in famous-people restaurants dream of returning one day as celebrities themselves. Many in all kinds of establishments are actors or screenwriters when they're not waiting tables. Sometimes they'll try anything to get noticed: a waiter once tried flogging a movie script to a group of film censor board members while they were meeting at a Toronto restaurant.

Sometimes, it is all the waiter can do not to rush over and beg the attention of a celebrity. Waitress Carolyn Meehan lost it when k.d. lang came into the pizza parlour where she was working. She ran right over: "I think you do a better rendition of 'Walkin' After Midnight' than Patsy Kline ever did," Meehan gushed. Lang left a note with her tip to say how much the compliment meant to her. "I fall to pizzas," it said.

Restaurant staff learn how to spot important people even when their faces aren't immediately recognizable. "You can tell the minute they say hello," according to the owner of a ritzy Italian restaurant, who says he specializes in picking class from crass. "There's what sounds like a genuine warmth in their voice, an expectation that they will have a good time. They have no need to show you who is in control because they know they are. Their manners distinguish them."

Not just their manners. Maitre d's do judge these books by their covers. "You get to tell when a piece of jewellery is really important or when it is just for show. People of importance wear their clothes comfortably and the cut just seems to be right on them. They never wear their clothes or jewellery as if it were a sign. You can spot an Armani suit on a woman and you can spot the woman used to wearing it. Chanel has knock-offs, but when it's the real one, you know."

A Montreal waiter also looks at the suit: "Most VIPs look like VIPs. There's a difference between a regular going-out suit and an 'I'm here' suit," he says. "These VIPs aren't showy, but they have a presence. It's not that they look dressed up. They just are."

A headwaiter in Palm Beach is so attuned to jewellery that he can tell the level of society by what is worn and how. He is impressed by a woman wearing real gems that match the outfit (sapphires on a blue dress, for instance), because that suggests she has a variety of stones. Another waiter swears by shoes: he can predict how much a customer will spend on wine

25

by the shoes alone. Spotting the spender is a common sport among people who run big-name restaurants and restaurateurs claim a good spotter can guess the tab as soon as the customer enters.

Once a restaurant becomes known as a place where important people dine, that reputation stays forever, and it's money in the bank. While driving around Los Angeles a year ago, someone pointed out El Coyote restaurant because it's famous as "the last restaurant Sharon Tate ate in before she was murdered by Charles Manson."

Sharon Tate ate her last meal there about twenty years ago, before I thought anyone actually expected to see a real star in any of those places. We were satisfied just to see glamorous pictures of them on the wall at places like Gallagher's near Broadway, where the signed photos indicated that stars were the restaurateur's best friends. After all, only very best friends would leave pictures of themselves attached to the walls to make people think that they are always there in person—except, by unfortunate coincidence, the night that you are there.

Lately, I've begun to wonder exactly how those pictures came about. Did the celebrities bring them along to dinner and present them to the restaurateur in gratitude for a meal? Or did the restaurateur just happen to have a photographer standing by at the ready, in the hope that a celebrity would happen in? If the picture doesn't turn out, does the star get a free meal so he'll come back and try again? Would you be insulted if you thought you were a celebrity and no one asked for your picture?

The name of New York's Les Celebrités restaurant on Central Park South is taken from its décor: the walls are hung with a rotating exhibition of paintings by such show-biz notables as Gene Hackman, James Dean and Phyllis Diller.

Remember when restaurateurs named sandwiches and specials after famous people? In Winnipeg, there was a deli that featured Brisket Bardot. Then there's the new wine from Washington State called Marilyn Merlot. A few years ago I saw an aperitif in an Edmonton bar named after the Ayatollah Khomeni. It was called The Ayatollah Cola and the menu promised that it was "a drink that shows no mercy."

Anyway, the food in most celebrity restaurants is not important. You go to see famous people and dish the dirt, not dirty the dish. I hope you see them if you go. I can only dream.

Swallowing Conglomerates

f you have ever wondered if The Establishment is alive and well, or at least alive and eating, you have only to poke your head in the door of any of your city's downtown business restaurants.

Business restaurants are boardrooms with waiters instead of secretaries. Business people eat at them when lunching has little to do with dining. That is just as well. The food in business restaurants usually tastes as if it is cooked by comptrollers.

Eateries that attract expense-accounted lunchers often dress up like private clubs. Panelled, cloistered and decorous, they are designed to satisfy a hunger for power. For the price of lunch, a person can rent a table for a few hours and be treated as if he owned the place.

Business restaurants look the way banks did in the last century, except they have modern electric lighting. They are often hotel dining rooms, commonly interior spaces without windows. The lack of daylight lends the desired sense that the world outside is irrelevant to the vital discussions taking place at the tables in this important room.

If the walls aren't wood or rich, dark wallpaper, they are discreetly decorated in pale colours and hung with pictures you'll recognize: usually hunting scenes or landscapes. They are chosen on the basis of efficiency: once seen, they do not need to be noticed again.

Hy's Steak Houses are a string of boardrooms with food. Bastions of business, they embody all of the clichés of the mercantile lunch. At the Toronto location, the ambience is stately and posh. The walls are lined with hardcover books with earnest titles; the floor is covered with floral broadloom of the dark jewel colours traditionally associated with old wealth. The walls are dressed, the lighting is low and the large tables are laid with starched white cloths and classy napery. The customers wear worldly expressions and suits with power shoulders. Like the room, the customers radiate a feeling of solid permanence.

Some places are so clubby that preferred patrons have the same table reserved in their name every day at lunch and it is off limits to anyone else. The table is as secure as the family pew. When Winston's, the legendary Toronto business restaurant was run by John Arena (who retired in 1992), he ran it, unapologetically, like a private club using a system he called "controlled reservations." The dining room had twenty-three tables, eleven of which were permanently reserved from 11:00 a.m. to 2:00 p.m., Monday to Friday. All were in one section of the room, well away from the kitchen, facing the entrance, so comings and goings could be casually observed. At the best of them, the customer could see the room without the

29

rest of the room seeing him. At eleven on weekday mornings, Arena's secretary called the offices of the tables' tenants to see who was coming for lunch. The tables of those who declined were carefully dispensed to non-members. Sometimes, eventually, desirable casual customers were offered tables of their own. Being a member of the club had other benefits: Arena regularly arranged theatre tickets and babysitters.

In my experience, women appear at lunch in business restaurants like Hy's about as often as kiwi turns up on the menu at McDonald's. On the occasions I have been one of those women, I have felt as self-concious as I would wearing a bikini on Bay Street, even when I pay the bill and sign it with one of those fancy French fountain pens with the testosterone heft of a business gift. A regular at Hy's reports that when he takes a woman to lunch, they are seated at a small and inconspicuous table for two at the far wall of an inside room.

Perhaps the headwaiter means to provide privacy for the non-business business lunch (for more on that, see Lunch in the Afternoon). More likely, the woman is seated where her soprano voice will not distract the men from the baritone business of lunch.

Should the fellas wish female diversion, they may move into the cushy bar where, over the fireplace, hangs a huge oil painting of a reclining naked woman, facing forward, her ample body openly offered, the fingers of her right hand indicating that delicate spot the naughty French call "le paradis." That painting, in that setting, reminds me of those Impressionist oils of picnics, where the men are dressed formally and the women are not dressed at all.

At mealtimes in these lunch lodges, patrons are greeted by name; their coats are whisked away; they are seated in their special chairs. Their valued presence is acknowledged with discreet courtesy by all the staff. In many such establishments, patrons need not bother with menus, because their customary meals come automatically. I once saw a waiter accidentally hand a regular a menu—the all-seeing maitre d' ripped it quickly from the witless waiter's hand in horror, apologizing to the businessman for the *faux pas* of not recognizing that he was above such tedium.

Generally, the meals are as predictably conservative as the establishment dress code—nearly everyone eats steak or roast beef—the food generally associated with blood sports like business.

Food is the least important part of the business lunch. Lunchers don't like to have to think about what they order. Complicated menus are a distraction. Cute cuisine like goat cheese pizza and food you fiddle with like artichokes vinaigrette are out of place at a business lunch. So is bad food. "Bad food is distracting," a businessman told me. Ingredients should be of high quality. They should sound swanky on the menu. But the dish itself should cause no great palpitations. They may eat beef, but never bouef bourguignon.

Once they find the perfect dish, some business people order the same dish repeatedly, as former Prime Minister John Turner reportedly did with Winston's steak and tomatoes.

The business lunch is one of the few meals that has remained untouched through the entire food revolution. In nearly every other restaurant, red meat is

31

consumed cautiously, drinking is down and hard booze is rare, smoking is furtive, cigars are abhorred. But the dinosaur lunches can still be spotted at these club-style business restaurants: begin with martinis, follow through with slap-em-silly slabs of meat, and finish with a Scotch and cigar.

A glance around the room at Hy's reveals business-men huddled happily over hard liquor, eating red meat kilned to grey. No woman is making them eat anything green or drink anything without alcohol. They are like kids let out of school, happy among their own and relieved that the world—at least in this place for this time—finally feels right.

Wine is not a big item at the business lunch. One executive dismissed my question about whether knowledge about wine marks you as a sophisticate and confers status by saying: "Posturing about wine marks you as effete, possibly a fairy."

Once the food arrives, it should be ignored. Customers must be cool and unhungry. There is rarely any comment on the preparation of the food unless it is in passing. Apparently, the less you eat at a business lunch, the more cerebral you will appear. And with just a little patience, the irritating eating part of the meal will soon be over.

A businessman does not like to confess to allergies or any prissiness about the food. But for the rare, adventuresome eater, the business restaurant is the place to have his demands met: his smallest wish becomes the chef's mission. (In an ordinary restaurant for ordinary folk like thee and me, a chef might react to a customer's request for an adjustment to the menu as Beethoven might have responded if he were told to lighten up the Ninth.) But for the powerful, professional rigidity is routinely relaxed. The chef at the Queen Elizabeth Hotel's Beaver Club in Montreal has replaced the anchovies in steak tartare with caviar—a tacky transgression confessed to me with the what-can-you-do? shame.

I once tested Winston's to see if they provided different treatment to the ordinary and the privileged. At one meal I dined with another woman, anonymously at lunch. We hated the first table we were led to—in a back room near the pantry. Our protest won us seating in the room of the righteous, but in the wrong section, at the back. There was only one other woman. "What is your pleasure," the waiter begged to know, handing us a huge, hard menu. None of the tables around us had menus; ours made us feel like the tourists we were. My pleasure was cream of oyster soup followed by calf's liver. Hers was smoked capon followed by grilled salmon. He pressed some of the restaurant's signature pâté on us. The pleasure at nearly all of the tables around us was steak and baked tomatoes. We paid $102.42 for it, with two glasses of wine.

Later that week I extended a dinner invitation to a man I knew would be recognized. Arena spotted him, remarked on the length of time since his last visit, and swiftly moved us from the plebeian table where we had been placed to a favoured booth at the front of the front room. Arena interviewed my guest at length about our wishes, and effusively set about preparing a special dinner, cooking it tableside with a flame bright enough to read the menu by, had we needed to see one.

We started with a shared seafood risotto with enough protein in it to feed several villages in the

33

Third World; later, some Dover sole for the lady and lovely swordfish for the gentleman. At the end, he insisted we have a hot raspberry soufflé for dessert—although by then I was so full I wanted nothing more than to sleep in the soft velvet booth.

The waiter made a deep cut in the crusty top of the hot soufflé and poulticed it with heaps of fresh cream and raspberries. Dessert wine came with it. I wondered if they could hear me purring in the next booth. What a meal. At $96.60, what a price.

Membership has its privileges. And one of the best is ease of payment. Commoners like us pay at the end of the meal. Restaurant royalty leave on a handshake with the maitre d'. They are billed monthly, at the office, where presumably a secretary, who has dined on tuna salad on brown, takes care of the paperwork.

Each facet of the business lunch—the privileges, the look of the room, the food—are vital tools to the messages business people feed each other.

The business restaurant is the sort of place to go in order to show people that you can afford to go there. For that reason, high prices are an asset, suggesting the substance of the restaurant and of the host. Even if the food's not great, at least the prices are high.

I am further advised by my anonymous source on these matters, Deep Brief, that the restaurant must be conventionally mainstream and never madly eccentric. Anyone with a hope of succeeding in business would not take a lunch partner for a low-cost cuisine like say, dim sum. Deep Brief explains that business regards eccentricity with suspicion. (Business people seem to talk about "business" as if it's a real person who needs placating.)

34

Elsewhere, eccentricity may be regarded a sign of creativity, but business appears to find it somewhere this side of madness. Deep Brief warns: "To choose a flaky restaurant may bring your judgment on other matters into question."

Some define a good business restaurant by its tables. These must be large enough so that briefcases may be opened and notes taken without their edges being dipped in the butter.

More important than size is the table's distance from its neighbour. The space must promote a feeling of privacy, an assurance that you can't be overheard. "The single most important thing about any business restaurant is the configuration of the room. You must be able to talk without being overheard," according to one bank executive. "Confidentiality is everything in business," he whispers.

Some dining rooms manage to achieve a cloistered feeling like that of the "cone of silence" lowered over people's heads in the sixties TV sitcom "Get Smart." High-backed booths and deep banquettes, like the ones in posh hotel dining rooms, are used to achieve this effect. Winston's had cushy booths with the walls built at just the right height so conversation couldn't be heard from one to the other. Each table had its own telephone line. Tadich's Grill in San Francisco is loved for mealing and dealing because of the way tables are curtained off, a style duplicated in Toronto's Senator Steak House.

The business lunch requires a special kind of waiter. He (it is almost always a he) must have the discreet prowl of a panther and the pacing of a Sherpa. In the short and frantic hours of the business lunch, the waiter must serve two masters: the customer and the restaurant manager. The manager is keen to have him sell as much wine and booze as possible, which means he will be trying to pour your wine and coax you into a second Scotch at the same minute you and your guest are coming to the crucial point of the discussion.

The balancing act among manager, waiter and customer has tried the very best of lunch waiters. According to one veteran of the business lunch wars: "The cardinal rule of serving the business lunch is: don't rush them to order, or rush the meal. It has to be the customer's agenda. Business people order just to make the waiter go away. Usually at first they want a drink, fast, and then to be left alone. When they order, it must be quickly and without complication.

"Never, ever clear one diner's plate when the other is eating. It makes them feel like you're controlling their meal." The waiter advises that the way to get the best service is to "tell the server (before you order) what time you have to be out and let him or her pace the meal."

A good waiter knows that the bill must be brought as soon as it is requested: it makes business people crazy to have to wait for a bill once they've decided to go. However, if it's there before it's requested, people may, quite rightly, feel pressured to pay up and clear out.

A financial adviser says, "The business lunch is about status: who you are seen with, doing what and where are vital information in business. You can send signals that way, so you must be careful."

The happy businessmen with their Scotch and steaks contrast with the eat-for-success gurus who insist that what you order and how is vital for business success. They argue that the food may be seen as a metaphor for the way you conduct business. If the message is fiscal restraint, people may choose cheaper dishes, hoping to be regarded as moderate and fiscally responsible.

In Hollywood, the business lunch is virtually scripted. Anne Thompson, Los Angeles-based reporter for the *New York Times*, has written that "...nobody in the entertainment industry ever orders anything they might actually enjoy; it's raw vegetables, grilled fish and no martinis." She points to the running gag in Robert Altman's movie *The Player*, in which the main character orders a different bottle of designer water at each meal. An industry executive tells her, "The message is, 'I'm a lean, mean, business machine and this is how I do business.'"

The distance travelled for a meal confers status: the most important person travels least. There is sometimes an effort to deal with the issue by finding a restaurant in the middle, or one to which travel time is roughly equal for each party.

Although much has been made of the power breakfast, lunch is still the preferred business meal. There is structure in the ordering and progression of lunch. And it has the advantage of an easy end. ("Gee, is it really two o'clock? I have to go.")

Business people are cautious about the other meals: there is no pattern to breakfast, no conventional way of ordering the appetizer and main course so that coffee signals when the meal is at an end. Breakfast can feel rushed and bleary: time is tight in the morning. Furthermore, as one executive points out, "You can be a few minutes late for a lunch meeting, but breakfast business is all about efficiency and squeezing every second from a day. Arriving late for a business breakfast is an absolute no-no." In Europe, the idea of the business breakfast is considered uncivilized, and the practice is regarded as evidence of North American obsessive workaholism.

Dinner is equally unpopular as a business meal because it is difficult to end. "You can't really say at 9:00 p.m. that you have to go back to the office. As well, people want to drink too much at dinner and tell you about their personal lives," says Deep Brief.

Business dinners are usually based on obligation, when someone is visiting from out of town and you have to do the entertaining. For that reason, the business dinner often precedes a sports event. The Hot Stove Lounge in Toronto's Maple Leaf Gardens is frequently the site of these obligatory meals, because most of the tickets are sold to businesses that want to entertain clients and the tradition is to have dinner and go to a game. The male menu is beef, beef and beef. The vegetable selections offers fried onion rings.

People may also like to eat where they can be seen and be seen with. Making an entrance with someone may be like making a business statement. "You want the maitre d' to welcome you by name and say how glad he is to see you. It makes you seem important. That's why it's good to go to a restaurant where you are known. If other important people come over to your table to say hello it bolsters your credentials."

Unless you are among the privileged whose bill appears at the office and not at the table, the subliminal work of the business lunch is not done until the piper has been paid. There's even a strategy and philosophy about receiving the bill. "I don't look at the bill," says Deep Brief. "If there's a ten-dollar error, so what. Why spend a hundred and fifty dollars on a big lunch and then bicker for ten dollars? And never, ever, split the bill. It marks you as a rube."

Ultimately, the business lunch is not defined by what you eat or even what you talk about, but by how it's paid. "If the bill isn't tax deductible, it's not a business lunch," says Deep Brief.

"Who picks up the cheque is not the same as who pays. I may pick it up, but my firm pays. Or my firm may pay, then claim it, so the government pays."

His favourite lunch is when the other guy picks up the cheque, pays it, charges it to the government, and thanks him for the great meal.

Sweet Surrender

*N*ow that hard drugs and soft sex are forsworn, hedonists chasing a high have found a new naughtiness: desserts—luxurious, sloppy sense baths of sweetness. They are this decade's decadence.

Dessert-namers have lost no time in exploiting the notion with titles that read like X-rated movies: Chocolate Decadence, Lemon Escapade. I saw a cake called Better-Than-Sex Chocolate—in Edmonton, for God's sake. Maybe dessert isn't better than sex, but it might be a substitute. A woman bemoaning her single status reports her mother's advice: "If only you would look at a man the way you look at that cake."

Listen to the way people use words like sin, and accuse themselves of being bad when they eat dessert. (The chocolate mousse cake called Death by Chocolate suggests that the wages of sin have changed for the better.)

Twenty years ago, sweets were savoured silently, secretly, in circumstances as private as petting, and usually only amongst women at such carefully structured occasions like bridge parties and afternoon teas. Our pleasure turned these polite living rooms into the gastronomic equivalent of brothels. Everyone was having the same sensual pleasure, secretly pressing morsels of nuts and chocolate past our lips, rolling tiny treats around our cheeks, over our gums and under our tongues.

Sweets were smaller then, teensy, bitty things that could rest on a doily on a little china plate—nothing like the mammoth portions you need a fork-lift for nowadays. Melting Moments were a delicacy about as big as a ping-pong ball. They were a construction of hazelnut locked in crunchy meringue, their name derived from the way the meringue, connecting with a warm, wet tongue, melted in a moment. Roly poly had exotic Turkish Delight and an ethereal dusting of icing sugar. Either one of these could be secreted in one cheek, leaving your hands free to take an offered shortbread.

"I really shouldn't," we would say.

But we always did.

Now we are brazen, and restaurants are happy to lead us down the sweet garden path. They have dessert menus separate from the other courses— some are even printed on fancy scrolls, like the kinds used to announce prizes, and presented with the flourish that once was granted only to pricey wines. Waiters describe each sweet with a wink and a nudge, because dessert is the playful time of the meal. Diners who have worked through two courses large enough to feed a family, who need a third course like a fish needs a bicycle, protest weakly—for form— then order—for fun. It was always thought that women were the main customers for desserts. Waiters tell me that now men are, though they pretend they are ordering them for their wives.

"The men say 'no dessert'; then you put the menu in front of them. First they stare. Then they order. Why not? It's a cheap way of getting a rush."

At Scaramouche, a luxury restaurant in Toronto which has a dessert menu that reads as if it were authored by Dr Ruth, sometimes people order two. After a meal at Jo Jo's or Bouley in New York, how could you leave without trying the Melted Chocolate Cake (cake baked just until the outside is firm, it releases the molten, dark insides with the first prick of the fork) or the caramel constructions at The Cypress Club in San Francisco (walls of caramel candy form an architectural scaffold to the cream and nuts inside). "Desserts are our specialty," the waiter promises. And we nod, seduced.

Restaurants and coffee shops which specialize in desserts are among North America's most popular and successful restaurants. Even through the recession, as other eateries faltered and failed, the dessert/coffee shop flourished. The styles of these restaurants range from espresso bars with fancy desserts, or places that serve only desserts, to a plethora of every conceivable kind of doughnut shop. The amazing success of the doughnut shop also has spawned countless restaurants which trade on the popularity of the sweet: Donuts and Deli; Donuts and Subs are two in my personal collection of food odd couples.

It can't just be the apple-glazed cruller that is drawing the crowds. These coffee shops always seem to be full at all times even in the most unexpected location (including otherwise deserted industrial malls at night). Desserterias have taken over from nightclubs as the places we seek the sins of the flesh. At a small dessert/sandwich/coffee place in my neighbourhood, jazz concerts are held on weekends.

Throughout the western world there are people who have turned a favourite recipe into a home industry. One who turned dozens of them into an empire is Dufflet Rosenberg, who supplies Toronto restaurants with some of their best desserts. (The same restaurateurs who used to lie and tell you that their desserts were made by their sainted mothers are now happy to boast that their chocolate mousse cake comes from Dufflet's kitchens.)

Specialty cookbooks such as Maida Heatter's volume on chocolate and Rose Levy Beranbaum's cake collections have been among the best selling of all time. They are quoted, their recipes copied and doggedly followed.

In the eighties, dessert chefs became as famous as those who did the entrées, even more so than your Aunt Helen and her lemon pie. A head-hunting firm in England reported that top pastry chefs routinely demanded—and got—higher wages than those in charge of the main courses.

Students of cookery who seek special skills go to Tante Marie in San Francisco or Peter Kump's school in New York. San Francisco's Jim Dodge was renowned for his pecan torte with bourbon and his coconut cream pie. They were among the desserts that he produced when he was pastry chef at The Stanford Court Hotel. Joanne Yolles, of Toronto's

Scaramouche and a graduate of Tante Marie, offers Dodge's coconut cream pie, although she has long since wearied of it. But every time she tries to drop it from the card, customers howl. No wonder: it is a sweet cloud of coconut crunch and cream.

In the early part of this decade, the popularity of pies was boosted by the "Twin Peaks" television series. The investigator punctuated every observation with cherry pie and coffee, and sometimes he held meetings over a selection of pies. However, even that boost didn't bring pie to the level of popularity reached by tirimi su and crème caramel—the desserts you were most likely to meet on any urban menu in the eighties. Tirimi su is on its way to earning the name given crème caramel in Portuguese restaurants, where it is called 365 after the number of days it is served each year. Tirimi su, made with espresso-soaked ladyfingers and rich marscapone (an expensive rich cheese with the texture of face cream from Saks) may turn up stacked like a layer cake, or in an amorphous puddle like a loose trifle. When it's served in a stack, it reminds me of Black Forest cake, the dessert that seduced the sixties. How to tell the difference: tirimi su has no red cherry on top.

These days, restaurant tarts on the plate are as elaborately made up as tarts on the make. Every dessert is accessorized by a sauce—usually raspberry. (I have a theory that buried deep in the earth's core there is a reservoir of raspberry coulis and a pipeline from it to every restaurant in the western hemisphere.) There may even be two sauces undulating under the flashy sweets, sometimes in several colours—raspberry and chocolate, say—their contrasting hues spreading out to each side of the plate. If there is only one sauce, you can be sure it will be traced with a little line drawing in a contrasting colour. Hearts are a favourite decoration, as are chicken tracks, though some chefs drizzle the diner's initials in the sauce, the way your name is written on a birthday cake.

The decoration of dessert is the one legacy of nouvelle cuisine we not only tolerate but adore. Aureole restaurant in New York spins phantasmagorical sugar sculptures. Bits and splats of syrups drip across the plate; cocoa-dust freckles the rims. Dessert-plate art has been called "stick-up cuisine" because the shaky squiggles and splats make the plate look as if the chef was interrupted by a robber.

Some restaurants serve what is called the "composed dessert plate," which means that the item you ordered—a mousse, a piece of carrot cake or a bit of fruit—will arrive with lots of things you didn't order. But you will be delighted to see them: a clump of exotic berries, a slice of pound cake, a poached pear. The plate will be architecturally designed; some may look like Japanese flower arrangements. There may even be a joke or a story in the design, as in the naughty juxtaposition of two scoops of ice cream on either side of a long banana.

When desserts aren't arranged like murals or dusted like winter scenes, they are presented as retro comfort food in big bowls, like fantasy Moms used to make. (I say fantasy, because no one I know ever had a Mom like that at home. We just think everyone else did. In my day, in my home, canned peaches were dessert.)

Rice pudding, last seen in Greek diners of the sixties, reappeared fancied up in the eighties. Bread

45

pudding, a favourite of the English nursery set, turned up in upmarket North American restaurants, sometimes with booze that Mary Poppins would never have allowed.

Fashion has even threatened ice cream, and the taste for ice creams and funny fruit sorbets has reached a zenith. My neighbourhood restaurant sells sorbets of prickly pear, ugli fruit or passion fruit with red banana honey ice cream, and other upmarket add-ons. The wafer is replaced by an almond crisp; the canned fruit cocktail we used to spoon on our ice cream is now a berry preserve.

Titillating though they may be, they are not the point of ice cream. Its thrill comes from laying a creamy substance, frozen at 30°C, on a yearning tongue attached to a body with the interior temperature of 37°C. Flavours should be simple: vanilla made with real vanilla and lots of eggy cream; or chocolate, dark and luxurious. (The exception is pepper ice cream when it is made with fresh-ground black pepper and real vanilla; most of the flavours sold now aren't ice cream at all, but candy frozen into scoops.)

So after we tried many of the goofy ice creams in the early eighties, some of us began to ache for a return to the tastes we had known. Trend-sensitive restaurants began to supply them. New York's Stanhope Hotel served a three-scoop (vanilla, chocolate and strawberry) sundae; and the trendy Mesa Grill sold an ice cream sandwich at prices that once bought lunch at the soda fountains that inspired it.

Anyone who doubts that desserts are the signature of our times should have been at the fashion show presented a few years ago by a Toronto bakery, Desserts by Phipps. They presented their fall lineup as though it consisted of clothing instead of calories, each item held by a model gliding down a runway. The commentator touted the shimmer of their chiffons, the cleavage of their meringues.

Crème brûlée, crème caramel's crunchy cousin, is the dessert I will track into the next century. By that time, I expect to see it in a cornflake crust in a puddle of chocolate mint. In its original form, it is a dish of dense custard, top sealed under a translucent shell of caramelized sugar. You have to penetrate the crust to get to the cream—very symbolic that, and delicious. The crunch of caramel against the softness of cream is its glory. The play of contrasts is always the most dramatic for your palate. (Think of a scoop of vanilla ice cream with a hardening of chocolate. Dream of a chilled glass of wine in a tub of hot water.)

Contrary to its French name, the custard originated in England, apparently at Christ's College in Cambridge. Its origins may put to rest the reputation of the poor quality of both English food in general and college food in particular.

A caloric concentrate, the custard foundation is made like crème anglaise (your basic custard sauce), but with less sugar and more cream instead of the milk. Crème brûlée is now served in every flavour and combination; Bouley in New York has sold three; in various restaurants, I have tasted chocolate, coffee, strawberry, hazelnut and ginger, in and out of pastry, with cream on top and without. At Olives restaurant near Boston, chef Todd English bakes his brûlée in a scooped-out baby pumpkin, tops it with a cracking caramel crust and a splat of whipped cream. It is the best I can imagine, except maybe for Toronto caterer Dawn Berney's. She makes a killer custard with the highest butterfat cream she can find. When making a collection of brûlée for a party, she uses a small blowtorch to kiln the caramel crusts.

All over North America, dessert plates big enough to sleep two and feed ten are being served to one at the end of a three-course dinner. I think we would all be better off if restaurants offered just a sliver of those fantastic desserts for $1.50, instead of the skyscrapers for $5.00. That would be an act of mercy.

It is one of the ironies of our age that at the same time we eschew the teaspoon of oil on our grilled fish, we consume the equivalent of a tanker of butter when it comes to dessert.

There is an arrogance to people who order these big, boastful desserts. Though they seem to suggest a person out of control, the opposite is actually true; the eater is probably thinking, "I'm stronger than this huge dessert." In fact, they are ordering to assert how much in control they are.

Writer Barbara Ehrenreich thinks they get that moral strength from exercise. In her 1985 essay "Food Worship" she says, "Upscale people are fixated with food simply because they are now able to eat so much of it without getting fat, and the reason they don't get fat is that they maintain a profligate level of calorie expenditure. . . . Exercise is the yuppie version of bulimia."

Of course, there are as many theories to explain dessert lust as there are fat grams in a bucket of white chocolate mousse.

The suppression theory of sweet cravings holds that sugar lust is a substitute for the elusive sweetness of life, particularly the caramel pleasures of sex. This is a theory to fit the times. As casual sex gets scarier, for all of their dangers, desserts seem a safer sensual indulgence, recreation without risk, or at least with only temporary consequences.

Another theory holds that we turn to sweetness in times of bitterness. Restaurateur Bob Bermann of The Avocado Club in Toronto reported that dessert sales soared during the Gulf War. "We charted them. January 15 they started to go up and they fell off after it was over."

Of all the theories from fashion to sex that explain the popularity of desserts, the one that seems to be missing is the one that makes the most sense: the taste of desserts is fabulous.

Last Thanksgiving I was mesmerized by a pecan pie with a deep and buttery interior, a crust of perfectly roasted pecans, accompanied by a bottomless bowl of whipped cream. I ate my share, then I ate the share of the child beside me. It's hard to get happier than I was in those moments. There is no song like the song that sweet things sing.

Lewd
Food

High-yellow of my heart, with breasts like
 tangerines,

you taste better to me than eggplant
 stuffed with crab,

you are the tripe in my pepper pot,

the dumpling in my peas, my tea of
 aromatic herbs....

My hankering for love follows you
 wherever you go.

Your bum is a gorgeous basket brimming
 with fruits and meat.

nibblings from
"The Haitian Peasant Declares His Love"
by Emile Roumer,
translated by John Peale Bishop

The appetizing equation of food and sex is nothing new, but these lascivious times have raised our horny hungers to slobbering lust. The yellow pages of urban phone books decorate ads for escort services with pictures of food. Ice cream cones ooze suggestively while swollen tongues hang nearby to catch each drop. A flyer for an escort service in Manhattan draws clients with a luscious-looking woman licking a hot dog. The flyers are placed under the windshield wipers of cars parked near Yankee Stadium to redirect the thoughts of men who might have connected hot dogs with baseball. The best-selling sex guide, *The Joy of Sex: The Gourmet Guide to Lovemaking,* is named after the all-time best-selling cookbook, *The Joy of Cooking.* Sex has long been used to sell food, but the reverse is now promiscuously true: food is selling sex everywhere.

Some restaurant reviews ought to be edited by the vice-squad. In the heavy breathing of modern gastro-porn, chocolate mousse is described as "sinfully delicious," veal piccata is "orgasmic," boring old brown sauce is "hot velvet on the throat." American author Garrison Keillor says, "Sex is good. But not as good as sweet corn."

Are our sexual and our gastronomic appetites so intertwined? Oooh baby, yes! Yes!

Romantic negotiations have moved from the parlour to the table. In restaurants couples sit, their lips so close that the waiter can barely wedge a menu between them. And it's all happening while the soup gets cold.

None of this surprises Howard Boughey, associate professor of sociology at the University of Toronto. He thinks it's because simultaneous dentition (eating together) is sexier than sex. The professor says the partners are closer when they are sharing food than when they are sharing bedsheets.

"You see, physically their experiences are in tune," he says. "There's less difference between the male and female chemistry of eating than there is between them in the chemistry of lovemaking."

Anatomical and chemical differences may prevent men and women from enjoying the same feelings when they are making love, but not when they are eating. We all share the same equipment for processing food.

So when we put food in our mouths, our bodies react in unison, the professor believes. "He tastes. She tastes. He murmurs, 'This is good.' She murmurs back. He chews. She chews. He swallows. She swallows. Their two mouths are experiencing the same feelings, the same chemistry. It's very intimate."

"Yes of course," I say. "But more intimate than sex?"

"Absolutely," Professor Boughey insists. "In fact, I would say that couples are closer in the moment of simultaneous dentition than in the moment of coition."

I take the question to bistro owner George Gurnon, because the traditional keepers of food and romance are the French. He will not commit himself on the food-sex comparison for intimacy, but reports that plenty of both go on in his establishment. He often has to avert his gaze from tables where there is more steam rising from the chairs than from the soup. "It can be very embarrassing. But only to the staff. The couple couldn't care less."

I know what he means. In restaurants, my attention is often diverted from my food to people satisfying other appetites at other tables. I am sorry to say that sometimes what they are doing seems more interesting than what is on my plate. For example, I couldn't take my eyes off the mating meal at a nearby table at Mustard's restaurant in the Napa Valley in California. Riveted by the parry and thrust of the pair's mutual feeding, I could hardly swallow a bite all evening. They were making a honeymoon of dinner. First, they teased with appetizers: a whole elephant garlic, baked soft with olive oil. He fed her a clove at a time, releasing each from its papery container, squishing it onto a crisp bit of toast and coaxing it into her mouth. She answered with a spoonful of cornmeal stuffing, first prying it from its roast chili nest, then teasing it back into his mouth. They continued thus on their pornographic path, consummating the meal with polenta and goat cheese, the melting goat cheese draping the supple polenta.

There was as much activity under the table as there was on top. Her feet, freed of shoes, stretched out, her toes snuggled into his crotch. Their above-the-table demeanour suggested everything was normal, although it seemed hard for the fellow to hide the colour that crept into his face when her toe suddenly found its mark.

Gurnon says that some diners should be X-rated because they cross the line between propriety and passion. A glass of wine is sometimes all they need to forget that eating is public and sex is private. "Their hands meet across the table and they continue from there. Their passion takes over and that's it for dinner. Sometimes they pay the bill and leave, but other times the dining room becomes an extension of the bedroom. It starts with a long, languid kiss. Believe me, I've seen it."

Gurnon says this kind of behaviour is worse in hotel dining rooms, which get whole schools of spawning couples. Apparently the knowledge that bedrooms are nearby seems titillating, suggesting a dessert that is not on the menu.

"When I managed a hotel dining room, there was this one couple who didn't even finish the bread basket before they called me over and asked if the meal could be served upstairs," Gurnon says. "We served it course by course, always giving enough time between. We waited until he phoned down for each course before we took it up. Even then, the waiter waited a long time at the door after he knocked, to give them time to pull themselves together.

"With each course, the intervals between the knock and the answering got longer and longer. By dessert, they didn't answer the door at all."

Room-service waiters learn to be very good actors. They know about timing orders and realize that the timbre of the knocking should be just loud enough to be heard without being intrusive. If they are admitted to the room, they must learn how to set up dinner and open a bottle of wine while remaining poker-faced and never acknowledging the flushed cheeks and bothered bedsheets. A hotel employee once told me that the best room-service waiters are those who see nothing, hear nothing, and later tell all.

The food of romance is no mere backdrop. It is the symbolic essence, the seductive tool, the meaty metaphor for love. There should be no need for words. The plat du jour may be all the chat du jour that is required.

Sociologists point out the primitive patterns from which we take our cues: in the animal kingdom the male brings a morsel of food to his intended to tempt her taste buds onto other branches of nourishment. And they point to modern times when human suitors—male and female—present boxes of chocolates, the hard and soft centres suggesting better things to come.

The endorphin theory holds that chocolate stimulates the centres of the brain that make you feel happy and sexy. It is called a theory because no one can say for sure that it is true: it's just an example of all the wishful research that has been done on specific foods as aphrodisiacs. For millennia people have taken to swallowing juniper berries, garlic, the intestines of sperm whales and ground beetles (now there's a turn-on). Still, there has been little success in making the science of nutrition serve the art of love.

The food that works best is the food that turns on your imagination. For a psychological view, I consulted a psychiatrist who sometimes counsels couples. She said, "What works is what you think will work. The head is the most important sex organ."

Perhaps some are aroused by Jell-O because it jiggles so suggestively. Molluscs and oysters have traditionally been thought of as aphrodisiacs because they are suggestively shaped and are squirmy and slippery. Warm custard is believed to have a soothing effect on men, its soft milkiness making them vulnerable and reminding them of childhood. The psychiatrist calls this The Edible Complex.

Some dishes are arranged to be visually suggestive. Jane and Michael Stern's cookbook *Square Meals* offers lovers a candlelit cake with a pineapple ring and a banana in its centre, the fruit tumescent with mayonnaise.

But imaginative lovers can make of foods what they will. A woman thinks that spaghetti served to a loved one suggests bondage, while another may lose her heart to the slippery seduction of hoummous. Spaghetti is not a dish often used in romance because negotiating its strands can be cumbersome and tomato sauce on the eyelid is a distraction. Couples in the early stages of seduction are usually very conscious of how eating makes them appear to the object of their affection. One young woman described her courtship this way: "It was in the earliest days when we were still eating pizza with a knife and fork."

I have favoured soup as a good first course, but obviously not soup with long noodles in it. Soft sensual mixtures that can be pressed against the palate often provide the best fodder. The texture of food becomes very acute to the horny—unless an argument arises and the food turns to ashes in the mouth.

The psychiatrist says she and her boyfriend favour the artichoke as their personal billet doux. "You don't eat them as much as undress them. You pull their leaves apart, taking each in your mouth, stripping it. You do this one leaf at a time, working your way into the interior of the flower to its soft, giving heart."

Professor Boughey says attitudes are revealing: "Lovers can tell a lot about their partner's sensuality by the way they eat their food. What you want to say is, 'What I'm doing to this chicken thigh is what I would like to do to yours.'" He and I toyed with some categories of lewd food.

Any food that must be dug out of crevices with the fingers: lobsters are lovely. So is watching someone coax the buttery, soft stuffing from the interior of a golden roast chicken.

Though the bird's suggestive posture—legs akimbo and all—might make some men drool into their soup, I find that the act of tearing off the legs can suggest an inappropriate savagery. I feel the same about the skewered and grilled chicken hearts offered by the delicatessen down the street.

But the professor argues that aggression can be stimulating and adds a further category of action foods: those that require ripping, tearing, and movement of the mouth and arms. This includes loaves of bread that must be torn apart before they are shared or meat that must be ripped from the bone with the teeth, rather than cleanly sliced with a knife.

He comments as well on the seductiveness of dripping foods: the sight of butter glistening on an intended's chin would incline a suitor to lick it off. (I wondered if it might incline the suitor to hand the intended a towel and call a taxi.)

The style of food is important because heavy foods are antithetical to lovemaking. That may be why breakfast is the one meal never used for courting: who would want to get into bed after Eggs Benedict? (Breakfast is also too intimate to act as the backdrop for ending a romance. Dinner is too suggestive: the night and a couple of drinks may slacken your resolve. Lunch is where you say goodbye.)

Contrasts between textures are very evocative and mean that some dishes you might otherwise scorn as chaste can fit the bill. Cheese soufflé and crème brûlée are metaphors for mating because both have crispy outer shells that yield creamy soft interiors.

The traditional romance of the French restaurant may be based on rich sauces that are at once soothing and seductive. Spicy ethnic foods are stimulating because the blast on the mouth sets up reactions that mirror emotion: the lips tingle, you suck in air, tears come to your eyes. If the food is intensely spicy, the eater pleads for release from an onslaught of stimuli. Here, note how talk about food comes close to sex talk. "How does that feel?" "Is it good?"

Sharing an affection for the harvest with the author of the poem quoted above, the professor suggests that soft, ripe, blushing fruits end the meal. But everyone agrees that if you have been heeding the advice thus far, dessert shouldn't be necessary.

Lunch in the Afternoon

I have learned that every weekday noon, people everywhere are engaging in a meal that doesn't fit into any of the four food groups. Commerce might be the excuse, but the reality is romance. The women's movement has been a boon to the practice, because now men and women can be seen lunching together without an eyebrow being raised. The woman might easily accept the invitation without knowing its subterfuge. The message comes with his courtliness. That message is: Me Man, You Woman. An unexpected invitation brought this to my attention.

In my line of work, I am accustomed to asking people out for lunch. I usually choose the restaurant, order the food and pay the bill. The people who eat with me seem content to have me do so.

On this occasion, the man who suggested lunch preferred that he take charge. I, happy to be spared the effort, became curious about him. He had been a topic of conversation among my fellow workers. He was worldly in a suave, mature way—in his sixties, we guessed. We speculated on the contrast between

59

his sophisticated demeanour and his apparently conventional family life.

When he and I met in the restaurant he chose, we didn't discuss any of this, of course. Our conversation was notable for the safety of its topics—the appalling state of the economy, the worrisome state of the restaurant business. From avocado mousseline until Spanish coffee I learned no more about his personal life than I knew before we met.

Yet the encounter seemed remarkably personal in its chivalrous tone. He was courtly in a traditional way—the way I imagine that women were taken out for a meal before the Dutch treat made it all so egalitarian. For all the lunches, breakfasts and dinners I have shared, it struck me that I never get taken for lunch that way—or dinner for that matter. He made the decisions: the place (pleasant, continental-style, furnished with male waiters), the table (large, clothed and well-appointed), the wine (good quality, ordered without fuss).

Once he had consulted the menu and me, he instructed the waiter on my behalf: "The lady will have the mousseline, roast beef, followed by the crème brûlée, and I will have the same."

I was surprised at how much I was enjoying this passé style. At the end of the two-hour meal, there was no question that he would pay the bill. It seemed clear that there was no way to even raise the issue. When we left the restaurant, he guided me with his hand just brushing the small of my back, and, as he put me into a taxi and gave the driver my destination, he handed me a small silk flower.

And that was that. We thanked each other for the lovely lunch, we both expressed our wish to do this again soon. But we never did and I thought no more of it. Well, not much anyway.

A few weeks later, I ran into a woman I knew through work, just as I was returning to the office from lunch. She was flushed, happy. She was carrying a small silk flower in her hand. When I remarked on her obvious pleasure, she said, "Oh, I just had lunch with ———."

It was him. Then I knew: ——— is a married man who lunches, "dating" at the safe meal. But to what end? Sex? Companionship? Just lunch?

Of course, I was fascinated. I began a sort of mini-poll—surveying other men. None of them admitted to engaging in the practice, but each of them assured me that he knew men who did. I was surprised at the expertise each had on the subject.

"It's perfect, don't you see?" said one man I surveyed. "A man lunching a woman on the excuse of business doesn't risk rejection. He can take her out a few times, have her full attention, have a nice conversation and if it never leads anywhere, he has had a nice time. Of course, there's always that chance that it will lead somewhere. Then Bingo! These days *she* might be the one to suggest it. That's what I mean about the rejection. If a guy lunches a number of women, there's bound to be a sexual harvest. It's perfect, just perfect."

According to a stockbroker in his forties:

*L*unch is the new hunting ground for businessmen. It's therapy, a way to express intimacy in a setting that's contained and safe—that seemingly doesn't affect your family or your own vulnerability. It's a safe way to explore possibilities and intimacy. For a repressed businessman, it's a way of keeping the lid on. That's it exactly. Lunch keeps the emotional mercury from spilling over.

A successful editor, married for twenty years, says:

The sham lunch has all the advantages of love in the afternoon, but without the remorse. There is no commitment and it has an easy ending because you have to go back to the office.

Lunch is the most dangerous meal because it comes in disguise. It can look just like a business meal and the real agenda is easily hidden. It's like the difference between a uniformed guard and a spy: the spy is scarier because he is hiding his purpose from you. If I invite a woman out for dinner, she might reasonably expect romance and sex, but not necessarily at lunch.

An old friend believes that:

The long lunch is inherently wicked. It's time stolen from the responsibilities of the day. The stage is set for sin.

It's for professional people who set their own schedules and can abandon the afternoon. The most dangerous time of the meal is afterwards, on the walk back to the office. Even though nothing may have been said at lunch, on that walk one may say, "Let's take the long walk through the park."

Nice days are deadly. There's that sense of abandon.

The overwhelming proportion of men in my survey appear to be resolved that the non-mercantile lunch is really about sex, that it's an interview technique when the man is looking for a partner. But during my research, I found one man who disagreed. He believes that the purpose of the lunch is romantic, though the romance may exist only in his fantasy. While the subtext may be sexual and romantic, the mealtime encounter may be as far as it goes. He claims lunch is a satisfying adventure in itself. He is happy to have the romance end there—outside the office, outside the rest of each partner's personal life.

He revealed that he lunched all the time, that he had been doing it for years. He agreed to tell all over lunch.

He chose a hushed hotel dining room near his office in Toronto. The room was big, the service discreet. He ordered venison, I ordered fish. I paid, he talked.

L unch is a way of having an intimate conversation with a woman in the daytime without worrying about what time you're getting home. It makes a gap in the middle of the day that I need to bring me down to earth. My days are very intense and I don't want to have to work at lunch or be phony.

I enjoy women's company more than I enjoy men's. By far. The conversations are more interesting to me—they are not necessarily about sports or business. There's an intimacy to them. Conversations with women wind up being about feelings, more emotional. They aren't at arm's length, as they are with a man.

There are things you can't talk about with your wife that you can with another woman. Lunch with a woman can be a venting process as well.

I avoid places that exude business, like hotel dining rooms, health club restaurants or real yuppie places that are bright, open and have plants all over the place. They're not soft or intimate. The environment I want has no constraints, visually or atmospherically, on where the conversation might go. I like steak houses sometimes, because they're dark. They usually have white tablecloths and the tables are far apart so you can talk without feeling someone is listening.

I wouldn't choose a very expensive place, because a place like that would raise expectations too high. Sometimes a woman feels that if you take her to a really expensive place, you are expecting a good return on your investment. It could make her cautious.

The first lunch might be at a business-like restaurant, then, the next time I'll suggest a more romantic, intimate place. Changing the style of restaurant like that sends a message to her. It's also a hell of a fast way for me to find out if she's interested. I wouldn't go to the more intimate restaurant for a real business lunch with a woman. It would be too threatening because the presumption of intimacy would make both of us uncomfortable.

There is an atmosphere in places that are good for these kinds of lunches: they tend to attract people who are there for their own purposes, rather than to be seen or to see who else is there. There needs to be a feeling of privacy.

There has to be room between tables to permit a personal conversation and to give you a sense of space from other people in the room if the conversation gets intense.

Lunch would usually be about one and a half hours. The process goes along for at least a year, but that depends on what happens. Often, nothing happens sexually, or even if it does, it's not for the longest time. It's a long, slow process that I find thoroughly enjoyable. It's the way things were before everybody just went to bed right away. Because it's without pressure there's time for soft feelings to develop.It's actually much better than dating. If you're dating, there's a shorter term expectation than if you're having lunch.

How you order is important—it's part of the way you convey feeling. I like to order something luxurious as a signal to her. You don't want the feeling of withholding pleasures, of disciplined eating, because that is the opposite to the feeling you want between you, the free feeling that will let you talk. Ordering sparse food makes you feel that restraint is the tone, and you don't want that.

I usually order a steak. It's decisive and tells her that she can have something bad, so she might order something with a sauce, or a dessert. Being free to do that makes us both feel unconstrained and undisciplined. That affects the conversation. It's hard to speak freely if the lead-up in ordering has been structured and disciplined.

You have to work quite hard in an hour and a half to bring the conversation from the impersonal—work, movies, etc.—to the personal. You have to cross the bridge from third-party conversation to first-person personal. It's hard sometimes, and the food and wine can help.

I always order wine immediately and wait about half an hour before ordering lunch so we can sit and talk. One bottle of wine is much better than two separate drinks: it's softer, more sensitive than hard drinks. Besides, you share a bottle, pour for one another, or it's poured for the two of you by the waiter. Wine is more emotional than hard liquor and a glass of wine poured from a bottle you share has more feeling in it than a diluted spritzer.

I never try to impress her with my knowledge. The kinds of feelings I'm talking about don't happen when someone needs to show off in a restaurant—ordering the waiter around, showing off with wine or food. Posturing is a killer to intimacy. The posturing guy wants all the attention on him. For this to work, the focus has to be on each other.

In an odd sort of way, you want the same kind of service that you'd want for a real business lunch. Efficient but non-interfering. You don't want the waiter breaking in at the exact moment you've finally started talking. You want that to be background—not someone hovering and constantly asking how everything is.

Anonymity is crucial. The waiters should act as if they don't notice you at all or have any sense that what is happening at the table is anything other than cool business talk.

A good restaurant, like the one that I go to, never shows any sign they recognize me. I hate it when the maitre d' addresses me by name at the door. They think they are flattering me, but in fact it pisses me off. I think she'll think that I'm there every day and there's nothing special about this.

I first began lunching in the last months of my marriage, about ten years ago. I was looking for an affair, thinking that would take the pressure off my unhappiness, but I was afraid to have one. Taking someone I was attracted to out to lunch was perfect. It was like dating, but without having to make any decisions. That caused me to take a real look at my marriage and to contrast the disparity between the intimacy you feel at lunch with the intimacy I felt in my marriage.

If you fall into something over a period of time, it's different than if you're proactive. I fall in love having lunch with people. There is always that potential. I knew someone who lunched with a woman for twelve years. When his marriage broke up they got together.

I can tell immediately by looking at the people if the lunch is really just business—by their body language. Their heads are a little closer together; sometimes they both reach for the salt at the same time—there's more look of unity between them than if it's non-personal.

I believe this is something an older man can do better—or at least someone who knows who he is in his career and has his feet planted on the ground. A thirty-year-old man is too anxious to have a sexual conquest; he doesn't see the intimacy as the goal in itself.

You can't use my name. Or else I'll never be able to have lunch in this town again.

The cynicism of the men I interviewed was directly opposite to the yearning this story engendered in women—mostly married women, I might add. They loved the idea that their company was inherently valuable just because they were women and allowed him to give vent to his "soft feelings." Their—or should I say our—hunger seemed to be for a man who is not avoiding intimacy but seeking it. He is the guy for whom the candlelight dinner for two was invented, where the talk is more deliciously satisfying than the food. One woman got misty-eyed at the thought of it; another said softly: "A man like that must really understand a woman's heart." A third simply said: "Give me his phone number."

Looking at Cooking

When restaurants emptied at the beginning of the nineties, economists blamed the recession. But I am wondering if what really happened is that everyone suddenly decided to cook at home with the equipment and cookbooks they had been collecting since the seventies. That's when we began to stockpile as if there was going to be a war: duck presses, blowtorches, industrial ranges and cold-storage units big enough for all the fur coats in Montreal.

We bought acres of stuff that could be used only one time for one thing. Did anyone ever find a second use for the laughable fondue set? Or for the divided artichoke plate with separate indentations for the tooth-scraped leaves? Even the famed Cuisinart is suspect. Most people never learned how to use it properly, with the result that most of us have been eating baby food for two decades of its popularity. The food processor was to cooking what the pill was to sex. It made things easier, but not necessarily better.

The pride of my personal collection is an electric

hot-dog cooker that heats by shooting an electric current through the length of the wiener. Once the wiener has been impaled on two metal prongs, the executioner flips the switch, the wiener quivers for a minute, then goes limp and sizzly. I notice that a variation on this appliance also executes the hot-dog bun. It is just another unique-purpose appliance destined for the gourmet graveyards of tomorrow.

To put all these appliances to use, we also bought mountains of cookbooks—on everything from Zen breakfasts to the haughtiest of haute. The books may take up less space than the appliances, but they whisper the same message: "Don't just sit there, cook creatively." The whisper became a chorus.

In the eighties, food editors in North America could hardly see daylight for the stacks of new cookbooks in their offices. In 1989 alone, the major publishers sent out more than a thousand new titles, just a portion of the total that included books from small publishers, fund-raisers, and the man down the street who wanted to tell the world about his way with bread.

I have penned a couple of recipes in my time—couldn't help it really. If you write about food or eating—especially if you are a woman who writes about food and eating—editors inevitably expect you to include a recipe or twelve among the words.

Writing recipes for publication is much different from trading them at a dinner party. Behind each printed recipe is someone who ran to the store for the groceries, measured each of the ingredients, tried the recipe, tried it again, and wrote down each step along the way. And cleaned up the kitchen. The recipe had to be typed, checked for meaning (does "two eggs beaten separately" mean you beat one whole egg and then the other or that you separate the yolks and whites, then beat each?), checked for accuracy, then rechecked in galleys.

The accuracy of each number, no matter how minuscule, and each letter is crucial. There is no measuring the chaos that can be caused by the most minor mistake. My experience has been that people who will forgive egregious failings of character in life, turn satanic if you goof in a recipe. Spell a name wrong in a news story and few will bear a grudge, but slip a digit in a cookie recipe, and life becomes a living hell. Who can blame the victim who has lost time and ingredients—expensive ones, if they've included stuff like shellfish, pure chocolate (or, given today's prices, more than a single egg)?

I once wrote a recipe for gingerbread that produced a material with a density usually reserved for bomb shelters. There was no quelling the tide of fury that issued from readers across Canada, people who had spared a few minutes from busy Christmas preparations to make and feed the stuff to their trusting children.

So I sympathize with author Carole Walter who put the wrong kind of flour in a cake recipe in an otherwise lovely dessert cookbook called *Great Cakes*. A later edition bore a sticker announcing that it was the "corrected version," a kind of exhibition of her shame comparable to the scarlet letter once affixed to an adulteress. But mistakes can happen to the most experienced testers. In 1992, *Gourmet* magazine sent letters to subscribers and issued press releases and reprints after an ingredient that was potentially poisonous slipped into an innocent cookie recipe.

The hazard of writing a reliable recipe is that other people will rip it off and claim it as their own. The issue of copyrighting recipes is often feverishly fought. The notion that recipe writing is a craft and the tendency to undervalue it as a profession has fuelled the wrath of cookbook writers, who know what it takes to develop and test a new dish. The hotter the fashion for cookbooks, the hotter the debate has become.

Once a baked dessert is part of a community, it is very hard to ascribe ownership of the original. Such disputes are usually kept within families (I know I had that coffee cake for the first time at Trevor's, and blood might be drawn over whether the hard sauce was inspired more by Aunt Sally or Uncle Frank), but the monetary value of these recipes in modern times has brought these disputes into the courtroom. In the late eighties, two U.S. corporate giants endured a bitter legal battle over the origins of a cookie that was crispy on the outside and chewy on the inside. Each side claimed the right to copyright the cookie. And so a search for the cookie's origins was on. It was finally traced to a small Mennonite community in rural Ontario—the community whose recipes author Edna Staebler has been recording for years in her books *Food that Schmecks* and *More Food That Schmecks*. After several years of legal wranglings, her testimony helped settle the case, and as I write this, the story is being dramatized by Toronto filmmaker Gail Singer in a movie called *The Cookie Wars*.

A real cookbook junkie can tell, just by reading, whether a recipe is worth trying. Good ones "taste" that way in the reading. See "granulated garlic" in a list of ingredients, and there's a dry feel at the back of the throat, just as "fresh" makes your mouth think it's just had a spring-water rinse.

Some of the world's worst recipes have the names of celebrities and politicians attached to them. Politicians who barely see their kitchen tables and have had about as much practice with food as I have with a filibuster (isn't it filled with red jelly and served in the morning with coffee?) are often asked to contribute to fund-raising cookbooks. There is great comedy in *The Meech Lake Soup Cookbook* (take Jane Crosbie's recipe for seal flipper pie—please!) and the *Blue Book*, a dusty collection of recipes from Progressive Conservative members of parliament. When politics is the spice, the names of the dishes have more flavour than the food. The menu at a fund-raising banquet made mock of political parties, serving Chicken Catch-A-Tory and N. D. Pea soup, claiming the soup was free, but the croutons expensive.

Even athletes are in on it these days. Swimmer Mark Tewksbury, gold-medal winner at the Barcelona Olympics, presses on us his recipe for beef. "When I eat red meat, it really helps my performance," he assures us, as if we wanted to argue the matter.

Ingredients and recipes have their fashions. One of the world's most honoured cookbooks is by Alice B. Toklas, companion of Gertrude Stein. It's most famous for its hashish fudge. Originally thought quite daring, these days the truly sinister dish might not be the fudge with the hallucinogen but the cholesterol-laden Oeufs Francis Picaba. The recipe calls for eight eggs, which are broken into a bowl and mixed well with salt but no pepper. They are poured into a saucepan—not a frying pan—and turned over a low flame, with the slow addition of very small quantities of no less than a quarter-pound of butter (and more if you can bring yourself to do it). It takes a full half-hour to prepare this dish, and the eggs aren't scrambled, but because of the butter (no substitute accepted) they have a consistency that Toklas admires as "suave...that perhaps only gourmets will appreciate."

Current stacks of dessert cookbooks are balanced by a mountain of diet cookbooks—more each year as our fascination with "lite" eating continues unsated. While diet dessert books have pitched their low-fat woo, sales have been low, likely because readers want a dessert to be naughty. On the other hand, a book that flaunted its contempt for the health movement sold well. *The Bad For You Cookbook* is full of passé preservatives and wicked fat.

One reason the cookbook stacks are so high is that most people think they have at least one cookbook in them. This probably began with *The Joy of Cooking*, which is based on the recipes that Irma Rombauer's mother turned over to her, and which has outsold the Bible, achieved mythic status, and sparked hope in the heart of every cook able to put pen to paper. (And given the desktop publishing revolution now under way, it's a good bet the number of attempts won't decrease any time soon.)

Although it has not been revised since 1975, *Joy* continues to sell well. But the mainstay of the food revolution is *The Silver Palate Cookbook*, named after the small New York catering firm where it began. The Silver Palate book can be credited with making the exotic commonplace, having caught the imaginations of the eighties' eating epoque, probably because it had the temerity to list wild rice under "Basics." The chicken in raspberry vinegar is a staple of the gourmet movement, while chicken Marbella (with prunes) is now traded in the same way meatloaf with onion soup mix was in my mother's time. The fame of the dish is international: when I tried to surprise a Los Angeles visitor to Toronto with The Marbella (as it is familiarly called), she said, "It's better cold."

Next time I'll cook her something from an Alberta cookbook, like *The Best of Bridge*, maybe frozen peanut butter pie or crunchy fish, which gets its texture from corn chips. The Calgary publishing company of the same name began as a hobby for a group of women who collected the recipes that they served at weekly bridge meetings. Their husbands thought the project was cute, until the first years of "cute" netted a million dollars. The success of the series is more noteworthy than the recipes they contain.

Jean Paré's Company's Coming Publishing Ltd. in Calgary rakes in nearly seven million dollars a year, also from a series of cookbooks which are sold in spin racks in corner and hardware stores. Each has its own theme (cookies, salads, squares), its own colour (fuchsia, turquoise, purple) and each features a photo of Mrs Paré wearing a blouse colour co-ordinated with the cover.

My grandmother fed a family of seven with no cookbook; my mother fed six with one: *The Settlement Cookbook*. I have hundreds of cookbooks. I order dinner in. Because I would rather collect and read cookbooks than use them, I buy cookbooks with unappetizing recipes, the ones that never make me want to get up and try something. The best is probably *Entertaining with Insects*, a one-hundred-page paperback book that gives a whole new meaning to "good grub."

Even people who can't cook feel the need to write a cookbook. In the course of building my collection, I spoke with a man in Minneapolis who was planning his first cookbook, *The World's Horrible Recipes.* The book was to be aimed at people who hated to cook and failed miserably whenever they tried. Michael Nelson's philosophy was "It's better to succeed at being a bad cook, than fail at being a good one." He felt that he was making a contribution to food literature. "There's no other cookbook on the market that offers this self-help. Most cookbooks shy away from bad recipes." He expected to find a unique position in the marketplace because "people can buy cookbooks of good recipes any old time."

Nelson's list of recipes already included hamburger Jell-O, minnow cookies (fold minnows gently into batter), liver pudding and wiener-water soup. None of the recipes will be tested. "I may be a crummy cook, but I'm not a fool," he said.

I will buy his book as soon as it's out. It will go to the top of my stack.

But I can't match Diane Watson and Doris Eisen, who are real cookbook collectors: Watson has more than 2,000 cookbooks, but she can't say for sure because she doesn't count them ("Who sits and counts their books?" she wonders). She also tries to avoid cooking, and collects books for the love of reading and collecting. Eisen owns 4,500 cookbooks and still dedicates her spare time to her restless search for the perfect home-made croissant. For some, the search for the best recipe is the reason they buy. To them cooking is a craft and a recipe is a method of polishing it.

"Eisen once brought in an absolutely fabulous croissant," reports Alison Fryer, manager of The

Cookbook Store in Toronto, supplier to collectors like Eisen and Watson. Toronto's Cookbook Store has been there for ten years, thriving, while other stores succumbed to apathy and recession.

But like many of The Cookbook Store's other clients, Watson never cooks, and eats out as often as she can. She finds nothing inconsistent in her collecting books about cooking. Cookbooks and cooking equipment aren't so much about food as they are about collecting. An alien visiting this planet would think that people buy cookbooks for reading and gadgets for storing.

We collected all these cookbooks and gadgets and then we went out for dinner. Ironically, the percentage of our food dollars spent on eating outside the home increased dramatically during the same decade that we were collecting.

Of course the most gripping recipes are those that are talked, not written: recipes traded with the testimonials for their goodness. I like to think of the practice as mouth-to-mouth recitation.

One of my favourite places to find these recipes is at Weight Watchers' meetings, because the deprived talk about food with a hunger no cookbook can match.

This one is from an area manager whose family lived in Montreal near restaurants that sold that city's fabulous smoked meat, but who couldn't afford to eat at any of them. She remembers: "My mother would ask the owners for the ends of the corned beef briskets that were too small for making sandwiches. She would carry them up to our tiny apartment and put them into a pan with a pile of sliced onions. Then she would sauté them. Now I know this sounds weird,

77

but just listen. She'd add a can of tomato soup and the juice from a jar of gherkins. Then she'd put the lid on the pan and let it all bubble away for a bit until the fat from the smoked meat melted through the onions and flavoured the tomato soup. You can't imagine how good it was."

The homey comforts of the talked recipe is partly behind our enchantment with cooking shows on television that have increased in popularity since Julia Child first dropped an onion on the floor of the set in the sixties. In Canada we started even earlier, mesmerized by the Kraft commercials and the mellifluous voice of announcer Bruce Marsh asking that we: "take two bags of miniature marshmallows, melt and mix with a large jar of crunchy peanut butter." The commercials were as entertaining as the drama they sponsored.

Entertainment is still the message of cooking shows. We remember Julia Child's various series not so much for the complicated recipes but for her husky big voice and her calming way. People who quickly abandoned her recipe for chocolate mousse, long remembered how she would pick up ingredients that had fallen on the floor, dust them off and mix them in. The Galloping Gourmet was a hoot with his glass of wine and one-liners. We loved watching him invite someone from the audience to try his dish at the end of the show, even if we never cooked the recipe. The modern cooking guru is Jeff Smith, The Frugal Gourmet, a former preacher who delivers his gastronomic sermons with evangelical commitment. We watch the singing Italian, Madhur Jaffrey's travelogues on India and "Yan Can Cook"—all for the fun of watching. At the end of any of them, I usually remember only enough to realize that it sounded good, and am hard pressed to remember exactly how to cook the dish. Obviously that's why some of them offer a box number where serious cooks, not just cooking voyeurs, can get the recipe.

Historically, of course, talked recipes came before books. The laying out of recipes in print was a departure from the oral tradition. My grandmother from Russia couldn't read or write, so she learned only those recipes that were told to her. They used few ingredients and few techniques. The long-winded recipes we see now are a luxury of a literate society and almost unlimited choices.

Ironically, with all of our cookbooks, videos and gadgets, the most enduring recipes are those that are spoken first, then written on scraps of paper, stuffed into pockets and purses and that way passed through friends and generations. These are the recipes that are cooked, not just collected.

Brave
New
Food

Sometimes, when a food becomes very familiar, we forget that a brave person was once the first to try it. Have you ever wondered what prompted the first person to eat an egg? Did he or she think, "I wonder what the white thing that just fell out of the back of that chicken tastes like?"

In 1820, when the tomato was still shunned as a treacherous and poisonous aphrodisiac, Robert Gibbon Johnson ate one on the steps of a courthouse in Salem, New Jersey. His act is entrenched as one of the most singular acts of valour in gastronomic mythology. Other early adventurers shared his courage: the noteworthy pioneer who first ate a lobster and the daredevil who first thrust a raw oyster down a trusting throat.

I don't mean to detract from these pilgrims, but I believe the modern taster working her way through the maze of foods produced in corporate labs might one day be seen as brave. For example, I wonder whether any one of those pioneers could meet the demands made of the modern food writer, whose duties sometimes require tasting the questionable concoctions produced by the food conglomerates: the ice cream that contains neither ice nor cream; the tofu cheesecake; the artificial sweeteners that move from being cloying to tinny in a split second, without passing "sweet."

I have encountered these, and others, in the line of duty, sampling them under the close scrutiny of people representing the corporate kitchens in which they were spawned. I have eaten the produce of endless test tubes, and the stuff that results when taste is entrusted to marketers instead of eaters. At one (unfortunately) unforgettable lunch, a particularly vile sweetener had been slipped into each of four courses, presumably because the marketing department feared we might miss any subtleties. It was particularly frightening in the strangely corrosive pink emulsion that dressed the salad.

Through the years, I have learned to make a distinction between good and bad corporate foods that comes down to this: the good packaged foods are the ones made with such simple ingredients that you could, if you wanted, concoct the dish yourself, with ease. Two good examples are cream of mushroom soup and macaroni and cheese. These are examples of corporate cookery that can be much better than you make yourself.

I sometimes fear that the current fanaticism for fresh foods has denied many of us the pleasures of good corporate cookery. I join with Alan Comfort of Nova Scotia whose wife, a fresh-food fanatic, has for years prepared him dinners of fish pulled just that afternoon from the sea, accompanied by a salad of leaves grown in an organic garden. He confided one day that his fantasy dinner is "a bowl of corn flakes and an Oreo cookie."

People like Comfort are the backbone of an anti-nutritional underground—a counter-culture backlash. There are many of us. A cookbook of recipes taken from the backs of boxes and sides of packages has sold well. A couple of years ago, *The Toronto Star* ran a kibbitzy piece on jelly moulds and got volumes of mail begging for more. *Vogue* magazine's April 1992 piece on back-of-the-box recipes brought grateful letters from readers saying thanks for the memories of Nestlé's Toll House cookies, Lipton's onion soup and sour cream dip, chocolate wafer/whipping cream refrigerator cake and Ritz Crackers mock apple pie. The campy craze probably has caused much rejoicing in the tidy departments of recipe development. I hope they are celebrating with a bowl of onion soup dip. Perhaps we all might start a movement to eliminate the term "made from scratch," surely a revolting thought, when you think of it.

Corporate foods are bad when they are pretentiously gourmet—like the squooshy chicken tetrazzini or godawful beef Wellington offered in frozen-food counters—dishes that only taste right when fresh and properly made. (If the idea that you can have these complicated kinds of dishes without the complications seems too good to be true, it is.)

Packaged foods are also offensive when they are given fancy names, but have had all the stuff sucked out of them that made them good in the first place. This is a particular feature of those low-calorie, pre-portioned items. To be good for you, corporate foods are presented as being free from life-threatening substances like fat, sugar, salt and additives; the very four basic food groups necessary for a packaged food to taste good.

People who assume that professional eaters are above any chemical concoctions, presuming that our refined palates reject them out of hand, might be surprised at how many of us, when we're alone, turn out the lights and find a corner in which to eat a plate of canned spaghetti or a bowl of tomato soup. It's because of the way we were brought up, when home-cooked food was more likely to involve compounds made from the contents of cans and packages than homey casseroles and fresh baking.

For example, as a child I ate my weight in tuna casseroles that involved canned green peas and meat-loaf made with Lipton onion soup. They were mother's milk to me and a godsend to my mother. Even today, I know there is no substitute for a tin of SpaghettiOs or for asparagus sandwiches made with canned asparagus and toasted white bread. In the winter I like to spread the bread with high-fat Cheez Whiz—the brightness of the orange against the pure whiteness of the bread cheers me somehow.

I still prefer canned baked beans over any made from dry beans, and I'm not alone in this. Furthermore, I've checked a lot of refrigerators of self-styled foodies and all of them contain dubious substances like catsup or something equally sinister.

I still eat Kraft Dinner, though less of it since I learned how many calories it contains. One whole box of Kraft Dinner—of which I have mindlessly eaten twelve gazillion in my life, not to mention the other twelve gazillion I am directly responsible for insinuating into the bodies of children under my care—has

1,276 calories. (Mind you, if I'd fed it to them raw out of the box, it would have had only 828 calories.) Our consumption alone translates into enough kilocalories to maintain a longshoreman through an Arctic winter. It had even more calories when we thought ourselves sophisticated and mixed it with sour cream and called it noodles Romanoff.

When protein was a big concern and three beef meals a day were thought to be ideal, we slipped cottage cheese into Kraft Dinner the way we added Vitamin D to milk or fluoride to toothpaste. And there were flavour additives as well, including catsup or maple syrup.

Kraft Dinner has also been used as an economic barometer. In July 1991, *The New York Times* noted that the recession was bottoming out, using as evidence the levelling off of Kraft Dinner sales. During the period of deepening recession, sales had increased.

And then there are the recipes you make with corporate food—more recipes than there are raisins in a silo of bran flakes. Food companies hope that we will use their products as the foundation of our cooking, thus enhancing them and extending their sales potential. They recognize that although the number of times in a day you might want a can of Campbell's cream of mushroom soup is finite, the possibilities of incorporating the stuff into sauces and casseroles is infinite. They hire developers to generate the recipes that appear in booklets or ad inserts.

Take Rice Krispies. In the fifties, when the name of every concoction ended in "surprise" or "treat," the cereal was rescued from its morning-only slot, and, thanks to Rice Krispy Treats, snap, crackle and pop became part of our afternoons. The recipe coincidentally contains mountains of marshmallows and margarine that are produced by companies in the same conglomerate family.

Rice Krispy Treats have fuelled decades of fantasies for marketing folks, who dream of copying its longevity for their own products. I have at hand *Cooking with Campbell's*, a red-and-white hard-covered book that contains recipes, each of which takes its flavour from canned soup. There's a cunning gingerbread cake made with tomato soup, as well as a peanut parfait that requires a can of condensed cream of chicken soup, salted peanuts, and a tablespoon of honey.

I have a loose-leaf collection called *Cooking with Coca-Cola*, published in 1991. It includes a recipe for Family Pot Roast that calls for a cup of Coca-Cola. According to the introduction: "Coca-Cola and spaghetti sauce mix give a unique flavour to the saucy meat gravy." (I have to take their word for it; it's one I can't quite bring myself to try.)

Many of the recipes specify Classic Coca-Cola. Coming up with a vegetable recipe that uses the stuff must have been a challenge, but I think they've risen to it with their sweet-and-sour cabbage which calls for half a cup of Coca-Cola blended with vinegar, brown sugar and bacon drippings, among other ingredients.

And pretty as a picture is the illustrated Southern Belle Salad, "the old-time favourite for a ladies' luncheon." The quivering moulded dish lets us ladies enjoy an artistic blending of a can of cherries, a package of cherry gelatin, a cup of Coke, lemon juice, cream cheese, and pecan or walnut halves.

For dessert there is Cuba Libre Chiffon Pie, a blend of rum and Coke suspended in gelatin and brought forth in a pie shell ("Graham cracker or chocolate cookie crust or baked...").

Despite the assumption that packaged foods are definitely down-market, the reality is that they can be healthier for you than some fresh foods. I wonder if one day we will discover that many packaged foods are safer because they are more closely scrutinized: contents must be labelled. But there's nothing affixed to the side of an apple to tell you what's been done to it.

We have an unshakeable notion that fresh is fine. But all the time manufacturers have been sterilizing the contents of their packages, producers have been doing nasty things to produce. Since Johnson proved that tomatoes won't kill you, humankind has been subjecting them to such tortures as radiation, genetic engineering and spraying. Today, a field tomato could glow blue in the dark and we would still think it was healthier than a packaged potato chip.

The future of food adventure rests with the folk who brave the produce sections. Next to the unknown future of edibles that might have come from the laboratories of Dr Frankenstein, additives are starting to look pretty tame; better the devil you know. With genetic manipulation of fruits and vegetables, it is up to future generations to discover how food alterations alter them. That may make even brave adventurers, with the high-wire courage of the first person to eat an egg, think twice.

A Few Takes on Take-Out

Researchers claim that working women are the reason prepared foods are popular. I don't think it has anything to do with working; it has to do with people who hate to cook—for any reason.

In the early eighties there was a fundamental shift in the food revolution. The skill had changed from knowing how to cook spiffy dishes to knowing where to shop for them. Chic food stores became the topic of conversation. At dinner parties, we would trade information about where to get the best bagels, the finest chocolate, the most fabulous smoked salmon. The advantage to these stores was that the food didn't even need the effort of assembly: it was ready to eat as soon as you paid for it.

The measure of a high-quality food shop is the speed with which you open the packages. The best of foods rarely make it to their destination. I have eaten many of them as soon as I was back in the car. I have eaten most of the breads and the dense, darkly syrupy chocolate cookies from Harbord Bakery in Toronto with one hand on the wheel, the cream puffs from Café Valerie's small crowded bohemian restaurant in London as I negotiated the escalators into the subway, the cream shooting out one end while I bit into the other. I've enjoyed the smoked salmon from Zabar's in New York (the salmon described by Woody Allen as having the texture of his true love's skin) in the back of a cab. Zabar's is a free-for-all, a New York fairy tale. (I once heard a story about a couple who met and fell in love at the salami counter. When I asked the clerk behind the counter if it was true, he shrugged, "Maybe. You know how long you can wait at the salami counter.")

In the days before it was fashionable to admit to, nay brag about, catered dinners, I grew adept at making store-bought food look home-made. I learned to take my own soup-pots to restaurants and catering companies, to twist the symmetrical edges of store-bought pie shells so they would look amateur.

I even rearranged the architectural piles of scalloped potatoes. I got good at it and felt that the creativity I brought to undoing professional artistry as significant as the artistry itself. I accepted compliments on Dinah Koo's Persian chicken so often that I have come to think of the dish as truly my own, swelling with conceit over my inspired combination of sweet apricots with savoury chicken flesh.

In time, I came to resent the cost. Food from shops costs almost as much as it does in a restaurant, but you don't get the restaurant. In fact, most of the stuff in many food shops originates in home kitchens, where a housewife, anxious to start a career, begins selling her favourite cookies to the food shops. If you go to the back of the shop you may find your next-door neighbour delivering from her station wagon. The cookies you once got for free with some gossip now are yours only at fancy-food-shop prices.

This penchant for grandma's recipes has created an industry of home-cooking and biggest among them has been mustard. During the eighties in home kitchens throughout North America, alchemists in aprons mixed mustard seeds with honey, with tarragon, with mayonnaise, hoping to turn it into gold. There were more recipes than there were grand-mothers.

My friend Jackie hated to cook, but I could never convince her that she might be better off buying food from shops and pretending it was hers. The bravest among us, Jackie had the then shocking idea that she had a right not to cook.

When Jackie married Arnold, she became the first of our gang to set up housekeeping and, simultaneously, the first to throw off the shackles of cooking. From the day Jackie returned from her honeymoon, her meals were assembled, rather than cooked. Most were simply ordered in.

None of us thought of challenging Jackie on this; we considered ourselves modern women who didn't have to do what our mothers did. But when she was criticized by members of our mother's generation, Jackie defended her practice by rationalizing that a ten-dollar pizza was cheaper than a three-course dinner and probably more nutritious. Even ten years after she married Arnold, she was still proud that the only thing she ever learned to cook was a roast of beef (but I once saw her make a salad).

Though she established her errant ways during an epoch when being "a fabulous cook" was one of the requirements of the Accomplished Woman, Jackie moved untouched through the entire gourmet movement. She would sit at our tables and laugh, "You guys are crazy," even as she ate our beef Wellingtons and coq au vins.

When the fashion passed and the rest of us, exhausted by its demands, abandoned our Cuisinarts, she took credit for clairvoyance, bragging, "I was ahead of my time."

Jackie particularly favoured meals that had been pre-planned, pre-cooked and pre-packaged, so that there were no decisions, no surprises, nothing required of her beyond the application of heat. Of course, she adored TV dinners. Our scorn for them didn't faze her; perhaps just to mock us, she argued that they were evidence of the Advance of Humanity, sort of like the freeing of the slaves.

A career dieter, she was a sucker for the wave of low-fat, frantically nutritious frozen dinners. I thought of Jackie as the target of Lean Cuisine, the image the manufacturers hold in their heads when they sip their Crystal Light, plot menus and section off the portion-control compartments in the little tin plates. I knew she would warmly take to meals that have the sole advantage of having a caloric balance calculated in some stainless-steel lab, far from the nasty smells of a real kitchen.

When I went to visit Jackie in Los Angeles in the spring of 1992, nearly a dozen years of safe and happy eating had passed since I last sat at her table. I had no intention of breaking the pattern. We planned a feed of garlic chicken at Versailles.

As fate would have it, I landed during the April riots. There was an air of panic at the airport but I determinedly rented my car, and headed for Jackie's apartment, past the raging fires and whizzing bullets. However, I hardly considered that events that threatened a city might also overtake our long-held dinner plans.

But there was no getting past the curfew that forbade any movement on the streets after dusk. Jackie pointed out that even if we made it to the restaurant before nightfall, we would never get back for breakfast. I reluctantly abandoned my dreams of garlic chicken.

Trapped by law in Jackie's kitchen—about the only way a feeling human could be coaxed to her table—we were forced to scratch for sustenance in that gastronomic wasteland of packaged meals. The only unfettered food was a bundle of weary carrot sticks, bought at the local shop that cleans, cuts and packages them for the Busy Career Person. They cowered in a corner of her vegetable drawer, flaccid from dehydration, blotchy with age. Every other edible was artificially flavoured, coloured or otherwise corrupted. A plastic tub of mean-looking macaroni salad shared the drawer with the carrots.

Her cupboard held a can of low-cal pre-puffed popcorn at $2.99 for the same handful you would take from your mate at the movies, a jar of low-calorie jam, a box of irradiated milk. Some calorie-reduced peanut butter with a scary oil slick on top seemed better suited to an environmental assessment than a meal.

I wondered how we could have chosen such different paths, she and I. We were raised in the same period, our birthdays within a week of each other. We tasted our first lipstick the same year, drank root beer at the same drive-in. We ate our first corporate packaged food together, Kraft Dinner at college (actually called KD by the cognoscenti), frozen fried-chicken dinners too. I remember we once held a serious discussion on whether fries are more authentic served with vinegar or gravy. She held passionately to the view that gravy was best—like a person who really cared.

I opened the freezer compartment of her refrigerator and found it fully loaded—a cryo-crypt of mean cuisine. There was a concrete iceblock of boeuf bourguignon, a freezepak of chicken tetrazzini and several impenetrable rectangles of veal piccata. Her small cupboard held a year's supply of packages that needed re-hydrating—enough to keep her for five years in case of nuclear war or earthquake. Among them was a two-year-old package of Mexicali Sauce with Beef Enchiladas, from which so many of the vital ingredients had been sucked out that the entire meal would fit into a jeans pocket. From another of her weight-loss systems, a package of seafood and noodles promising—"Imitation Crabmeat with Natural Crab Flavour." On the back of the package it said: "The great taste of this entrée is made possible by the use of modern technology. It brings the flavour and goodness of freshly-prepared food to your dinner table."

I felt a tight knot where my stomach used to be. For a long moment I considered taking my chances on the street.

But that sort of bravery is out of my league. We settled on the tetrazzini, laid over a toasted Cheddar-flavoured rice puff. There is this about Los Angeles at night, even when there aren't riots: just being there makes me think of packing the car trunk with dehy-drated dinners and heading to the hills. If Robert Gibbon Johnson could try a tomato, I could manage one night of futurefood.

No Guts, No Glory

I count myself among those who believe that offal is not so terrible. Some offal is lovely, especially if you don't know exactly what you are eating. Sweetbreads sound docile, even cuddly. You can eat them fricasseed, as long as it never enters your head that you are chewing a thymus gland. The word "gland" puts me right off my feed.

Liver makes many people quiver. They will never eat a sliver of liver, no matter how long eternity lasts.

The heyday of liver was in my youth, when it was served in every diner. It was thought to be life-giving because of its rich iron content, and Weight Watchers required it be eaten at least once a week. It has been deStalinized in the last decade because, like all organ meats, it is high in cholesterol and because of further concerns about the dangers of too much iron. Currently, the organ is being attacked because of its function as a filter: some argue that eating liver incorporates into your body all the toxins even the cow's body didn't want.

In every couple, there is one person who loathes liver and one who loves it. Restaurateurs have turned that little piece of culinary sociology into profit by offering it on the menu so the one who loves it can order it and the other one can say yuck and order something else.

I was once in a delicatessen that featured sandwiches called "Liver Come Back To Me," with onions for $4.95; "Liver When You're Near Me" had tomatoes and the same price.

My favourite liver was served in a restaurant in St Paul, Minnesota, where it was cut thick as a steak—maybe 1½ inches—then barbecued just until the squish left the interior and the colour was still red-pink. It was tender and delicious. Italian restaurants do a lovely job with liver, which they call *fegato*, and which they slice very thinly, and cook fast and light so that it's pink inside. Now that diners rarely serve liver and onions, or when they do, rarely find customers to take them up on it, Italian restaurants are the best place to have it.

In brasseries and bistros, you can find delicious dishes made with animal underparts. Apparently we are happier to eat offal in such settings because the menu in French makes it all sound exotic. Andouillettes sound a lot better than a double offal whammy of ground-up stomach lining stuffed into intestine.

Brain has the texture of tofu and a very bland taste, so it does need a boost. Le Trou Normand in Toronto does a smart job, serving it in brown butter and dotting it with capers. The nutty flavour of browned butter is important, as are the capers. They also serve it as a salad, whole in an oval with leeks and tomatoes under and cider vinegar over it. Those who prefer to hide their brains can have them folded into a tasty omelette. A book called *Unmentionable Cuisine* by Calvin W. Schwabe, first published in 1979, lists twenty-six recipes for brain, including brain in coconut cream and brain tacos.

If you don't understand French, you'd be smart to ask what you are eating in a French restaurant. For example, you might want to know that the dish that made headlines at Paul Bocuse's Lyons restaurant a couple of years ago was Chicken for Two in a Pig's Bladder.

I think tripe is fine offal. I never tire of its soft gristly texture and its flabby taste, partly because I rarely get to eat it. Tripe is seldom served in North American restaurants: too many customers resist the notion of putting the lining of a ruminant's stomach into their own. People who don't like tripe say that eating it feels like biting the inside of your own cheek. (People often talk about it in terms of feel rather than taste.)

I have found terrific tripe in unexpected places. I'll bet the biggest dish of tripe in the world is served at Tony and Lucille's Italian restaurant on Wooster Street in New Haven, Connecticut; there, it comes in a huge heap in a bowl big enough to bathe a baby. The tripe is stewed in a perky tomato sauce and served with spaghetti on the side. The Plaza Cafe in the centre of Sante Fe, New Mexico, offers a knock-out breakfast of beans and hominy, stewed with large chunks of tripe. The stew is covered with a red hot sauce made from green and red chilies, the way we pour maple syrup over pancakes. It is a dish well known among the locals and has been served the same way for forty years.

In France, the dish has been elevated to an art form. The version known as *Tripes à la mode de Caen* is so honoured it has its own Academy Awards, the Norman Confrérie de la Tripière d'Or, which since 1952 has been conferred only when judges are convinced the ruminations are right. Properly cooked, the dish includes calves feet, calvados and cider and is baked for ten hours in a cool oven, long enough to allow the tripe to relax and absorb the flavours of the liquids. The calves feet are removed before the dish is served.

Chicken hearts are common in Middle Eastern cuisine. They are often skewered and barbecued, a procedure which lends a rather brutal note to the meal. I am otherwise very fond of them, but they must be cooked properly. If they are underdone, as is often the case, the hearts continue to bleed onto the plate and their texture remains uncomfortably organic.

When people tell me that my fondness for animal parts is baffling, I answer that food fetishes never make any sense to anyone. Schwabe begins his book with the following quote: "Modern Man, despite his frequent temptation to claim his foodways are based on rational considerations, is no more rational in this than other men, for it makes no better sense to reject nutritious dogflesh, horseflesh, grasshoppers and termites as food than to reject beef or chicken flesh." In North America, we shudder at stories of raw monkey-brain eating in China, of slug swallowing in Africa, of blubber chewing in the Arctic. I nearly gagged on my tripe when a dental hygienist told me that she and her husband were served a freshly splayed frog when they were asked to dinner in the Thai countryside.

It's all in the way the dish is described. North Americans routinely feast on cow muscle hung to age until it is nearly putrid; Eastern Europeans eat sausages made from blood. We decry the repellent-sounding foods of others, even as we savour the flesh of a large sea crustacean whose mushy grey insides tighten and whiten when they are heated. Gourmets wax poetic about the slimy green and red content of its thorax. In fact, we're happy to pay a fortune for a creature that looks like an overheated insect on steroids, when it is served to us in ritzy surroundings. We willingly don a child's bib, wield an ice pick and a pair of nutcrackers, dip the flesh in melted mammals milk and savour it because it's called lobster.

An Angst of Confessions, Comforts and Fetishes

I really shouldn't be telling you this, but people tell me all sorts of strange secrets about how they eat. It surprises me that they do: why reveal intimate details to someone whose job it is to repeat them?

Some of these confidences show the puritanism about eating that has overtaken us in the last two decades. They have the flavour of confessions about sex that might be made to a priest: full of remorse, shame, and the feeling that desire has once again grabbed you by the throat and, dammit, got the better of you.

"I shouldn't be eating this," moans the person across the table from me. She describes how she monitors every mouthful, calculates each nibble, weighing her transgressions. At the end of the day, she tells herself that tomorrow can be better.

"I'm a secret midnight eater," says the slender woman beside me at the lunch counter. She is eating a chaste fruit salad. "At night I eat sandwiches, desserts, everything. It's my time for myself. Then I pay for it like this."

Most of these self-flagellating confessions reveal our obsession with slimness. One of the most poignant was made in an interview by the fabulous jazz singer Diane Schurr, blind since childhood. She was also overweight as a child. On losing one hundred pounds, she said: "The blindness never bothered me as much as the weight. That was a real handicap."

Some have reported with glee that losing weight was the silver lining in a tragedy. A food consultant who was hospitalized for six months after a truck hit her car broadside told me: "The good thing is I've lost twenty-five pounds."

A woman whose husband of ten years left her for a younger woman—my friend called her a "flimsy" because "the tramp's not good enough to be called a floozy"—lost fifteen pounds in the anguished weeks after the news. She said: "I felt like hell, but I was never so happy in my life."

We are as phobic about fat on our plates as on our bodies. The man sitting beside me at a dinner party is still worrying about a breach two days earlier: "I had some lamb the other night and all the next day I could think of nothing else except how that greasy fat was lying in my veins."

I believe that if he had eaten raw carrots with his meal, he could have eaten the lamb. I told him that rough raw foods like carrots are antidotes to many sins of consumption. If you eat them, no matter what other foods you send down afterward, you will lose weight. If you eat enough to turn the palms of your hands yellow, you will look like a fashion model. It's that easy. Raw carrots are magic.

People have crazy notions about food:

- A civil servant, the son of a minister, confides that he finds unpeeled tomatoes an abomination. The peel casing is vulgar, he says, and he feels that people who eat it show an illiterate palate.

- A slender woman whose job is to promote fresh fruits and vegetables, sometimes eats a mountain of mashed potatoes, digging a well in the centre and filling it with creamed corn.

- Red jam can be eaten only with white toast. White toast must have red jam on it. Red jam must be strawberry, possibly raspberry, but never silly fruits like plums. Jellies are even better than jams because they have no seeds. Seeds are torture to the texture-challenged.

- It sometimes seems that the world is more divided about Marmite than about communism. There are people (the English) who adore Marmite and those (the rest of the universe) who regard eating it as only somewhat this side of perversion. The English seem to feel the same way about the North American affinity for peanut butter.

- The distaste for specific foods is profound and unpredictable. The same people who will eat handfuls of raisins may loathe them in muffins. A grown man says he has been unable to eat them, plain or cooked, since he was a child and his brother told him that his parents kept rabbits so they would always have a plentiful supply of raisins.

- Oysters may be cherished by most of the world as an aphrodisiac, their shape and texture pleasantly suggestive, but a scientist of my acquaintance confesses that he loathes them.
  "Avoid them like the plague," he advises. "They are filter feeders. Never eat filter feeders. When you eat an organism that filters thousands of gallons of water for its lunch, you eat not only the oyster but its sex organs and its last meal."
  American writer Roy Blount, Jr. writes of his suspicions of raw oysters and his solution:

J prefer to have my oysters fried
'Cuz then I know my oyster's died.

The fetishes extend to vessels.

A woman from North Winnipeg explains that orange juice must be drunk from four-ounce glasses, while milk can only be taken from eight-ounce ones. Neither drink will taste right in the wrong glasses. Exploring this, I have noticed that people are more than passing strange in their attachments to vessels—certainly more than plates and cutlery. I've been told that water cannot be drunk out of a cup and must be taken from a glass, because it tastes "thick" out of a cup. The impenetrable wall of a mug hides the water and takes away the clear, light and cool taste that you'd get in a glass.

Some people are rabidly against drinking tea from a mug, believing it is only properly taken from a cup with a lip that curves out to meet theirs. I think to refuse to drink coffee out of a mug is against the spirit of the times and wonder why people seem to hold undeserved hostility towards mugs, angry at them for no other reason than the fact that they aren't cups with saucers. Mugs deserve some attention these days, since they have become, like T-shirts, billboards of opinion. They may indicate the bearer's feelings about Christmas (Bah, Humbug) or state an emotion that one is too shy to say (I love my Mommy).

I prefer small mugs and I fill them only halfway up, so I can keep refilling them with hot, fresh coffee. This quirk has been interpreted as a lack of generosity by those whose own quirk requires that mugs—or cups—be filled to the brim.

I think of coffee in the same category as purses. They are indulgences that are completely unaffected by any weight concerns. Unlike any other item of clothing, except maybe handkerchiefs, purses are unrelated to weight. Same with coffee: it feels like an indulgence and it has no calories.

I like coffee best all by itself. Unlike tea that goes well with a dry cookie, too many foods ruin the taste of coffee, sometimes as badly as artichokes ruin the taste of wine. Bananas, tuna fish or peanut butter make coffee taste vile. Since I love the taste of coffee, I loathe the flavoured, candy coffees that are everywhere. Supermarkets are selling cherry coffee and cans of flavoured iced coffee. What an abomination!

A woman reports that she is greatly affected by the temperature at which coffee is served to her. She tells me that she doesn't mind drinking it cool if it has been allowed to cool in front of her, but she is angered if it is served cool to her in the first place. Is there anything else we insist on being so steaming hot when we take it into the soft tissues of our mouths?

People seem to have all sorts of fetishes about storing and making coffee. When you buy a pound of coffee from Caffe Latte in L.A. they give you a little piece of paper that says (in capital letters): DO NOT REFRIGERATE; DO NOT FREEZE; BREAK THESE RULES; WE BREAK YOUR KNEES.

Coffee is such a symbolic drink used for hospitality or an excuse for a break or for extending a meal that people who don't drink it feel at loose ends. One woman told me: "When I refuse the coffee at the end of a dinner party, people are always offended. They seem to think that they've done something wrong that has made me want to leave. Coffee is just a way of winding down the meal and punctuating it, so the hostess is not left with a feeling that you've eaten and run. So I always ask for a Kahlua and that seems to satisfy them."

The belief that a particular food, alone or in combination, is health-giving or health-taking is nothing new. My grandmother believed that if you drank a glass of milk right after a glass of orange juice the war between the bland and acid in your stomach—the very core of your being—could cause death. An article in a 1961 *Coronet* magazine proposed that ingesting opposite tastes and textures at the same time—hot and cold, sweet and sour, crunchy and soft—might cause digestive upsets or even personality changes. A woman in Nova Scotia told me she is convinced that the combination of lobster and milk is possibly fatal.

People also have odd notions about the magic in food that makes them think better. Such people claim to be paralyzed while their fussy brain cells bang their little knives and forks on the table, petulant until they are fed the one substance—be it tea or tofu—that triggers them into action. American chess champion Bobby Fischer has considered freshly squeezed orange juice so important that in matches held in Vancouver in 1971 he had a special squeezer assigned to him. English champ Tony Miles used to drink two litres of whole milk before and during a game; Mikhail Botvinnik brought his own Thermos of coffee to a game because he was dissatisfied with the stuff that was brewed for everyone else.

Anatoly Karpov's love of blueberry yogurt sparked the Philippine Food Fight of 1978. He ate it at regular intervals during his games, a habit noted by his opponent Victor Korchnoi. During one tense match, Korchnoi observed that the yogurt appeared without Karpov's ordering it. In an open letter to the organizing committee, Korchnoi's representative argued that the yogurt might be a signal and demanded the talisman be regulated. The organizers agreed and ruled that the yogurt had to be served at prearranged intervals and that it always had to be purple.

Some fetishes are psychological, based in childhood. Many people say their food fetishes were founded in poverty. Even if they have long been able to afford caviar, they still crave the nearly free meals they used to make from condiments in restaurants: the two slices of bread they paid for that became a catsup sandwich, the catsup soup made with the boiling water provided for tea. Mustard and cracker sandwiches were common in the Great Depression, as were mashed potato or onion sandwiches.

White bread has been much maligned—sneered at in public—but it is consumed in secret. There are foods that can only be made with white bread, for example peanut butter and jelly sandwiches. Or asparagus rolls with Cheez Whiz. Toast made from white bread is special because the high sugar content gives the surface a caramel sweetness. I love the way cafeterias slather white toast with butter, then serve it with bacon and eggs. White toast was invented by the taste gods as a vehicle for butter.

White bread is medicinal. Nearly every mother I have ever heard of, including me, serves white toast to an ailing child. My children get it in increments: dry when they are really sick; lightly buttered when the fever has broken; with sugar, cinnamon (cinnamon toast) and cocoa when they need their strength for a full recovery. I supplement the toast with other proven health restoratives: ginger ale, canned fruit cocktail and Jell-O puddings. (Chicken soup has had the advantage of the world's best press from an agency of Jewish mothers and needs no more from me here. Anyway, it only works if it has lots of noodles in it to absorb the demons that caused the illness.)

I hear many stories of the miracles of white bread (sometimes called bimbo bread) toast: a man I had just met told me that whenever he was sick his mother served him buttered white bread toast sprinkled with sugar. He developed an unnatural attachment to white bread and grew into adolescence living off a gastronomical delight he called Klikshit: a can of Klik luncheon meat, mayonnaise or Miracle Whip, and sweet pickle relish, mashed together and served on white.

White bread is only one of the casualties of politically correct eating, which can easily conflict with our apolitical cravings. A woman, crazed for coffee, could not ease her hunger with Bridgehead, an organic coffee grown by a co-operative. Although her husband responsibly insisted it be kept in the house and, she says, "I know I should drink it," she also knows that "it is just not good." She also confesses that she has her suspicions about taboulleh and wonders whether people eat the tart and grainy Middle Eastern salad because it's responsible to do so, not because it's good. Because she had been so open with me, I gave her the food secret of a family physician, who told me that after he had spent three days in a spa "eating lightly, exercising and feeling great," he stopped on the way back home for a line of Italian sausage—"not the lean home-made kind either."

I am often struck with the degree to which reactions to taste and texture are personal. Although we are all born with similar taste buds and nerve receptors, foods titillate or torment us differently. For example, I love rice pudding, especially when it's made by Ethel Shuken of Toronto using a recipe from a New Jersey diner run by her grandfather. This is a soft sea of eggy custard in which islands of sweet rice are deliciously suspended. Just holding a big bowl in my hands straightens the world on its axis. I said that to a woman who gagged and shivered in disgust: she could never eat something that had "things" in it. Every food she eats must be of uniform texture: custard is lovely, but rice pudding is "distracting." Tapioca drives her nuts.

I like to eat orange segments long after they have been left to dry. I first learned this from reading M.F.K. Fisher, who preferred her orange segments dried on a radiator: if you bite into them after letting them dry by either method for a few hours, the segments crunch through the membrane and the juice squirts. It's the contrast between the papery tough membrane and the sweet squirty juice that gets me.

Watching a teenaged boy pick a dozen raisins out of a sticky cinnamon bun, I asked him what it was about them that bothered him. He said it was the way they crunched and were mushy at the same time, "like eating an eyeball." His view of eyeballs reminded me of the scene in the movie *A Day in the Life of Ivan Denisovitch,* where the starved Denisovitch is served a bowl of gruel with an eyeball in it. It was several weeks before I could look at a raisin again.

Occasionally, people will confess, not just to some food misdemeanour, but to food sin in the first degree. Richard Nixon is "fond" of cottage cheese and catsup. Ronald Reagan really likes those black Jelly Bellies. But my friend Faye loves chocolate—not in the way you or I might prefer the flavour of chocolate to, say, the flavour of coffee. Faye loves chocolate the way Chopin loved George Sand, or the way Othello loved Desdemona—not wisely but too well. A day rarely ends when she hasn't had at least one piece of chocolate. And there are many days when she has bagfuls. If she has her taste buds set on a particular chocolate bar or box of candy, she will go to the ends of the earth to find it.

"It's such a nice feeling. It's a very personal experience. That's why I sneak it, I guess. The guilt is part of the pleasure, and I feel guiltier the older I get. I don't remember this lovely sense of wickedness when I was younger."

When Faye returned to Nova Scotia for a family affair a few years ago, everyone had made a special chocolate dessert for her. At her sister's there was amaretto chocolate cheesecake. Her sister-in-law made a two-pan chocolate cake with a soft interior and a very moist and rich fudge on the outside. At her friend Goldie's there was a chocolate mousse cake with a chocolate cookie crumb base and chocolate shavings on top. When she was alone at Goldie's during the day, she kept opening the refrigerator and taking edges off the mousse. The theft was discovered when Goldie noticed chocolate crumbs on the floor. Of all the chocolate desserts she encounters on a home visit, she dreams most of the steamed chocolate pudding with hard sauce served to her by a friend. It is a recipe that she has never been able to duplicate in her own kitchen, though she puts the chocolate batter in a coffee can (Choc Full o' Nuts), gives it a foil dome and steams it in a pan of water, just the same way as her friend does. "I kept getting glue, not steamed chocolate. I knew then that I was put on this earth to eat chocolate desserts, not to make them."

The idea that food fetishes and obsessions are more related to what's between your ears than what's on your plate is hardly new. People eat nuts and crunchy things to bite back their anger; others crave sugar to replace the sweetness they feel is missing from their lives; the vulnerable may seek yielding, slippery foods.

Which brings us to that most personal and mysterious category: comfort food. Melzeta McAlman, head dietician of the hospital attached to the Rikers Island prison is quoted in the *New Yorker* as saying, "...it's nothing personal, but [inmates would] just as soon be having dinner someplace else. I like gentle flavors and gentle seasonings. Something soft. That's a daily challenge—to keep your food homey and loving when you're cooking for so many unhappy people. I like to believe that if I can just cook something wonderful, then maybe somebody won't feel so bad about being in jail. Maybe they'll feel for a minute like they were 'just visiting'—you know, like in Monopoly."

A comfort food usually attains that status on the basis of the memories it carries. If cornflakes warmed your tummy when you were six, they will warm your heart when you are sixty. A woman who holds a responsible public job and is raising apparently normal children reports that when the world is too much for her, she takes a can of processed baby pears, slides into a hot bath and eats the fruit with a baby spoon.

I find overweight people loath to confess their affections: having committed the apparent social solecism of being outside the fashionable silhouette, and sensitive to the evidence in our mass culture of how much they are despised, they do not feel entitled to profess the need for soothing-by-food (unless they're crazy about carrot sticks).

Let this stand as a plea for foods that bolster us when life takes more than it gives. Sometimes, there's not much else you can count on: a cheese and peanut butter sandwich when the budgie has died; salami and catsup, mashed potatoes, and corn when you've lost the account; bananas and sour cream when the hard drive crashes.

Ice cream is the food I turn to when I need food kindness: vanilla or dark chocolate, maybe with a few nuts, although if I really need gentleness, the nuts are out because they just slow me down. I must eat the ice cream from a large bowl so I can make a hill and leave a moat around it for the frozen cream to melt into. I have a dress code: I must be in a bathrobe and wedged securely into a corner of the couch. If I stay there long enough, I will feel right in my skin again.

I like to think that there is, at least, this refuge from an unrelenting world with too many flavours and too much friction. Husbands may change, constitutional crises may come and go. But ice cream is forever.

Word
of
Mout**h**

S omeone who spends as much time at tables as I
do watches a lot of people eating, and over the
years I have become curious about the different
ways people use their mouths. You can spot a real
eater with their first mouthful. There is a moment of
quiet when the food is laid on the tongue; a beat
while the flavour and texture register; and another
before it shows on the face.

Equally, to watch self-conscious eaters is to watch
a rape of the mouth—they push little morsels past
tightly pursed lips, opening them only long enough to
say "I really shouldn't have done that."

At a lunch counter in St John's, Newfoundland,
which specialized in fish and chips, where the fish
was fresh Atlantic salmon and the chips were fat, I
watched a man with a carefully knotted tie perform
delicate surgery on a plate of very hot battered fish.

This is what happens when fish is fried in batter:
the batter crisps and hardens under the onslaught of
the boiling oil, sealing in the steam that has been

forced from the moist fresh fish. The wet heat waits under the batter for the over-anxious eater who can't wait, who must bite the bundle fast, before the batter turns flaccid.

But this patient, tidy man painstakingly separated the batter from the flesh, letting the steam escape and the fish cool, while the rest of us at the counter agonized in anticipation of his first mouthful, when he opened wide, letting the steam fill the cavity, placing the morsel in the middle of his tongue and closing his lips to chew.

I have always wondered what happens next—in the space behind the face after the lips close around the morsel. The following is a collection of answers based on my own observations and those of experts ranging from oral pathologists to psychoanalysts.

The mouth begins at the lips and extends just past the uvula to the glottis. The mouth may look small from the front of the face, but inside, its curves, alleyways and undulations give it a huge surface area that is more in proportion to its importance to the functioning body.

The mouth is by far the most sensitized area of the human anatomy: there are more sensory receptors around the mouth per square inch than anywhere else. The mouth, lips and cheeks sparkle with neurons known as Krause End Bulbs. They are tiny receptors, ultra-sensitive and highly charged, that transmit the messages of taste, texture and temperature to the brain, and are found in only one other part of the body: the genitalia. But the mouth variety are sensitive to heat, cold, taste and pressure in a way genital receptors can only envy.

This supports the theory (mentioned in Lewd Food) that eating together can be more intimate than sex. According to the University of Toronto professor from whom it comes, "Simultaneous dentition is more intimate than coition." A concept well worth repeating.

The map of the brain shows a constellation of receptors, vast areas devoted solely to receiving oral impulses. In fact, more brain space is devoted to receiving messages from the oral neurons than any other kind. The mouth is ten times more sensitive than the skin, able to discern even the shape of objects.

The lips are the gatekeepers to the mouth and to the digestive system. They are acutely sensitive, highly suspicious and very protective. Once substances are past the palate and up against the glottis, they are sent automatically down to the stomach without appeal. Therefore, it is up to the lips to be vigilant and spare their owner undue pain.

To carry out that task, lips are armed for detection better than any other part of the body. Touch a piece of butter lettuce to the lips and they will prepare themselves differently than if you had pressed a cashew nut against them. Brush a feather lightly to the lips and a thousand neurons spring smartly to attention to record and relay the feather's effect on the lips to the brain.

A pair of lips can also best discern temperature. Bring a soup-spoon close to the lips and if that soup is hot, they will sound an alert to the brain before the lips actually touch the liquid. A mother can find out whether her child has a temperature more accurately by using her lips than her hand.

Lipstick affects women's ability to taste in two ways. First, the oils and other components mix with the food and alter its flavour. The second reason is mechanical. A woman trying to protect her lipstick will tend to place the food well back in her mouth, passing over the front of the tongue. In doing that, she overshoots the sweet receptors at the front and will have less sense of sweetness than if her whole tongue wrapped around the morsel.

Aside from what we learn from our own lips, consider the information we glean about one another when two pairs of lips touch each other.

Dr Howard Book, chief of psychiatry at Toronto's Women's College Hospital notes that:

K issing is extremely intimate and the way a
person kisses is revealing. Is the mouth open?
Are the lips held tight or left soft? Perfunctory
kisses are closed, but not tight; the lips are
left soft. To a psychiatrist, intercourse without
kissing suggests concerns around intimacy. You
hear of prostitutes who won't kiss; that's because
of the personal, intimate nature of kissing,
though it seems ironic in that context. Think
of the effectiveness of all those old movies with
close-ups of kissing, how much more intimate
than the new movies with explicit sexual
intercourse.

A baby satisfies both its hunger for food and
its curiosity about the world through the mouth.
The mouth provides the first source of pleasure
from sucking, and the first source of pain from
teething. It is through the mouth that a baby
begins to autonomously satisfy hunger,
by sucking its thumb. It sends sounds through
the mouth that will bring loving and help. It is

through the mouth that the baby initially learns about security and trust.

Psychiatrists believe that we never completely grow out of this phase. The remnants of the oral phase of development remain through adulthood, in kissing and language.

The pleasures of eating remain constant throughout life; the rhythm of chewing is satisfying in itself, as is the fullness of the mouth. Although our bodies may be physically satisfied when we have sufficient food, we still get mouth hunger—a yearning for textures, tastes and fullness.

I have noticed that people who like food will keep it in their mouths for as much as twice as long as people who are eating just for function. Those who eat a lot of food very fast may be trying to fill up more than to taste. That is why real gourmets are often not fat: they don't actually eat more—they just keep food longer in their mouths, playing with the texture, analyzing the taste.

It is said that the eyes are the window of the soul, but we get a lot of our information about another person by the way he holds his mouth. Angry people display a lot of teeth; those who are needy seem to open their mouths more—sometimes they look like baby birds feeding. Tight people hold their lips tightly, as if they don't want anything to escape their control. There is a lot of information in a smile: we easily distinguish a cold or a phony smile.

Dr Book: "When I am giving information, I look into a person's eyes. When I'm trying to figure out what they are saying, I watch their mouths. This isn't just lip reading. I am learning from the way their mouths are saying it."

These are some of the things that mouths say:

An unpleasant experience leaves a bad taste in your mouth, or sticks in your throat. We have gut feelings, bitter feelings, a sour disposition; someone makes me sick to my stomach, causing me to eat my heart out. Sometimes I can vent my spleen, or spill my guts, but most often I simply must bite my tongue and swallow my words, unless of course I can suck up, and convince you to work it out by sitting down and chewing the fat.

Not only is the mouth the orifice through which we let the world into our bodies, it is the highway on which our feelings and thoughts come out. Just as unhappiness may cause us to put more food and drink into our mouths than we need—as if to give us strength—extreme emotion may make us vomit, as if we are ridding ourselves of the painful excess.

Certain foods offer emotional outlets. Crunchy foods for anger; steaks when you want to tear at flesh. Soft, baby foods—custards, buttery sweet cinammon toast—when you need soothing. (I am of the opinion that the English are the only people who really understand toast: it should be cold, dammit. That way the butter stays tidy and provides a comfortable background for fresh raspberry jam. Excuse me, I'm just going to the kitchen to check something.)

I think people's oral attachments may be seen in their choice of careers. I have a theory that people who make their living by talking—psychiatrists, lawyers, actors, dentists—can be expected to have an interest in tastes and textures that a businessman or mechanic does not. Of the food and wine mavens I hear from, a greater percentage are in those oral professions than any other segment of the population. (In the same way, many physicists and mathematicians have music-related hobbies, and some musicians actually enjoy mathematics for their leisure. The sense they are drawn to for pleasure echoes the sense they use in their work.

Cyril Sapiro, a Toronto accountant who specializes in bankruptcies, may dispute my theory, since he seems very attuned to mouth sensitivity. He keeps sour candies on his desk, because he finds that when clients suck them they cry less and for shorter periods of time.

A dentist explains that Sapiro's practice is soundly based on physiology: the sour taste causes an increase in saliva production, which causes the poor wretch to swallow more and faster, effectively distracting him from the pain of the subject that caused the tears. The principle of distraction is well known to pain-inflicting professions. "It would work the same way as a hard pinch on the ass," explains the dentist. (But it wouldn't taste quite the same, would it?)

Taste is vital to our pleasure and well-being. People who have lost their tongues complain more about the loss of taste than they do about the loss of speech, according to Dr David Mock, an oral pathologist. Clearly, the phrase "a taste for life" is more than a metaphor.

Many senses contribute to the sense of taste. Think of taste as a queen, gathering her handmaidens of smell, sight and touch to enhance her. Smell is the most vital among them. Wine expert Tony Aspler says, "The nose is considered by most wine experts as being the organ of taste. It's more like a muscle and gets better as you work it. The importance of the nose will be remembered by anyone who was told to hold your nose when swallowing bad medicine, so you won't taste it." Aspler reports studies that show men's taste acuity is best at noon, while women's seems to peak later in the day—around four or five in the afternoon, when they might be preparing dinner, say. (Another of those nasty bits of trivia used to keep women in the kitchen, tasting.)

Smell is also detected through the mouth. As food passes over the palate, aromatic substances send their tiny molecules north to the nasopharynx to be appreciated intra-orally. So we get to enjoy strong aromas like cognac two ways and twice as much.

Taste buds do not look so much like buds as they do bulbs. They are soft, like tiny uvulas, with a nerve that senses taste. They are located on various areas of the tongue, mapped out in clumps. Each area is dedicated to picking up a different taste. The buds at the front of the mouth discern sweetness; those at the sides of the tongue discover salt. The bumps at the back look like moguls on a ski slope and detect bitterness. A few random buds are scattered as well on the hard palate.

The ability to taste is a circuit involving the taste buds, the neural pathways to the brain and the brain itself. Interference anywhere along the way will cause a change to taste. Along the course of the tongue, the cranial nerves five, seven, nine, ten and twelve pass the messages along to the brain.

When food enters the mouth, it is mixed with saliva; as the solution slides around the gums, tongue and palate, each area, recognizing its stimulus, fires its acknowledgement to the cranial nerves.

For example, an egg roll would cut the following path. The plum sauce excites the sweet receptors at the front; soya sauce arouses the salt receptors at the sides of the tongue; the acid in the vegetables thrills the sour receptors on the top flat of the tongue. Pressure and temperature receptors scattered throughout the lips, teeth and palate signal the crunch from the wonton shell and the viscosity of the food mass. The brain, which has already recorded your sighting of the egg roll, confirms that information with the new data from your mouth and reports: "Egg roll. Safe to swallow."

The mouth can sense teensy differences in taste, texture and temperature, enabling it to recognize crème brûlée in its traditional form, or if the form has been altered to crème brûlée purée.

The sensations received by the bitterness receptors at the back of the tongue are treasured much more by adults than children. Campari and tonic water is a sophisticated drink that gets the ninth cranial nerve frolicking in a way that grownups adore and children detest. The acidic bubbles in the tonic water also stimulate the fifth cranial nerve at the front of the tongue. The combination is so stimulating, it is a wonder that people drinking Campari and tonic can keep their tongues quiet in their mouths!

Textures on the tongue have traditionally been considered more refined than a blast of taste to the mouth, and as societies became more refined, so followed the foods. The most advanced expression of classic French and Chinese cuisines are found in the texture of their dishes. In the quenelles of France, the texture of the fish is completely changed to make it light and airy so that in the mouth it dissolves on the tongue, hardly meeting the teeth. Chinese cookery reveres foods for texture alone—simply for the pleasure of the way it feels in the mouth. Squirmy jellyfish or the slippery mushrooms called tree ears have very little taste, but their textures are intriguing.

Because taste is a chemical reaction of a substance (food) within a solution (saliva) stimulating a sensor (taste bud), there can be no taste unless saliva is present. A chili pepper laid on a dry tongue has little sting. Lose saliva, you lose taste. People with disorders that result in dry mouth lose much of their ability to taste, even if nothing has happened to their taste buds as such.

Like all chemical reactions, taste is activated by heat. Warm food will have more taste than cold. The closer the temperature of the food is to body temperature, the more the flavour is enhanced. Extremes of either hot or cold interfere with flavour perception.

Hold a very cold substance in your mouth for a minute; let it rise to body temperature and you will notice how the flavour lifts. Ice cream might feel better cold—at -2°C on a 37°C tongue, it feels lovely in summer heat—but if you want its full taste, you must let it melt to meet the temperature of your tongue.

But beware of very hot foods. They can scar the tissue, and even after the food cools, you may not be able to find its flavour.

You lose taste when you eat chili peppers either because the pepper causes a burn and cauterizes the buds or because so much sensation is going to the brain that the circuits get overloaded and shut down temporarily.

(The pain from spicy food may be long-lived and the hurt linger after you've finished: the mucous membrane is as sensitive at one end of the alimentary canal as at the other. From this, spice insiders have developed the term "flying ax handles" to describe how your body reacts the next day, or, as they say, it leaves one with a "heinous anus.")

Some foods retain high temperatures better than others and, unless you are wary, can be a great threat to the sensitive tissues of the mouth. Pizza burn— used in medical texts to describe a specific and recognizable burn of the sort that occurs when people take a reckless bite of pizza without testing the temperature—is the fault of the cheese, a foodstuff that holds heat very well. Shrimp, on the other hand, get cool immediately: they are the bane of many a waiter rushing a plate from kitchen to customer.

The top of the tongue, the gums, and the hard palate are covered by keratin, which acts as protection and makes them the least sensitive areas of the mouth. (Nitroglycerin pills are placed *under* the tongue where they will be absorbed very quickly, because that location lacks keratin and has a superficial blood supply.) A person who eats lots of spicy food will develop a thicker keratin coating and be more able to tolerate spice. Similarly, a smoker loses some of his ability to taste, because the heat from smoke causes the tongue and palate to become calloused; the callouses cover taste buds, which become less sensitive.

People who enter chili pepper contests and swallow bowlfuls of jalapeno peppers do so successfully because they learn how to bypass the sensitive tissues. They throw the peppers onto the parts of the palate where the sting registers least strongly; the best method of all is to toss the peppers right to the back of the mouth, onto the soft palate, then swallow them quickly.

The feel of foods in the mouth–known to food companies as "mouthfeel"—greatly affect our perception of how they taste. Often, diet foods don't taste right because they don't feel right: diet cheesecake tastes odd because there is a reduction of the fat that produces that silky feeling. Improvements in technology have created morally fraudulent substances that simulate the feeling of fat. When they are very effective, as is the chemical Simplesse in ice cream, the stomach is left to decide if it has been cheated.

An off-putting, soggy potato chip is a case of bad mouthfeel—though the chip may taste fine. Mouthfeel is a very big factor in boxed snack foods and food companies pay intense attention to it, trying to codify its various components. For example, they distinguish between crispy and crunchy: crispy is at the front teeth (a crispy cracker snaps at the front of the mouth); crunchy at the back teeth, like an apple.

The mouth is a cesspool, a swamp of bacterial flora and fauna. The only thing that keeps us from getting more infections and diseases is the war between the bacteria: they keep each other in check in what is a virtual civil war. This makes kissing and eating among the most dangerous activities in the world. You are ten times more likely to get a bacterial infection in your mouth than you are to get herpes or

AIDS or even to die in an airplane crash, and most of us take out insurance for that.

Taste buds die off as we age and we need more stimulation to set them going. The taste buds of children are particularly sensitive and perceive small differences in flavour much more readily than those of an adult. Perhaps that's why children are so picky. If they don't like something, like spinach or broccoli, it can be really revolting to them. Furthermore, children are very acutely attuned to texture. For example, many kids loathe tomatoes, complaining about squishy seeds and the toughness of the skin, qualities to which most adults may be oblivious.

The sensitivity will fade as a child's mouth ages. The decrease will allow him to tolerate and eventually even enjoy flavours and textures he once loathed: at six months, the flavour of spinach is anathema; at eighteen years, he can take it or leave it—in many teenagers food seems to pass through their mouths without touching down—in adulthood he may seek variety in the kinds of spinach he savours and the care with which he dresses it. He should choose wisely and well, for too soon comes the day when the mouth is just grateful that the spinach requires no chewing.

Training
Meals

One of the biggest changes in eating out is the proliferation of children in restaurants. When I was a child, we went to restaurants only to mark extra-special occasions and the restaurant had to seem equally special, which meant fancy. Fancy included the French restaurant where I ate onion soup (which was good only if it had more cheese than soup), or the hotel dining room with high ceilings and hard bread rolls (as good for table croquet as they were for eating), or a steak house where the rule was Astonishing Excess followed by cheesecake with bright blueberry topping. We often went out for Chinese food on Sunday nights or after events, because Chinese restaurants were about the only places open in Canadian cities after 9:00 p.m. Food was never ordered in, unless it was deli. Pizza was something romantic that Sophia Loren ate when Cary Grant wasn't pitching woo.

When I was a kid, I measured how fancy the restaurant was by how long it took for the food to come—the longer the wait, the fancier the restaurant. In those days, the menu of one place we ate in carried the warning: Good Food Takes Time To Prepare. I guess they wrote that so parents wouldn't have to keep saying it. Anyway, it wasn't true: the best food at that time, an Oh Henry! bar, took only a minute.

You could also tell fancy restaurants by their amenities: the more amenities there were, the more rules. You couldn't roll your used gum in the cloth napkins. If there were candles, you couldn't accidentally let the corner of the menu creep near the flame.

The best thing about fancy restaurants was that the waiter would serve a basket of bread without saying "Don't fill up on bread." Those were still the days when the customer was always right and to be accorded rights by an adult wearing a uniform seemed amazing to me. Going out to dinner was just about the most marvellous thing that could happen.

By the time we grew up, restaurants were part of everyday life and so our everyday children came with us. The fecundity of baby boomers meant that children and their parents stormed restaurants en masse and not a sugar cube or bread roll was safe anywhere. People who had considered restaurants a bastion of adulthood resented this. The matter of children in restaurants became a hotly debated topic dividing the population of North America.

There was no such controversy in Europe, where the issue had long been settled. In England and in Germany children are obscene and not heard; in Portugal and Italy, however, they are everywhere at all hours.

In fact, restaurant staff in Italy or Spain seem happier to see your children than to see you. In North

America, on the other hand, children are tolerated, though I've found few waiters who are glad to see them and many who regard them with horror. A Montreal server would rather have a couple in a contretemps over the escargot than have to deal with children. "I hate kids in restaurants," he says. "To me, people fighting at a table aren't nearly as irritating as a baby crying."

Although as a child I ate in restaurants on only a limited number of occasions, my children have spent virtually unlimited time in them, thanks to the era in which we live and to my job. While other children may have found their mothers at the kitchen stove, mine found theirs behind a menu. Each of the four children who has passed through my hands has spent more time in restaurants than your average waiter.

This does not mean that my kids were more restaurant friendly than anyone else's. But it was worth travelling the road that brings a human from wanting a glass of Tang to craving a cup of black coffee from freshly ground beans. (Once it's travelled, they rarely go back. An adult committed to cassata and cornichons fast forgets the joy of bologna and mayo on white, the hard thrill of frozen Cheez Whiz, the pleasure of a Lifesaver left to dissolve in the cheek, the allure of the petroleum-based pie topping.)

Still, my children did not always appreciate the wonders that were open to them and they often behaved in childlike ways. Children are children, in restaurants and out: babies cry, toddlers toddle, teenagers sulk. One can find dining rooms that are amenable to any of these stages, but they are rarely the restaurants you want to be in. In that regard, I have found the teenage stage easiest: teenagers who have been taken to restaurants all their lives have learned to stray outside the hamburger-pizza-taco triangle of the usual diet and may even be quite adventuresome. (The sight of an adolescent straining spinach pasta through braces is quite riveting.) Otherwise, they can easily be quieted with a Walkman.

It is the earlier ages that I found most challenging. When mine were at the food-tossing stage (they toss, you retrieve), I searched for restaurants where the decor featured plastic modules that could be hosed down, but avoided places where a lucky throw might mean a breadstick in the Pommard was interrupting another table's seduction dinner.

When a child is at that stage, he or she can out-smart the best-intentioned staff. At one eatery, the waiter thought he had solved the problem by spreading a sheet of green plastic under a child's chair. The tyke, for whom a green plastic spread signalled "throw garbage here," responded with Pavlovian predictability and promptly did just that.

The most important rule for little kids in a restaurant is that they must be served immediately. Kids don't have a normal sense of the order of dinner. They prefer to eat dessert first. That is frustrating for parents who mean to use sweets as a buy-off: the dessert menu is a bribe for finishing the okra. Beyond that, children are most likely to eat (in the following order):

- Anything incarcerated in batter and fried until its shell turns to acrylic;

- Any variation on breakfast-food basics—cereal, eggs, white bread toast and catsup, in any combination and at any time of the day, except

127

at breakfast, which is when they want pizza (a balanced breakfast being defined as a piece of pizza in each hand);

- Store-bought birthday cake. If you are in the restaurant to celebrate a birthday, do not bring a homemade cake. "Bought" is what's needed here: cakes with more style than substance, essentially edifices of icing. Children prefer store cakes as a revolt against all the adorable little bunny-shaped cakes that Mommy slaved to make;

- More food, even when they still have stuff on their plates. It isn't that they are afraid that they won't get enough, but that their siblings will get more. A restaurant with good portion control can go a long way to help here, but no matter how careful, no restaurant can overcome one child's determination to torture a sibling and a parent by insisting they were dealt with unfairly;

- Solid items, like hamburgers or egg rolls, but never soup. Soup is always too hot, and once a child begins to blow on it, chances are the blowing will extend to her brother. Soup used to give my children a chance to remind adults that in some countries it is polite to slurp soup. Then they did. Minestrone is deadly because a child will edit out the beans and vegetables and arrange them on the table. He will pick out all the beets in borscht and repeat "Yuck, I hate purple food" so often his sister will pick up the refrain.

While it is wretched to have nasty children seated near you, I think, on balance, children get a bad rap. From where I sit, there are lots more nasty grownups who should have been left at home. A slurping, sloppy child at least has some appreciation for the feel of food and his nastiness can be modified by ice cream. Served more of what he wants, a drunk only gets drunker.

I was once in a restaurant, sitting with a very mindful child, when another diner walked past, patted her on the head and said, "You're a very well-behaved little girl." The child answered gravely, "Thank you. You were well-behaved too."

Role
Call

The terms "waiter" and "waitress" have become issues of linguistic correctness. The resulting censure of the former as servile and latter as sexist has sparked an earnest search for a word that works for both. But so far the efforts have been clumsy. The multisyllabic "waitperson" is a mouthful. (The menu of a restaurant in Providence, Rhode Island says: "Food Allergies? Notify Your Waitperson Immediately.")

There is no help from tradition. *Garçon* is not only pretentious, it is inefficient. Every year, we see waiters from new and various parts of the world, but never from France. In an effort to avoid offending either sex, one trendy place calls them "waitron," a robotic word that offends nothing but the ear. There is a movement to change the term to server, a spare and dutiful word that limits the scope of a person's responsibilities.

I wonder, as I watch waiters struggle with this modern identity crisis, if they wish that they were back in their heyday, when everyone knew who a waiter was and what a waiter did. In the era of fancy restaurants and flambé, a cunningly tossed Caesar salad or a cleverly boned Dover sole was the measure of the man. Tableside performance really counted for something. Then, steak Diane was the Zorro of tableside derring-do: the flight of onions, the writhing of raw beef, the woosh of booze when it hit hot copper—those showed the breadth of the waiter's virtuosity and gave him a place in the world. He knew who he was and what was expected of him.

It's easy to say *him* here, because in those days, there was no question that the waiter was a "him." No one expected women to work in fancy restaurants: they had jobs in coffee shops and (if they were older) in the carpeted luncheon grills of department stores.

The fact is that ritzy restaurants still use male waiters almost exclusively. Women get the lunch-hour sore feet and men get the dinner-time big spenders. The demand for inclusive names now means only that we want to pretend that women have equal rights to wait upon the drunken expense-account customer, the yuppie show-off and the big tippers.

I think the debate misses the point. If we could figure out what a waitperson does, perhaps we could decide what to call him, er, her, um, them.

Is the waitron a server? A salesperson? A performer? A parent? All of the above?

The Parent

Just like the first person who waited on you, the waitron is your parent. A friend who reads *Psychology Today* says this theory works for her, that we are intimidated by waiters because they have control over our experience at table, just as our folks did. She illustrates the theory of Waiter Control by telling about the experience of a forty-year-old friend who, having conquered the scepticism of family and co-workers, finally made it to the executive suite. When she took a young male trainee to lunch, the headwaiter said "Good afternoon, sir" to him, leered at her, and ushered them to a table, watching him for approval. The waiter handed *him* the wine list, as if his gender alone bestowed on him the expertise to know a Pommard from a Pepsi.

Many times, waiters, in true nursery or baby-sitter style, have addressed me in the third person (Are we happy today?), as if my tummy belongs to someone else. Would madame wish another roll? Is madame done with her blancmange? More than once, by the end of the meal, madame wanted to knee him in the groin. (The way a grownup would.)

Men are made to feel like tots too, though not usually by tip-hungry waiters in high-end restaurants. In a delicatessen with a staff whose rudeness is its trademark, I overheard a man ask the Wagnerian waitress what was in the goulash. She ticked off the main ingredients, impatiently, as if any fool should know: tomatoes, meat, vegetables, no not too many carrots, no not spicy. When he asked what was in the cabbage rolls, she answered, "You know, you look like a nice man. But you've gotta grow up!" He ordered the goulash and cleaned his plate, every morsel. He probably flossed his teeth right after dinner, too.

Waitpersons have weapons of intimidation—big weapons that make you feel small. You don't want to mix with a pepper mill that looks like the leg of a

Jacobean table. It is said that these mammoths were invented because customers persisted in stealing. (This is true: customers steal everything from soap in the washrooms to cloth napkins from tables; one Italian restaurant stopped using the clever little spoons for tirimi su because the customers filched them.) Aside from promoting honesty, the spice grinders can be wielded by waiters who mean to keep you in your place.

Pepper grinding and Parmesan pushing appeared in ordinary restaurants in the seventies, and since then, waiters have held us in thrall with their rituals: our meals are barely on the table when they grab the grinder, hold it over the plate, and demand "Pepper?" Sometimes they don't ask. If you go along meekly, like a child who lets her parent sprinkle wheat germ on her cornflakes, he will rush back to the kitchen to tell the other servers about the dopes at Table 4.

Worse than being like mothers, waiters can be like mothers-in-law: even if your mouth is full and your plate is half-empty, they will break into your most private moment to ask if the meal is satisfactory. Should you ignore the waiter—in favour, say, of your date—you will be brought sharply back when he insists on knowing that everything is to your liking.

He also asks if you are ready for dessert, not because you've exhibited any signs of sugar deprivation, but because he'd like to free your table and restock it with fresh customers who will leave another tip and (this is probably his dream!) allow him to grind pepper on their crème brûlée.

Like your mother, the waiter can tell when the storm clouds are gathering and the diners are unhappy with the meal. "I guess it's the way they get silent, the air around the table gets dark," explained one waiter.

Your parent may have distracted you with a promise of an extra hour of television. The shrewd waiter has a comparable strategy. "The best way to keep a complaining table quiet is to give them something free," he said. "You can do this without their demanding it, if you're smart. You can tell when they're mad. It's written all over them: they're not eating and they're not talking." It works the same way your parents put the dessert on the sideboard to coax you into eating your turnips.

The Actor

There's an old joke about two old friends who run into each other. Says one, "I'm an actor, how about you?" "Me too," answers the other. "What restaurant are you working in?"

A waiter told me he sees his service as a performance and the performance he delivers depends on the stage: "At an informal restaurant, such as a pizza parlour, you're personable, cracking jokes, playing the part of being the customer's friend, as if you could be sitting right down with him, because you're that much alike. In fancy restaurants, you are reserved and very polite. After all, giving the customer status is what fancy restaurants are all about. You just pretend, that's all."

Some bestow the benediction of status using a technique known as the School of Positive Strokes: the waiter tells you that whatever you have chosen is terrific (and you, pleased that he has recognized your talent and sophistication, are keen to order more).

"Great choice," he says. "I've seen it in the kitchen and it looks terrific!"

In fact, whatever dish you order is the best; the order in which you want it served is evidence of breeding; and the wine you choose reveals genius. No kidding, your selection may spark a revolution in the way the experts marry wine with food.

The committed actor will persist with stroking, even in the face of appalling choices. Once, when urged to try a restaurant's chicken, but unsure about which to order, I asked for the creamed chicken as an appetizer and chicken Cajun as a main course. Any fool would have noticed the redundancy and surely the waiter did. Nevertheless, he said it was the perfect choice. "You're pushed to gush," says my source, Deep Tongue, who confirms that "excellent" is a big word in waiterspeak.

Sometimes vague names on a menu are a boon because they make the customer ask for an explanation and give the waiter a chance to perform a monologue. ("Timiri su or not tirimi su. That is the confection.") Some waiters make a recitation of the specials sound as if it were an event that should be broadcast live from the Met.

Says one such, "We always memorize the specials to the point where we can describe their ingredients and preparation. I always pump up the product: I loved to be able to say 'served with a fine coulis.'"

Just as the pacing of the play belongs to the actor, the timing of your meal is the waiter's. A good waiter will first off have earned the co-operation of the chef, the person really in charge of your meal.

When they are performing their services, some waiters have only two speeds—slow and stop.

135

Another may perform his part as if he were being governed by a stopwatch: He stands at your table, motor running, impatient while you choose. Or he may be a plate-snatcher, grabbing your table-mate's dish before the last bite has hit bottom, making you anxious to swallow fast, as if the point of the meal is to get it over and done with.

The Salesperson

Today's waitperson is a salesperson or, in the language of the hyped job description, a "sales host." A restaurant association executive says that he likes to remind his waiters that they should be order makers, not order takers. "His job as sales rep for the restaurant is to merchandise the food, to finish the job the menu started. He brings the printed word to life. If he increases your tab he increases his tip, thrills his boss, and boosts his stock."

When economic times are tough, every penny counts and once the restaurant has captured a paying customer, they will try to coax the bill as high as possible. The waiter is the agent for doing so.

Most are paid the minimum wage (which, for restaurant staff, is usually below the average wage) and boost their income through their tips. In that sense, and for other reasons, they are commissioned salespersons: some get a commission on sales and may be offered incentives. If they sell enough shrimp chantilly, they get a bottle of wine; flog the overpriced special and get the next night off.

You may recognize a few tricks of the trade.

Beverages, including mineral water, are always brought first so you will drink them and need another with dinner. Some managers insist their staff say "beverages" instead of "drinks" because it sounds classier.

It takes no more work on the part of the waiter to bring you a thirty-dollar bottle of wine than a twenty-dollar bottle. Therefore, if you order the cheaper bottle, he will try to upsell you. And beware of the house wine: people assume it's the cheapest but, often, it isn't. Note, as well, that part of the sell is in the way they pour the wine—constantly—so you will need another bottle at dinner.

It's a cardinal rule that the first bottle must be finished before the main course is served; the waiter offers the second bottle at that moment the first bottle is finished and the main courses are being brought. Timing is crucial: if the waiter misses the rhythm and brings the first courses before the beverage, diners will start eating and refuse more wine.

The Hungry Waitron

Some waiters know the menu because they have tried it themselves. At a restaurant in Quebec where I worked, the staff were fed before dinner, trying out some of the evening's specialties and finishing those left from the night before. It was my favourite part of a long day that stretched from 10:00 a.m. to midnight, hours that did a great deal to enhance my already overwrought appetite. I loved the abundance of food; I adored the constant play with flavours and textures. The refrigerator was as large as a living room and stacked with cakes, pâtés, fresh produce and chilling beer and booze. Just to stand in it filled me with warmth.

I found opportunities to eat beyond the staff meals. The chef was very particular that the plates being sent out of the kitchen were perfect in every way. If a slice of cake was not symmetrical, it was to be discarded; a carrot incorrectly carved followed it into the large round garbage bin. I couldn't bear the loss, so I ate them.

I once saw a waiter at Scoozi restaurant in New Haven, Connecticut, approach our table savouring the last of a morsel he had filched off the counter in the kitchen (or possibly from our plates).

My waitress source in these matters tries to avoid the practice of eating customer leftovers, but sometimes circumstances overtake one. "It's considered too gross to take something off a customer's plate, but there was this truffle cake in a restaurant I worked in. Each slice had a perfect big chocolate truffle on the top. If the truffle came back untouched, that was fair game."

She reports that most snatching happens after lunch. Many servers come directly to work without breakfast, and have little time for a meal before the frantic noon service. But once the last customer has licked his fingers clean and left, the hungry hordes descend. "We always ate after everyone had gone and I was starving."

At night, staff may be more inclined to drink than eat. My informant says, "The nemesis of lots of people who work in restaurants is booze. They've been serving all day and they figure they deserve a drink or five.

"You probably hear lots of rumours about drugs and alcohol in restaurants. With me it was desserts—especially the fresh fruit tarts at this fancy restaurant

I worked in. The tarts sat on fresh white doilies on a marble slab. They had thin crusts and custard and juicy sliced strawberries or fat little raspberries, all glazed. I'd finish whatever was there, especially if there were parts of three tarts. I gained about seven pounds the summer I worked in that place."

The Good Server

I love the waiters who get it right. They know the menu well enough to guide you through ingredients, steer you clear of food dislikes or allergies and gently point out that squid *en croûte* for the first course may not go perfectly with the beef Wellington for the second. Without asking, good waiters put the right order in front of the right person. I get the apple crumble and espresso, she gets the chocolate decadence and the cappuccino.

The very best servers form a protective, but invisible, net around you and your table. They are unobtrusive, but always available; reserved, but not aloof; friendly, but not forward.

The server must not be invasive or he becomes another personality at the table. The person with whom I'm having dinner is the only person I want to deal with. The server is there to facilitate that relationship, not create another one.

I like a server who pretends I'm right when I complain. All he or she has to do is hear your concern and assure you that action will be taken.

When a Toronto socialite complained about the tirimi su at one popular Toronto dining room, saying "it needs to be softer, smoother texture" (holding up her hands and rubbing the tips of her fingers against her thumb as if she could feel the texture it should be), the waitress answered: "I'm very sorry it's not right. Thank you for telling me. I will inform the pastry chef."

As it happened, there was really no such person. The "pastry chef" in that fancy restaurant is also the salad chef, the soup chef and the sous chef. He is Abdul from Somalia who follows the recipe and puts it on a plate. In the waitress's words: "As if I'm really going to tell him. But I had to tell her I would."

The best server co-ordinates all the roles: the protective and nourishing parent, the consummate actor able to provide the entertainment that is the point of eating out, an excellent salesperson for the boss's goods and services, and, best of all, the vital link between the eater and the cook.

I want to be taken good care of the way I think the Queen is taken care of: by staff who don't cross the line and intrude. The melon comes and goes; the coffee is hot; no one says to the Queen: "Hi, I'm Bruce and I'm your server." The good waiter orchestrates your meal without your knowing he is there. He has no airs, no agenda of his own beyond enhancing your meal.

In Arrivaderci, an Italian restaurant in Toronto, where I was dining with another woman, we got fawning service. When we asked the waiter what was the special of the day, he winked and said "me."

At Fenton's a waitress dressed in a tuxedo, and looking like a skinny man, took all her instruction from the man's side of the table. She moved there right away, as soon as she spotted him, not even standing in the middle as is the custom. She leaned right over my date and asked, "What kind of wine will you be having today, sir?" as if her real question was about what kind of (extremely personal) service she was dying to perform for him.

When she returned, the top buttons of her blouse were undone and her presentation of the wine should have been X-rated. She wiped the neck of the bottle slowly and poured his wine in a teasing little trickle, watching his mouth closely while he tasted it. She treated me with excruciating politeness, with the kind of flawless deference cops exhibit when writing out your ticket.

Which brings us back to names.

What do you call a date who flirts with the waitron? Never again.

What do you call a topless waitron who seduces your date? Tipless.

Prepare To Meet Thy Menu

Menus are advertisements, written to entice you into buying the food on it: simultaneously an invitation to eat and an invoice to pay. A menu is a brochure, a carefully planned and targeted pitch; the diner is its mark. Seems obvious, you think. But it is a fact of human behaviour that responsible consumers who show the utmost caution in every other purchase are suckers for menu sweet talk. If the menu promises "a delicious steak," most people don't say, "Prove it," or "Show it to me before I buy it." They say, "A delicious steak? That's for me."

Over the years, menus have become harder to understand. Once, when apple pie was on every menu in North America, you could order a slice and apple pie was what you got. Now you might be offered pommes de terre de trattoria with goat's cheese in a vanilla coulis.

Sometimes, as the menu drivels on about the spicy forcemeat in gentle casing with green salsa and the waiter brings you a hot dog and relish, the creativity in the writing exceeds the creativity in the kitchen. You can almost picture a collection of staff sitting around a bottle of Scotch, slapping their knees as they come up with each fantastic description. The Courtyard Cafe in Toronto's Windsor Arms Hotel, which closed with the decade, offered "marinated and grilled Washington State lamb and lamb sausage served with ratatouille flavoured with three vinegars, goat cheese, and haricot blanc flan." An uptown bistro had "genteel red snapper invigorated by Scotch bonnet essence."

Indecipherable menus mean you have to spend more time talking to the waiter than to your date. One diner, cross-eyed with confusion at the ingredients and complex dishes described by the waiter, asked for clarification. She was challenged haughtily: "Are you not familiar with Greg's cuisine?"

Menu fraud is very common but it is rarely noticed, and almost never challenged. Pork scallop is often substituted for veal scallop, because pork's white flesh looks more like the milk-fed veal we expect. (Older veal is cheaper and redder.) Margarine is often substituted for butter or butter may have so much air whipped into it that it has the colour of whipped cream and the flavour of lard. It should hardly be served as butter. A common deceit is to describe frozen items as fresh. Press a waiter for proof that the "fresh fish" really is fresh, he will reluctantly allow that it really means "fresh frozen." I once got into a discussion of Talmudic proportions about the freshness of the orange juice described as fresh on the menu of a Toronto deli. I ask the waiter if the juice is freshly squeezed. He says it is. I order it. I taste it. The liquid, a bright orange, is cloying, horrible, oversweet, just like juice made from concentrate. I think I'm the one being squeezed, I tell the waiter. He counters: Well, the juice was squeezed not that long ago in Florida and the oranges were fresh then—that makes it fresh squeezed.

Dessert menus are written in extravagant, sexual language to exploit the notion of eating sweets as enticing naughtiness. Some will list more choices than there were of main courses or appetizers. The sheer variety can make you giddy. I once overheard a man at the next table in a New York restaurant hold the towering dessert menu in front of his face like a deck of cards and say to his co-diner: "I'll see your Decadent Chocolate Mousse and raise you two Lemons in Love."

It is the word processor, not the food processor, that has changed the modern restaurant menu. Just by pushing a button, the day's bill of fare can be changed and easily distributed. Menus—and prices— may change daily. Restaurateurs pretend that menu changes are in their customers' interest, but, after economics, the most common reason they are changed is because the chef gets bored with the old one. Creative by nature, a good chef needs variety to fuel the imagination. If an owner forces him to do the same thing day in and out, he gets stale, and the very talents that make him valuable are stifled.

It is surprising that with menus so easy to print, we still get filthy ones that are graphic maps of what the kitchen has been offering all week. I once got a dirty, worn menu in a restaurant that had been open less than a week. I wondered if the owners had rented grubby menus to make it look as if they were long-established.

I don't mind menus covered in plastic. Although it seems an unappetizing material, it is often welcome because of its association with protection and cleanliness. The plasticized cover is also useful for preserving those celebrated spelling fumbles, like "rabbi in mustard sauce."

Handwritten menus are used by cozy bistros and trendy trattorias to give a homey, personal feel. However indecipherable, they are better than the bistro menu scrawled in faint chalk on a distant blackboard in a dimly lit room. But some reveal more about the menu writer than about the kitchen: you've probably encountered those with handwriting that suggests a homicidal maniac is in charge of your dinner. Spelling mistakes, either printed or handwritten, don't mean a thing. They are put there on purpose to make you think that the chef cares more about cookin' than spellin'.

Many people find modern menus more of a test than a treat. They might be embarrassed that they can't understand all that French or Italian on the menu, or they might be intimidated by the fancy descriptions of the dishes. They are the ones who say: "I'll just have what she's having." What most people want, even this far into the food revolution, is no trouble. They want the waiter to go away and come back carrying something good.

People tend to believe that customers are restricted to the menu, obliged to choose from that list only, and in the order dishes are offered—as if a menu is like a set of assembly instructions from Ikea. In fact, there is no by-law: if you want to, you can have two appetizers and three desserts. You can ask for half portions. Or you can decline to open the menu at all and simply ask for what you want. I have found most restaurants to be obliging in this regard.

Menu-makers give much thought to the design and to the organization of the items. Customers should think of the menu as a map of where the restaurant owner wants you to wander.

Certain colours are known to get your mouth up, so there are reds and yellows for steaks, pasta and pizza. They are warm colours. Fish items are often done in blues and greens—cool, ocean colours.

The most colourful menus are usually found in coffee shops and in diners, where there are photographs of the meal you can expect to have. Some menus are designed like postcards so you can send them to friends to show how you're living it up.

The top right-hand side of the menu is where the eye falls first and is traditionally responsible for 50 per cent of sales. A careful restaurateur will put there the dishes he wants to sell, the ones that bring the highest profit. They are further flagged by order: the items he wants you to have most will be listed first and last, because people's hunger usually hooks onto the first dish or the last one.

The same thought goes into pricing the items, which are usually $5.95 or $2.99 because those seem so much less than $6.00 or $3.00. In the glory years of the eighties, even numbers—$18.00, $22.00 etc.— were common and there was some experimentation with eccentric pricing like $12.34. When the recession made diners cautious about prices, restaurateurs quickly lowered the costs of the main courses. In the eighties, they were creeping up to $30.00, in the nineties, they are below $20.00. However, most customers haven't noticed that the prices of appetizers and desserts have either stayed high or gone up.

Always read the menu posted outside a restaurant before you go in. You can find it in a glass case or in seriously ritzy restaurants cloistered inside the foyer, resting on a gilded easel. In spiffy places, the menu will have tassels and no pictures; the prices will have lots of zeros and no mercy. The cover of the menu will be tooled leatherette and very large—almost as big as the prices. They are useful for hiding your ashen face when dinner is a three-digit disappointment. (In the days when Longchamps in the Empire State Building was the snootiest and most expensive restaurant in New York City, visiting Boston musician Ruby Green lowered the bed-sheet-sized menu, and staring undaunted at the haughty waiter, said, "Tell me, my good man: are these prices or serial numbers?")

The proprietor means to lead you into temptation with the menu in the same way travel agents entice you in February with colour brochures of the Caribbean. Ignore the lure and take the prices and the hype as a warning. Otherwise, you may go in, make friends with the headwaiter, eat the crackers and crumple the napkin before you realize that you have no interest in the chef's seven ways with kidneys (and couldn't afford them even if you did). Then you have to come up with some excuse for leaving without ordering.

Some waiters act out the menu in pantomime. At the chic Park Bistro in Manhattan, the waiter showed me where the skirt steak corresponded to his abdomen by pinching a wad of flesh under his rib cage. Other waiters I've only newly met offered up their sirloins and thymus glands. At Happy Seven Chinese restaurant in Toronto, the waitress, frustrated by her lack of English in her efforts to explain a dish made with beef tongue, compensated by pointing to her own tongue. When I still didn't understand, she grabbed her tongue and practically laid it on my plate.

Waiters often have difficulty explaining the menu to the customer because it is written in a language foreign to both the waiter and the customer. For example, French restaurants like to act French by writing the menu in French and offering no translations, even if everyone knows that most customers don't read French. The sophisticated diner might be expected to have some familiarity with French food, because it is assumed that French is the language of food. Any fool with a spare hope of being thought worldly knows a *frite* from a *figue* though he may be forgiven for being baffled by a dish like *Tripes à la Mode de Caen* which requires knowledge of geography—of France and of the cow.

At a lodge in Quebec's Laurentian Mountains, the waiter actually recites the evening specials, singing a song of light puff pastry and soft, creamed lobster; of scallops still connected to their roe, cradled in lemon grass and honey vinegar. The words sound as good in his mouth as the food later tasted in mine.

Menu recitation became a solemn table ceremony during the eighties. Obviously, restaurateurs had not seen the Gallup Poll showing that 64 per cent of adults preferred to read about the specials on a list attached to the menu, while only 11 per cent preferred the waiter's performance. (I have seen no surveys about how many people prefer the blackboard placed over the table of the couple who break off their romantic gazes to glare at you as you helplessly squint into the dark and try to figure out whether you are being offered pesto or piscatore.)

When the waiter recites the specials, listen for the order in which they are recited. The principle of order of ingredients applies even more strongly here than it does on the printed menu. The dish he mentions first is usually the one he is trying to sell. A man who has owned many restaurants tells me that when a customer is given a list of specials—either written or recited—she is most likely to remember the first offering and the last and forget the ones in the middle. "If the waiter says it right, the first suggestion gets a hungry customer fantasizing about the dish. It makes her mouth start to water and she is still dreaming about it as he describes the next few. When he stops, she will remember the last one he said and likely will choose either the first or last. I always put the dishes I wanted to sell the most in that order."

The term "special" should always make you wary. Customers tend to think (to hope?) that special means the food and the price are better than usual. Don't count on it. The benefits are weighted in favour of the house: the special may be so called because the chef got a good price on the ingredients or because the kitchen just needs to get it out of there. It doesn't mean the food is bad, just that it's quickly dated. On Saturday night, if the restaurant is closed Sunday and the kitchen has ten live lobsters, the waiter will offer it as a special, working to make it sound better than anything else on the menu. "The special tonight is the broiled lobster in a light saffron butter zabaglione."

Make sure you get the price of the special. It is a curious fact of human behaviour that responsible consumers who show the utmost caution in every other purchase are suckers for restaurant food which is mysteriously missing a price.

For example, most of us assume that the unpriced restaurant special will turn out to be a bargain. But beware: it is a common, though creepy, practice to boost the special a few dollars higher than the other items on the menu. The waiter rarely offers the price unless you ask and customers seldom do. Cossetted in the glow of wine and fellowship, we don't notice the tab until the bill comes. By then, it is too late: the meal is consumed, the evening is over, and we pay, feeling caught. Vicious taxes and tipping have boosted the prices even more and the bill is an unappetizing shock. Now, isn't that special?

Some items are especially good profit-makers for the restaurants, and waiters are encouraged to promote them. Like appetizers. You're hungriest at the beginning of your meal, and appetizers have grown bigger in recent years, both in size and in price: they often are nearly the size of the main course and will cost between five and ten dollars, although spiffy restaurants will send them up to twelve dollars.

A waitress once told me, "If they seem hesitant about ordering an appetizer, I suggest they share a Caesar salad or something else." Not only are appetizers profitable in themselves, restauranteurs have found that if you enjoyed the appetizer, you are more likely to order dessert.

Bruscetta is the modern con. Restaurants usually offer bread. That's free. But waiters now suggest bruscetta as they approach the table. It's a high-profit item: a bit of bread, a smear of olive oil and some chopped tomatoes hardly cost the restaurant, but it will cost you, usually about the price of popcorn and a drink at the movies.

A server may try to get you to add extra side orders to your main dish, by offering them casually, as if they're a gift that the chef wouldn't want you to miss. You've ordered the grilled veal chop—the first item on the monologue of specials. "Would you like a few mushrooms with that?" "Or the asparagus?"

Add-ons often are slightly exotic-sounding—artichokes, wild mushrooms—because they can be marked up higher than can an item as commonplace as broccoli. "Would you like a shot of sherry in that soup?" the waiter asks, and you, seduced, agree. The shot of sherry will cost the restaurant twenty-five cents and will cost you three dollars plus tax.

Even those restaurants that list every other kind of dish on a printed menu, like the waiter to sell desserts, the biggest profit-maker of all (aside from alcohol). Because dessert is considered a luxury item, people expect to pay for it. The ingredients of a chocolate mousse may cost the kitchen four dollars a cake, though many restaurants—these days, even fancy hotel dining rooms—buy desserts from wholesale bakeries. The cake will yield eight pieces at six dollars a slice. Kind of makes your teeth hurt, doesn't it?

The waitress: "We always try to get people to order dessert. Those cost about five dollars each and they go stale fast. I find it best to wait a minute before I offer dessert. If I try to push it right away as I'm clearing the main course, people are really full and they'll say no. But if I wait a few minutes, their curiosity and hunger will return."

Restaurateurs are increasingly concerned about the politically correct and ecologically responsible menu, highlighting the low-fat heart-saver meals, line-caught tuna or the promise that the paper the menu is printed on is recycled. Is it just my imagination, or is it true that menus with the most righteous main courses usually have the most extravagant desserts?

Some menus include a thorough list of ingredients for people with food allergies, in an attempt to beat government agencies before they bring in regulations. It is commonplace to see a notice warning those with food allergies to alert the waiter; these cautions protect the restaurant as much as the customer. A customer writhing on the floor with a nasty reaction to anchovies may deter others who are contemplating the Caesar salad.

Some restaurants still like to include a covered and mysterious dish usually called the Menu Surprise. What is surprising is how often it is ordered; customers think it's fun and expect to get something unusual. "Unusual" always turns out to be a dish made with ingredients the kitchen already has on hand. The only surprise is the price, which is the same as that of the other main courses, for which you didn't have to play mouth roulette.

Menus are about choice. In an Italian restaurant I once argued with the waiter about the steep price of the pasta. We had wanted some as a first course—a not unreasonable expectation in an Italian eatery—but the stiff price was a deterrent. Why don't the two of you share one, suggested the waiter. But we were in a restaurant in the first place so that each of us could have what we wanted. Sharing food is what you have to do at home.

The menu can be an effective diversion. If you're out for an awkward dinner with the boss, your son's fiancée or any one of the people we invite because we don't know what else to do with them, you will find that the menu offers lots of possibility for cover-talk.

The best menu in an unfamiliar restaurant is the plates in front of the other customers. Walk around and take a peek. You can even ask. You will almost always get a helpful answer, unless you have interrupted a fight or a seduction, in which case you may get an answer with more flavour than you expected.

This is particularly recommended in Chinese restaurants. The thing about them is that even after you uncover a new find, you are still lost because there seem to be two menus: one for Chinese people and another for the rest of us. I always get a case of Other Table Envy when the food travelling past my table to those of Chinese eaters looks so much more interesting than what's on my plate. I can never shake the feeling that within this restaurant is a secret country to which I, an Occidental, have no passport. Without one, I am doomed to a life of deep-fried chicken balls slathered in sweet-and-sour Day-Glo. Pointing to another table or ordering by number is the only way to ensure you and the waiter understand each other.

All menus have their tricks. No matter what the cuisine, the diner must proceed with caution, to measure the food against the menu, scrutinizing it with the careful eye of a Ralph Nader, not the hungry heart of a Romeo.

Waiter, There's a Flaw in My Soup

I have complained for years about how customers never complain in restaurants. I think we take it on the nose too often. We blame ourselves when the wine tastes odd, shrug when the veal is tough. We sympathize with the chef when the soufflé sinks (poor fellow must be having a bad day), and quietly endure sneering headwaiters and lying menus ("farm fresh" lettuce, "homemade" desserts).

When we find the gumption to protest, we're quick to accept the restaurateur's lame lies: he was short-staffed; the cook is sick; it was an off night; he's really sorry. Gosh I hope you'll try us again.

Then we pay the bill and tip on top. We're even afraid not to tip.

I think the reason for not complaining is that we see the waiter as a sort of parent—standing over us, coaxing us to eat what's put in front of us. The stories of less fortunate children that we absorbed with our Pablum have stuck, and as adults, we feel like ingrates if we don't gobble everything. The chef and his surrogate, the waiter, cast their terrifying shadows across our plates and we submit, snivelling cowards that we are.

We cosmopolitan consumers, who righteously return a faulty toaster to a department store or fight like Clarence Darrow when our rights are violated in traffic court, turn to tofu at the threat of a waiter. When was the last time you returned a bad meal to a careless kitchen?

You're not legally obliged to pay for a meal you don't like. If you take a taste or just glance and find it's not what you expected or want, you can send it back free of obligation. In Canada, the convoluted law known as "invitation to treat" allows that a verbal contract has been entered into between you and the restaurateur: he promises to give you good food and you agree to pay. That law is rarely tested because going out to dine is seldom one of those events you want to litigate. (The cost of a couple of hours in a lawyer's office may make that bad meal seem cheap— and almost palatable.)

Everyone has a terrible story about how he or she was mistreated in a restaurant. About 90 per cent of the calls I get from disgruntled restaurant customers are about service, not food. They include excruciating stories of humiliation, rudeness and carelessness. There's the woman in Halifax whose server spilled the Coke on her, then charged her for the drink. There was the Vancouver party of four who were asked to leave their table and move to a smaller one so the manager could seat a party of five. There was the Saturday brunch when I waited forty-five minutes to be rewarded with Eggs Benedict which had been warm—once. The other people at my table were finished their main courses when the waiter reappeared to take away my cold, hard eggs. I asked him to get the kitchen to make the next ones immediately so we could eat our meals together. His answer: "Why is it when people come out for brunch, which is supposed to be a long, leisurely meal, it's rush, rush, rush?" You can add your own story of in-your-face attitude and make-my-day service.

Restaurateurs may argue that the mood we bring with us into the restaurant affects our response to the service. That may be true, but it is also true that I arrive at the restaurant vulnerable to the ministrations of the staff. And a professional staff can do wonders to modify the mood. Restaurants with frosty welcomes (you could store furs in some of them) or perfunctory farewells should be struck off your list. They could take a lesson from the traditional Japanese restaurant where greetings are shouted enthusiastically from the sushi bar when the customers enter and exit.

When the issue is bad food, it might help to complain. But not often. In a perfect world, the waiter would apologize, whisk the plate away, and return with a perfect one almost immediately, or at least before the others in your party are finished dessert.

But it is axiomatic that a rude waiter who serves you a bad dish will also handle a complaint badly. Should you marshal your feeble resources to complain that the dish is not hot enough, most waiters will remove it and replace it under the grill only until the top crusts over.

You can demand that the entire dish be replaced. But the horrible truth is that bad restaurants make bad food and if one dish is off, the replacement probably won't be any better. Complain effectively about lukewarm soup and it will be succeeded by a warm salad. Furthermore, the waiter will want his revenge on you because you have made him face the cook.

Better him than you. Don't ever take the dish into the kitchen yourself. Ten years ago, at the Taku Hotel in Whitehorse, a customer complained that his breakfast was cold, and the waiter returned it to the kitchen. Cook James Collins shook a bottle of Tabasco on the mound of eggs and potatoes and returned it to the waiter, saying "Hot enough for you now?" Enraged, the customer carried the dish into the kitchen to confront the cook, who ran him through with a chopping knife. The customer died on an empty stomach and the cook is in jail serving a life term.

A few years ago I shared lunch in Il Posto, a spiffy Toronto Italian restaurant, with an editor from New York who was seeking advice on Toronto's best Italian restaurants. I was fond of Il Posto's liver and recommended it to her. She ordered it rare. It came well done. Brave in her company, I insisted that as professional eaters it was our duty to return the unsavoury liver to the kitchen. She hesitated, I pressed and she did. In fact, she felt so empowered that she returned the kitchen's second try at the liver, which was rare but tough. The owner was a fierce woman who hadn't read the manual on consumer rights. After a humiliating confrontation in front of rows of cowardly onlookers, none of whom took our part (maybe they didn't like liver), we were tossed out of the place.

Food critics have recourse. I complained in print while my dinner mate scratched Il Posto from her list of Toronto's best.

Don't be afraid to show your anger. When a restaurateur tells you he's just having a bad day and begs your forgiveness and expects your credit card, tell him all about your bad day. Then remind him about your bad meal. Unless he backs up his sympathy with an offer of a reduced bill or a replacement meal, to hell with him.

Which leads me to a particular category of restaurant: the new restaurant that makes no allowances for its inexperience.

When I go to a play that is in previews, I pay less than I would once it is in regular run. Why can't restaurants do the same? There are precedents. When La Cité Bistro opened in Manhattan in 1989, the management discounted the food 15 per cent for the first six weeks. Park Avenue Bistro in New York did it for eight weeks.

"We used the discount as a signal to the customer to say 'Please excuse us, we're practising on you,'" La Cité's manager, Dennis Martin, explains.

That should be the attitude everywhere. If there is to be no compensation or warning that the restaurant is not up to speed, if it is welcoming customers and charging full price, it is ready to be reviewed. Like any enterprise offering a public service for profit, it must expect to be assessed publicly. Until he has it right, a restaurateur should practise on his relatives, not on recession-weary and unsuspecting diners.

Whether the restaurant is new or old, you must take a stand. Show no mercy towards bad food or lousy service. Don't leave a tip. Tell the owner or manager you will never come back (and don't). Tell your friends about your experience. Word of mouth is still the most effective advertising (good or bad) for a restaurant. And while you're still furious, write a letter documenting your complaints to the restaurant owner and copy it to your favourite nasty restaurant critic.

Get 'em while there's still time for them to come out with their hands up.

A Few Futile Complaints

I get steamed about:

- Cold salad served on plates hot from the dishwasher.

- Hot food served on plates cold enough for salad.

- Waiters who let my dinner cool on the counter while they chat up a tipping customer.

- Restaurants where they fill my cup with one of those appalling candy coffees (Irish cream, almond or some such) without asking me first.

- Hot drinks served lukewarm. It is vital to serve coffee very hot. No matter what the temperature when I drink it, I am offended if it is served cool. Coffee is equally revolting if it is served boiling hot, because you know that's just what it's been doing—boiling. Coffee must never taste cooked. Many restaurant chains have rules about how long coffee may stay on the burner before it is thrown out—a shocking twenty minutes for some—but coffee shouldn't stay on a burner at all. Once the brewing is done, it should be stored in a Thermos.

- I hate tea served in metal pots that have been designed by a misanthrope to pour hot liquid down your forearm and settle in the crook of your elbow.

- I hate tea bags served outside of the teapot on the excuse that some people prefer to control the strength. (An Englishwoman visiting in Canada was so horrified by the practice that she went home and described it as "tea in the contraceptive manner.") Tea should be steeped inside the pot and its strength regulated by a separate pot of boiling water.

- Milk served icy cold from the refrigerator but meant for tea or coffee cools the coffee right down and gives it an odd kind of scumminess. The only time I have had the milk warmed without asking was at the St Thomas Street restaurant in Richmond Hill, Ontario.

- I detest baked goods that have been reheated in the microwave because zapping by the inexperienced who often staff restaurants can so easily compromise the texture: bread crusts get tenacious, interiors turn gummy. Pizza is revolting when it has been microwaved: the cheese releases its water, the crust hardens in protest. My particular microwave sin is the ruining of pecan pie, my favourite dessert. Those pernicious rays cause the custard to run and the pecans to turn to hot little bullets.

I also dislike:

- Plates that are overdecorated with squiggles and squooshes and underdecorated with food.

- Restaurants that serve gargantuan portions so that you'll think you're getting good value. Food served in those amounts doesn't mean the restaurant wants to give good value, just bad vaudeville.

- Hard-to-open packets of butter and envelopes of sugar in pricey restaurants.

- Hard butter that tears delicate bread or sits like pebbles on hard rolls.

- Restaurants (most of them) that serve terrible bread that can only be redeemed by butter. Bread is often the first thing you eat in a restaurant. Because it makes such a strong first impression, why don't more restaurants pay attention to it?

- Polyester napkins that don't absorb. Your hands slide right off them and they slide right off your lap faster than napkins made of cotton or linen.

- Diners who leave big purses or briefcases beside the chair so the waiter keeps tripping.

- Invasive music in restaurants. The best background noise is the steady buzz of conversation. Loud music in a busy restaurant makes conversation impossible. Loud music in an empty restaurant has a desperate sound. Most music interferes with conversation—the main reason you are there in the first place.

- The restaurant pedant who has to explain things at length to the waiter or chef, helpfully bringing everyone up to the mark. "In Paris," he will say, "I had this dish *al dente* with a shaving of truffle." His table-mates and the waiter must suffer in silence. I include in this category the authenticity buff who calls the table to attention so he can parade his expertise on papaya or Pernod.

- Headwaiters who seat two at the room's tiniest table when the restaurant is empty and the couple could have spread comfortably at a table for four.

- Headwaiters who seat women near the kitchen, cash register, washrooms or otherwise below the salt.

- Waiters of my own age who call me "ma'am."

The Sum
Also
Rises

*P*eople talk as if getting a reservation and a good table in a popular restaurant is a great achievement. But I reserve my admiration for those who can achieve an exit without a hassle. Getting into a restaurant can be nothing compared to getting out of it when the meal is finished. Bagging the bill, checking its accuracy and performing the high math required for modern tipping can give you a bigger stomach ache than even the most malevolent meal.

A successful exit falls under the Law of Diminishing Attention, which holds that the waiter, who is often there when you don't want him (your date has just said, "The most exciting things about you are your..." and there he is, topping up your wine, extracting your praise for the blancmange) and, like a cop, never there when you need him (you have ten minutes to make the movie). According to the law: the more you need him, the harder he is to find. The chances of his returning to your table decrease in inverse proportion to your need.

To escape, you must capture the waiter four times. One: he comes to determine why you are waving now that he has brought you everything you ordered. Two: he brings the bill. Three: he retrieves it, along with your money. Four: he returns with your receipt. As a rule, the waiter has three things on his mind at any time: the fork for Table 3, the stew for Table 5 and the drunk at Table 11. At any point in the four trips, you are likely to lose him to one of those more pressing concerns. Any one of those concerns may trigger the law.

To get the ball rolling, motion to the waiter that you want the check by miming writing in the air. This will usually result in action, because it is the most rewarding part of his service to you: your signature translates into his wages. Calling in some foreign tongue, or even your own, may impress the cousins, but, with the waiter likely out of earshot (that could be two feet away in today's noisy restaurants) it won't get you what you want.

Once you have won the bill, read it thoroughly. In my experience, few people do. They are tired, drunk, or distracted by the company or by concerns about how checking the check will make them look to their table-mates. As one businessman told me: "It's incompatible with the meal and the hospitality to do accountancy at that time—it cheapens you."

Such a faulty philosophy is an invitation to restaurant scams. In one of them, the wayward restaurateur runs your card through the machine twice. You sign one chit; he forges your signature on the other. Both are submitted to the credit-card company, and at the end of the month the restaurant is listed twice on your tab. The same diner who didn't check his bill isn't likely to check the credit-card invoice at the end of the month. Even if he does, he may not remember whether it was twice or four times he ate at Chez Bistro Casa de Trattoria. The date is not a clue either, since many credit-card chits are not dated.

Presuming the restaurant has light enough to read by, check the bill to make sure everything is accounted for, but nothing more. If something bothers you, you are perfectly within your rights to ask to see the menu again to recheck the prices. When signing the chit, make sure you fill in all the spaces.

Vigilant people have ways of ensuring that their credit bills have not been tampered with. Some make secret squiggles on their credit-card receipts, so they can check later to ensure that the receipt matches the carbon from the credit-card company. One man tips so that his total will always end in two zeros. That way he can recognize his own bills quickly. For example, if the meal tab is $42.98, he tips $10.02, so that the total will be $53.00 even. Another man adjusts his tips every month so that the total will end with the number of the month. In January, his bills end with number 1 ($53.01); in February number 2 ($52.02); and so on.

Even this basic sort of bookkeeping can be challenging in a dimly lit room after a few glasses of wine, but it can be worth the trouble. At a popular restaurant, I once watched as a party of drunk diners paid the bill and left, leaving a written tip the waiter thought puny; he changed the tip and the total. Chances are the scam worked. Unless the diner compared his credit-card receipt with the company's bill when it arrived six weeks later, it is unlikely he would remember how much he paid or tipped.

Drunk or sober, people rarely know how much to tip or whether to tip at all. There is hardly a practice in restaurants that is more fraught with confusion. We fear that tipping too much marks us as hicks, or that tipping too little will mean we are considered cheap. We are not even sure which staff should be tipped.

Although a tip is supposed to relate to the service, few of us can find the heart to leave nothing when service is bad—"stiffing" it's called. Perhaps you worry that a waiter will miss the point and rate your character and ancestry, rather than his inattention or surliness, by the meagre tip.

He will. A waiter obtuse enough to give a paying customer a bad time rarely makes the connection between his rotten service and your refusal to reward it.

Some waiters claim they can predict our tips no matter what quality of service they offer. One in Montreal told me, "Canadians are so nice. You can ignore them and they'll leave 15 per cent. You can break your butt for them and they'll still leave 15 per cent." A popular joke in Florida goes: What is the difference between a canoe and a Canadian? Answer: Sometimes the canoe tips.

The Montreal waiter likes the challenge of diners from south of the 49th parallel. "American tourists are the best to serve because they recognize good service and they pay for it. Serve an American badly, and he'll leave nothing and yell at you. Serve him well and he'll leave 20 per cent and thank you for it."

Then there are the diners known to waiters as "country folk"—those people, unsophisticated in restaurant culture, who usually reveal themselves by ordering rye and Coke and asking telling questions like "What's a *beurre blanc*?" or "Is the salad included with the meal?" They always leave 10 per cent, according to the slick city waiter who defined them.

The notion of tipping up front is not only not done, any suggestion of it appears to arouse rage. A letter to Washington-based columnist "Miss Manners," asking about the practice of diners leaving some money on the edge of the table at the beginning of the meal brought a Mannerly haruumph: "What is this pre-tipping? Perhaps it is closer to what Miss Manners believes is known as protection money. At any rate, she does not like it."

Tips on tipping

The rule of thumb in a restaurant is 15 per cent for good service, 20 per cent if it was exceptional, although 20 per cent has become the norm in New York City.

Customers tend to tip 10 per cent or lower in places where a small tip is commonplace, such as casual family restaurants. In those circumstances, the low tip often penalizes women who make up the majority of servers in lower-ticket eateries. In a family restaurant, the waitress must work double time to bring your soup at the same time your child is crumbling his crackers into the ficus benjamina.

Ten per cent is also inadequate when the server has to keep running at breakfast and brunch. In Canada, where liquor laws prevent alcohol service until late in the morning, the server cannot benefit from the higher tab that alcohol sales produce. Furthermore, breakfast is a labour-intensive meal—

167

getting breakfast to your table may require twice as many trips as dinner—pouring juice, topping up coffee—and it all has to be done in a shorter time.

But there are occasions when 10 per cent is appropriate: at buffets or salad bars where you have done most of the serving yourself.

Do not tip on the tax. In Canada, you can calculate what you owe by combining the provincial tax and GST (although the result will be on the high side in provinces with whopping sales tax rates) or in the U.S. by doubling the state taxes, which vary from place to place. Or simply ask for the total of the bill before the taxes are added.

In Europe an automatic 15 per cent service charge is added to the bill, in order to save both the customers and the waiter from end-of-the-meal angst. But even that system leaves you with judgments to be weighed: should you comply with the custom of leaving a few extra dollars—or francs or kroner—in cash—on the table to acknowledge *special* service? The result is that few leave their tables without leaving something—even if the service was less than special.

I think most of us wish that tipping could be abolished, that the pain of the practice could be extracted from the pleasure of the meal. We wonder why restaurateurs can't pay the waitress a decent wage and free us from the responsibility of supporting her aging mother. In North America, we have clung hard to the notion of fee-for-service. Restaurateurs and many waiters argue that tipping helps keep prices of food down and encourages a waiter's zeal.

But what the customer giveth, the customer can taketh away. The tip can be freely used as a weapon, one that, increasingly, we should use in hard times, because it is the only part of the bill that we can control.

And that means also that the waiter loses out even when he gives good service. In Canada, after the GST increased already taxed restaurant bills by 7 per cent, some waiters noticed tips decreasing as customers shaved the tips to accommodate the new tax.

But the "7 per cent solution" was a boon to other waiters. Men—usually, it is men—who work in high-end, expense-account restaurants where customers automatically tack 15 per cent on the total bill, found their tips being carried upwards with the bill.

Nonetheless, it's doubtful that many waiters would prefer a higher wage in exchange for fewer tips. A waitress told Hugh Fearnley Whittingstall of the London *Sunday Times*, "Waiting tables is like performance art, and the tips are the round of applause at the end of the evening. You have good nights and bad nights, but if it was the same wage, week in and week out, you'd lose the incentive to perform, and it would get boring."

It is a tenet of food lore that "tips" is really an acronym of the phrase "To Insure Prompt Service." But, if that were true, money would have been paid at the beginning of the meal, not at the end, as is customary.

Some diners also refuse to tip on the alcohol. If it is a high bar bill, restraint is in order, but here flexibility is the rule. Sometimes just calculating 15 per cent of the food, without taxes or alcohol, results in a puny tip that may not be fair to the style of meal and quality of service. Note that in Canada the sales tax on alcohol is higher than the tax on food in restaurants. Make sure the restaurant does not include soft drinks and mineral water in your bar bill before they calculate the tax.

It does the waiter no good for you to leave the tip in cash on the table, while you pay the bill by credit card. Contrary to common belief, it rarely allows the waiter to pocket more money. In many restaurants, especially large ones, the waiter is required to "tip out" to other members of the staff—busboys, kitchen staff, bartender, doorman and sometimes even the owner. Distribution of tips is based on his total sales, not on actual tips received, and the percentage depends on the staff member's position.

If you want to do something extra for a special waiter, put your usual tip on the check and leave a few dollars cash on the table as well; just as if you were in Europe.

Habitués of sushi bars sometimes slide a few dollars to the sushi chef after the meal, in addition to the tip on the credit card.

When you pick up food for takeout, you will sometimes find a blank space on your bill, apparently for a tip. You, by reflex, may fill it in. Be wary: the tradition is for table service provided when you eat on the premises. You don't have to pay it when you're the person who's made it through the snow or rain to get the order. However, do tip 10 per cent on a delivery order.

Restaurants commonly place an automatic service charge—usually 15 per cent of the total—for parties of six or more. The practice has arisen because a group of diners, faced with a high tab of several hundred dollars, may tend to be mingy with the tip.

The restaurateur ought to tell you about the charge when you make the reservation, but many don't. I was shocked when our bill for dinner for seven arrived at the end of a three-course meal at Tabu, a trendy bistro in Palm Beach. The bill was a jolt, but so was the 18 per cent gratuity that had been added—the first notice of any automatic charge. Although he had the right to challenge the charge, our host clenched his teeth and paid.

Even more aggravating is the practice in some restaurants of leaving room on the bill for a tip in addition to the automatic service charge, arguing that the patron should be able to tip more for exceptional service. Of course you are under no obligation, moral or otherwise, to do so. But, by the end of the meal, diners are often too tired or drunk to examine the bill that carefully. They may not notice that the tip has already been added in; they see a blank space and react by filling it in.

Whatever the cause, enough people fall for the redundant tip often enough to encourage waiters to continue this nasty piece of work, which is called "double bagging." One waiter describes it this way: "It's as if you've gone hunting and got two birds with one shot." Some owners hate the practice because it leaves customers feeling that the bill was too high, but others may actually be in on it.

Restaurant staff who repeatedly treat you with kindness that suggests a personal interest should be thanked in kind. Remember them at Christmas or on their special occasion (marriage, birthday, etc.) with a gift—a bottle of wine, for example.

Praise is food for the chef. Convey your appreciation in writing to him or her: it means much more that way than being relayed by the waiter. Your words, delivered second-hand, are appreciated, but a kind, quick note is a record a chef can hold to his or her heart when the days are weary and the nights are woeful.

Unpalatable Truths

I have been involved in many lovers' quarrels in restaurants, both as a participant and as a witness. Some have been tender and heart-rending, others brutish and barbaric. They are all a terrible waste of good food.

In a fabulous Italian eatery, I witnessed a hissed battle at a nearby table, the fight reaching full volume as the first course was served. Through mouthfuls of romaine and olive oil she told him: "You've never told me an honest thing in your life (crunch, slurp)." His reply, strained through minestrone: "Oh yeah, you wouldn't know the truth if it hit you in the face (slurp, mash)."

I was surprised they actually ate through it. I find that when my teeth are clenched and my throat is closed, it is impossible to eat. Think of the years of restaurant fights we witnessed among the Ewings on "Dallas." No one ever managed a bite.

In restaurants where you have to pretend everything is fine, I've had to suck spaghetti through clenched teeth, swallowing my anger, wishing he would eat his words. I usually just push the food around the plate. And sharing never happens in a fight. I never, ever try his food. If he attempted to put his fork onto my plate, I feel no court would convict me if I stabbed him to death with mine.

I don't think couples actually go to restaurants intending to fight: they just plan to "talk this thing out over dinner." And, on the face of it, restaurants seem like a good place to carry on an ardent discussion. The setting imposes physical and psychological constraints on touchy topics that might get out of control if raised in private at home. In a place with no freedom of movement, no freedom to gesticulate or throw your arms around, no freedom to shriek at each other, you can stick to the topic, be more mature, right? It's why experienced negotiators like restaurant settings.

Together alone, an island in a sea of strangers, knees touching under a small table, a couple must focus on each other, staring straight into each other's eyes. Nothing need distract from the topic at hand. A waiter whose mission is to assure your pleasure will bring you everything you need and most of what you want. Alan Alda once told *Cosmopolitan* magazine that eating is one of the few things you can do together "that doesn't lead to divorce." That just shows how stupid even a heartthrob can be when it comes to the triumph of fury over food.

Restrictions, in fact, make restaurant fights not kinder, just more polite. Not less cruel, just quieter, tighter and meaner. Forced to confront each other, with any apparent escape cut off, emotions run hot, and words become weapons. (That's why restaurant fights are the likely source of such gut-wrenching expressions as "bite your head off," "venting your spleen" and the galling "eat your heart out.")

The strain of behaving in public, of appearing calm at the very moment emotions are struggling to break free, is stronger than the stress of fights in private: mimicking gestures and smiles of good humour when you're feeling venomous, pretending that dinner is lovely, thank you, when every muscle in your body begs you to plunge the bread knife into his heart. Or your own. No substance is as volatile as hate under sauce.

One waiter recalls the man at the corner table who snapped a warning to his date that she was making him very angry and perhaps she might help him prevent a scene by putting a cork in it. The woman quietly tipped the gelato onto his crotch and whispered through a thin smile: "Perhaps that will cool you off, darling."

The style of restaurant dictates the kind of fight. In, say, a Greek restaurant where smashed crockery is part of the exuberance, you feel at liberty to raise your voice and wave your arms. In the neighbourhood Burger King, with children shrieking and where a bit more noise would make little difference, you can slam down the fish sandwich and storm to the washroom without attracting attention. But in hushed and reverent temples of gastronomy, where customers feel obliged to behave as if they deserve their wealth, people fight quiet.

The last resort in a restaurant fight—marching out, head held high—is more easily achieved in an informal place, although it carries more impact in one that is fancy. In fast-food restaurants, the food is paid for before the fight, in spiffier surroundings, someone must remain behind to pay, trying to assume a combination of looks that tell interested witnesses "It really doesn't matter; I don't care; it was just a little spat; I'll never talk to that idiot again"—all in one.

From afar, it can be hard to tell whether a couple is fighting. There may be a special glow as they sit head to head in a restaurant. Candles flicker, faces shine, and the mood seems rapturous. Closer inspection reveals that those dreamy eyes are not locked in love, but in combat. The incandescence around the table isn't lovelight, but the kind of flare used to mark car crashes. The romance has turned to rancour. The loving couple is having a restaurant fight and the pepper steak isn't the only flesh that's burning.

Waiters get close enough to know a lot about restaurant rows. None of our avoidance strategies—like stopping mid-sentence when the waiter draws near—fool them a bit. They know clandestine combat better than anyone and often have special tactics to deal with it. A smart waiter will approach cautiously when he sees emotional steam rising from a table. But a really good waiter can actually help keep the fight under control, earning the gratitude of both management and the other guests. He achieves this by putting a rhythm on the fight with well-timed interruptions. "May I bring the wine, sir?" "Would you like some dessert, madame?" The questions must be carefully weighed. The smart waiter would never interrupt with the standard-issue waiter query: "Is everything to your liking?" because someone may answer.

A waitress says, "When a couple is fighting at a table, they may think they are being discreet, but all the staff know because the server tells them. We have to keep the kitchen informed of what's happening at the tables, so they can pace the meal. If the kitchen's not happy with you—if you screw up their timing—you're going to have a fight of your own. I need their co-operation, so I'll tell them, 'There's a battle at Table 18. Hold the appetizers—he looks like he plans to take a layer of skin off her.'"

Other than that, she doesn't much mind fights and finds they provide some distraction from the routine. "I'm deadly curious about what the fight is about and who is saying what. Unless there's tears. If someone is crying, I just stay away."

Montreal waiter Angus Duff wonders why anyone cares if a couple is fighting. "In Europe, people love and fight at the table all the time. It's part of life and no one takes much notice of it. In Canada, we've turned restaurants into a sterile haven that demands special behaviour. It's silly. I like to let people do what they are doing, unless it disturbs another table."

A waiter who deftly handles a fighting table may be well rewarded. Though you might expect that a preoccupied couple will stiff the waiter, their tips are often bigger than usual—perhaps because they feel badly about the tension. The waitress calls it a Guilt Tip.

Skilled maitre d's know how to prevent skirmishes. The customer who comes with a mistress at lunch and his wife at dinner must be greeted as if he hasn't been there in weeks.

The burden often falls to the maitre d' to juggle tables to prevent newly estranged couples from encountering one another when each is locked in candlelit rapture with a new love. At Sonny's in London,

177

where Mick Jagger sometimes dined, people in the restaurant watched with great interest as he ostentatiously ignored former lover Marianne Faithfull.

They remind me of the couple in Toronto whose courtship and marriage had included many restaurant romances and restaurant fights. When they split up, they actually divided custody of the restaurants they frequented (she got The Hazelton Café, he got Fenton's—both of which barely outlasted the final decree).

Even if you are very careful, other people can get embroiled in your argument. A woman once admitted that she couldn't help overhearing the argument at the next table, nor could she resist offering her opinion. When the man went to the washroom, she turned to his dinner date and said, "Dump him honey."

I once shared a table with a competitive couple who were in the last throes of a short and volatile marriage. The fight was precipitated by the waitress, who innocently put a Bodum coffee pot between them, so that they could share. The lever had not yet been pushed down. He slammed it down immediately. She could barely contain herself and issued the first volley. "Darling, the Bodum method requires some patience," she said with malicious sweetness. "You must wait for the coffee to steep before you push down the lever." He countered silkily: "My sweet, I do believe I know how to make coffee." After several exchanges, he rose to address the room: would we set his wife straight about the Bodum? No one looked up. No one answered. The other diners were studying their plates as if they expected to have to answer questions about them. The fighters left, taking the argument onto the street where, unfettered by the rules of a restaurant, it later became—well—grounds for divorce.

Sometimes just going out to eat can start a fight. One man reports conflict over the kind of meal. "My idea of eating out is a long, leisurely, indulgent night over food and drink. For her, indulgence in food and drink is tied up with restraint and guilt. Inevitably, she eats more food and drinks more wine than she planned. Then she gets mad at me because she thinks I put her in the position where she was forced to do that. Her anger at herself gets passed on to me."

Restaurants are even better for making up than they are for fighting. One battling duo look forward to going back to turn the experience around. They find it a turn-on. Referring to Le Select, an Edmonton restaurant where they have fought twice and made up once, he said he found that making up in the same place they fought to be quite heady. "The place was so infused with mutual meaning," he explained.

I prefer to return to places where the food has better flavour than the memory of the fight. The best dishes to order include soft, sweet foods that restore the taste of happier times and heartier appetites. Do not order kebobs on skewers.

Alone
Together

*I*f we are to go by statistics, the number of people eating alone in restaurants has increased enormously. Although our attitudes have changed, I doubt that we are yet fully comfortable with seeing one person eating at a table for two, nor are we comfortable doing it ourselves. There was a time when women never ate alone, but that time ended when women began to travel—unless we learned to eat alone, we would be sentenced to night after night of room-service meals. Room-service meals are a joy the first night, depressing after that. Eating alone is like that: a relief or a burden, often both.

I eat alone a lot; sometimes because I want to, especially at home on cherished nights when everyone else is out and solitary eating seems like a holiday. I like the opportunity because all rules of etiquette are suspended: I can do it in front of the TV set, with the plate on my lap, or straight out of the casserole or take-out bucket.

I can grab spaghetti in handfuls while standing over the sink; drink noodle soup right out of the bowl and slow slurp long noodles; eat sausages in whole baked potatoes, as if they were hot dogs, squirting catsup along the meat; suck the ends of chicken bones without causing someone at the table to gag. I feel reckless and grateful that 't takes so little to feel footloose and free.

So I am of two minds when I read articles about treating yourself well when you are alone, with a proper setting, a placemat, even a candle. The idea is to set the table as if to say, I'm important all on my own and I don't need someone here to justify nice china. These articles miss the point. Treating yourself well when you're alone might just as easily mean sitting around in your jammies eating ice cream with your hands. Eating alone has its own singular pleasure in self-gratifying selfishness. Who needs a placemat?

Sometimes I eat alone because I have to: in restaurants when I am travelling, and at home when my lunch date cancels and there's no one else around. Just after my marriage ended, I often had no one to eat with but I enjoyed the solitude. However, my friends felt sorry for me, and I began to wonder whether my pleasure in eating alone was evidence of a character flaw. (When you're first separated, you think everything you do is evidence of a character flaw.)

Some people won't eat alone, no matter what. Once, as I was sitting at a cafeteria table at the Chicago airport, a man came up to me and asked if he could join me for dinner. "I hate eating alone," he explained. He started to put his plates on my table even before I answered. We talked amiably until he finished dessert and drank his coffee. Then he thanked me and left. Although I've never seen him since, I imagine him in a thousand airports sitting with a thousand strangers just so he won't have to eat alone.

I understand his need for a companion while eating in public. Dining alone in restaurants is different than dining alone at home, because other people see you doing it.

I have long admired the fabulous M.F.K. Fisher's essays. She said that the two best ways to enjoy dinner were first, with a group of no more than six people and second, alone in a restaurant with an attentive waiter. I feel far too self-conscious sitting alone in a restaurant, especially with an attentive waiter, to enjoy the food to its fullest. It is an activity filled with hazards.

For example, restaurant staff may ignore you. I once waited alone at a restaurant entrance for a table for one, while a couple waited behind me. The hostess looked through me, greeted them and turned to show them their table. When they protested that I had been there first, she laughed. "Oh, I didn't see you standing there."

When you eat alone, you are at the mercy of the staff. The server may be overly solicitous and destroy your privacy, or be frosty, because while occupying a table for two, you will be tipping for one. Or the server can make the meal a pleasure.

A waiter tells me: "Serving singles is an area that can get a waiter into a lot of trouble because it throws the usual pacing of the meal off. Everything must be quick. The person sitting alone has no one to talk to, so they feel the minutes between the courses more. The kitchen has to be faster and the waiter has to be on the kitchen. That can cause some tension.

"And remember: Alones are there to eat, so they are often a better bill than they would be as half a couple."

The trend is now to bars with stools at the front of the restaurant to accommodate the increasing number of single feeders. This is actually an old trend in disguise—a reinvention of the wheel. Although many restaurants now serve dinner for singles at the bar, which they call bar-counters, there is something about the line of backs hunched over a counter that is depressing. And I hate sitting on bar stools with my feet swinging. Balancing rice on a fork is all the steadying work I should have to do, and I want a back for my chair.

But the counters—at sushi bars, booze bars and diners—are all good places to eat alone; facing the cook or bartender is better than facing an empty chair. In fact, watching the grill cook at an old-fashioned diner is great entertainment. They have special skills, these acrobats of the diner stoves: breaking eggs with one hand while they flip the pancakes with another; building a mound of hash browns at the moment they spoon the cole slaw. Lunch counters are show biz: facing the stage, you can watch the drama of an egg white turning from opaque grey to solid white and hear the opera of onions squeaking from the heat as they are flipped and turned.

Sushi bars have chairs with real backs and are the easiest places in which to eat alone. The sushi maker is your companion, making each piece of food to order. Watching him manipulate tiny pieces of raw fish, vegetables and rice into shapes and mouthfuls is terrific fun. The menu at the sushi bar is not limited to raw fish and you can have anything you want—except for those cook-at-the-table things like sukiyaki.

Studies have shown that singles are happier eating at a bar when the bartender is a woman. Life has shown that everyone is happier when dinner is served by Mom, except Mom. She is often happiest, alone, eating a pint of Rocky Road straight out of the cardboard container.

Sociologists tell us that restaurants have become increasingly important for providing the sense of belonging that can be an antidote to the alienation of big cities. But people eat in restaurants for all sorts of reasons—some for a moment of peace and privacy, others because they are travelling on business or vacationing by themselves.

The worst enemy of the lone diner is the dreaded table for two where one sits like a teeter without a totter. Why can't designers develop better tables for one? Dining rooms should offer lots of choice—booths, counters, tables for one, two or four. And I think singles should be made comfortable in whatever part of the restaurant they choose to sit.

I have some advice for restaurateurs. I wish headwaiters would use common sense when they seat me when I'm alone. If I'm carrying a book or newspaper, I'll need a table with some decent light—not near the kitchen, cash register or washroom. And please make it a table large enough to open that book or newspaper. And please, please, not in the centre of the room, where I will be a focus for the other diners.

Your welcome should be kind, but not effusive; the server should be friendly, but not fawning. I appreciate respect for—and no comment about—my choice of reading material as a dinner companion.

At the entrance, don't ask, "Is it just you?" or "Are you alone?" Especially don't ask in a loud voice, so that every head in the place turns to see what loser couldn't get a date for dinner. There are better ways to determine how many people there are in a party. I like the approach at the New York restaurant Paris, Texas, where the maitre d' asks, "Will you be dining with the bartender tonight?"

I am getting accustomed to sitting at the communal tables that are being used in some hip restaurants. When, as in a Chinese restaurant, lots of different-sized groups are seated at the same table, lone diners find it easy to eat without feeling orphaned.

There is a respect for privacy at these communal tables: individuals share a common surface without social obligation, though proximity does lend opportunity, if you're up to it. When I'm alone, I like the food to be good, but not so fabulous that I feel frustrated because I don't have someone to share it with.

Some cities are better than others for cross-table talk. Even seated alone at a table for two, I found that in Santa Fe, San Francisco, Florence or in New York, people around me struck up conversations or responded when I did. In Boston, Toronto or London, you could drown in your soup and no one would give you a glance. In those cities, eating alone is solitary confinement.

The major benefit to eating alone is that you never have to share your food. While sharing food might be fun with an intimate, I hate sharing my drink. If it's my drink I'm being asked to hand over, I just say,

"Here, please have it. I was finished anyway."

On the other hand, I believe other people should not hesitate to share their food with me. I even wish I could lean over to strangers in restaurants and ask if I could just have a little taste of their dessert. That's because the food on other people's plates often looks better than what I have on mine. No, let me restate that: it almost always looks better than mine. (Just as the book being read by the person sitting next to me in the subway always looks more interesting than mine.) I find this is especially true in Chinese and Italian restaurants. In Chinese restaurants the menu's descriptions are indecipherable, so I become convinced that any dish travelling to a table where Chinese people are sitting must, by axiom, be better than what I, an Occidental, have ordered.

In Italian restaurants, it is common for the owner to take favoured customers under his wing and arrange special dinners for them. In those places, you indicate you are a member of the club by throwing away the menu. I am so filled with envy at these tables who are getting food I couldn't have that I want to lean over and put my fork in their plates.

The notion of sharing food is under assault because of germ phobia. People are so frightened of microbes, they are afraid to have even friends touch their food. I notice this when on assignment, where I expect to have a taste of everything that's been ordered. Not long ago, I thrust my spoon into the Designated Eater's soup and he recoiled. "Can I get you your own bowl?" he asked frostily. I'm offended when that happens, because I know I'm clean. Doesn't he?

We are expected to share platters in Chinese restaurants, but the practice is a horror to anyone unused to it. (The long Chinese chopsticks are ideally suited for extending your reach. Japanese chopsticks, on the other hand, are much shorter because the food is served in individual portions.) In *Reversal of Fortune*, the movie about the Claus von Bulow case, the lawyer, his staff and their client, the proper, mannered European, are forced into a typically raucous Chinese meal. Von Bulow's barely concealed horror at the ritual, his plea—"I wonder if I might have my own plate"—falls on deaf ears because the others are too engrossed in the ritual.

In a Chinese restaurant in Kentucky, a sign on the wall instructs customers to "Please share." But I noticed that everyone orders their own plates and holds onto them for dear life.

We used to be better about this, but now you have to have been married to someone for a year before you'd let him lust after your linguini. Sharing food with someone is an act of faith, maybe even of commitment.

Of all the prohibitions about food, the most strongly held seems to be about someone touching your food with their fingers. Someone's fingers on my food means my knife in their heart.

Sharing food is the basis of many seething hurts in relationships. A therapist in Los Angeles sees her husband's habit of poking his fork into her plate as a metaphor for their marriage. "He has absolutely no respect for my boundaries. He just sticks his fork in my plate without even asking. Think of what it means when a man sticks his fork in a woman's plate without asking—without any sort of foreplay. I don't think this is my problem," she says, her voice rising to a shout. "I think it is his. I've shared food with husbands before."

Some restaurants put a tax on sharing: five dollars for a shared plate at Guido and Patrick's in Boynton Beach, Florida. Ironically, this infuriating bounty always seems to be levied in places that have huge portions. While the meals are big enough to look as if they were meant to be shared, restaurateurs make it hard to do it by charging you for taking the logical action. They often apply other rules as well, such as no doggie bags. (Restaurants used to be better about giving doggie bags, but perhaps they've stopped because some places were finding that the number of doggie bags leaving the restaurant exceeded the local canine population.)

Diners can usually keep their forks to themselves until dessert-time, but that's when they go astray because they hesitate to order a whole dessert for themselves. They say, "Why don't you order and I'll just have a bite." So you order cheesecake and they begin taking "bites" until you wish they'd order their own.

The dilemma of sharing is illustrated by a woman whose marriage to her doctor husband has been bliss except at mealtimes. He is firm in his belief that the food on her plate is his to explore. In their twenty years together, she has been unable to alter his behaviour. (You think your doctor is indifferent?)

One night, as they shared a table at a trendy new Italian restaurant, the conversation was animated and his company a pleasure. As she took a mouthful of pasta arrabiata, suddenly a bay leaf lodged in her throat. She gesticulated madly, clutched her throat, tried to call, but no words came.

And no help came from him. He was busy—eating her spaghetti. Maddeningly silenced, she was forced to watch him polish off the remainder of her plate.

"There I was choking and all I wanted to do was choke him," she reported later.

He was unrepentent. "No point in wasting good pasta," he said.

Interiors

When I was in my twenties, first writing restaurant reviews, I thought restaurant décor was beside the point. In fact, I was sure that too much attention to comfort compromised the kitchen—the only room that really counted. If the food wasn't perfect, what was a restaurant for? And if it was, how could the room or the hospitality matter?

I had this argument with my mother who said that a restaurant should make her feel comfortable, welcome and a little pampered. If food was the only point, she could do as well herself.

Now that I am closer to the age my mother was then, I find in this, as in the occasional other thing, she was right. In the stage somewhere between my first youth and second childhood, I am as conscious of the feeling of the dining room as I am of the food, and grateful for safe, comfortable places where I can step out of the ring for a while and have responsibility lifted from me.

Restaurants function as sanctuaries, as nightclubs,

as pubs. They are communal public spaces where people can relax at the same time in the same circumstances, using the same tranquillizers and stimulants of food and wine. In this way, restaurants serve a vital social function, basic to a sense of community. In the big cities where most of us live, restaurants also serve as neutral territory for any kind of negotiations, be they business or romantic. A restaurant is neither your place nor mine—it is ours.

Whether or not any of this works depends in large measure on the feel of the room. This is a quality even more abstract and subjective than the taste of the food, but the importance of it does humble the importance of food. It's not that food isn't important; now, however, it matters most in a kind and nourishing context. A restaurant succeeds when it feeds all the sensibilities.

I rush to emphasize here that I am not talking about the kind of comfort and kindness that is associated with expensive restaurants. Some of those haughty rooms are the least comfortable spaces I have suffered. The pleasure of a room isn't easy to buy; it is achieved more through ambience than its appointments. What's on the walls doesn't count nearly as much as what's in the welcome.

It doesn't make poor food taste better, but it does influence my tolerance for food that is less than sublime, which is to say most food. At Splendido, a Grand-Go-To in Toronto, where the room is always lively, the service always confident and thorough, when I am served a piece of mediocre salmon (often), my feeling is: What the hell, at least I'm having a good time. If the atmosphere and the room were not a comfort, the commonplace salmon would infuriate me.

Hospitality Sweet

When readers call to complain about a restaurant, nearly always they are angry about the service, not the food. Diners may not be sure that they have been insulted by the kitchen, but they know for sure when they have been insulted by their hosts.

"If I'm paying all this money, I must feel a little spoiled," says a reader calling with a list of abuses, mentioning the goop du jour only at the end of her rant. She vowed she would never return. For most people, rudeness in a restaurant is irrevocable: once they've been badly treated, almost nothing will erase their anger, including a free meal.

Sightlines

The physical setting of the room can influence how well the warmth and welcome can be expressed. From such details as the way the tables are angled into the room to the colour of the walls (imagine the effect of a yellowish-green wall on a woman in the trying first trimester of pregnancy), to the less tangible atmosphere, we are undoubtedly very affected by the setting. So is the staff. If a restaurant is theatre, as so many have argued that it is, then the room is their stage.

A successful dining room delivers what it promises. A trendy, happening place ought to give you a hip view of the passing scene. When you go there, you want to feel that the price of your meal includes the floor show. The aisles may be wide enough to serve as a promenade; or they can be crowded with tables so close together that you and the people next to you are breathing the same air, the scents from your plate mix with the smell from theirs—your lamb kebobs with their tomato soup, their cross talk and yours—everyone shouting from one table to another, the yoo-hoos yodelled across the room.

According to Toronto-based international restaurant designers George Yabu and Glenn Pushelberg, "A successful restaurant has a hierarchy of tables, a mix of twos or fours and singles, some tables better than others. The good ones are where you can see and be seen, the bad ones take you out of the stage and put you off to the sidelines, unimportant."

In Malibu, Wolfgang Puck's celebrity-studded Granita is tiered like a nightclub with two levels and a wide entrance. Postrio, a Puck restaurant in San Francisco, has a wide staircase leading into the dining room, so newcomers can be scrutinized as they descend. Splendido in Toronto has stars painted on the floor to define a path, like a fashion runway.

But the kind of restaurant that calls itself Mom's should follow through with a "Hi honey, I'm home" kind of coziness, with soup that tastes like it has simmered slowly on a familiar stove. Homey can mean different things, of course. A recent joke is about a man who goes into a restaurant called Mother's, which promises a meal like your mother gave you. When he asks the waitress for the soup, she says, "Get it yourself."

I liked the days when you could count on ethnic restaurants to look corny. East Indian restaurants had pictures of the Taj Mahal: the classier the restaurant, the smaller the picture; Spanish restaurants had pictures of straining matadors and Greek restaurants, posters of the Acropolis.

But the restaurant revolution de-ethnicized ethnic restaurants. As national cuisines became upwardly mobile, they strained to pass for white, just like upwardly mobile people casting off trappings of their earlier lives.

Trendy restaurants look alike no matter what city, country, or what cuisine: minimalist if that is the trend or pine and ferns if fashion demands. They are decorated à la mode. The trendy restaurant is defined more by clientele (the overdressed and the underfed) and decor than by cuisine. The restaurant might be Italian or Thai, or a crazy combination of both. It all depends on what is selling that month.

There are no pictures of mosques on the walls at Byzantium, a restaurant serving Middle Eastern food in Toronto. It has gone high tech and high gloss, and there is no way to know that couscous will be served until you open a menu. The cheaper restaurants still trumpet their heritage and I still prefer them. We were not meant to eat hoummous off French porcelain.

Chinese restaurants may be the most seriously thought out of all, because they follow the philosophy of *feng shui*, and employ a *feng* (water) *shui* (wind) master to implement it. It is based on the use of positive and negative elements of nature to create a physical atmosphere conducive to well-being. Chinese restaurants have a characteristic look because they favour the happy colours of red and gold and because of the functions of waterfalls, mirrors and fish tanks. If a positive energy force is interrupted by a wall, a window may be moved to allow it to flow; if a negative force threatens, a mirror or fish tank may be added to deflect it. Positive energy is associated with good health and prosperity.

For a time in the eighties, trendy restaurants had open kitchens to show off the chef and the other workers making a strenuous effort on our behalf. They turned the diners into health inspectors and the cooks into performers and as such they were fun, though they made me miss the immediacy of the clatter and action of the open grills at the lunch counters that inspired them.

Putting the Din Back in Dining

For the past ten years, the trend in restaurant rooms has been noise and brightness. The two are interdependent: the brighter the light, the noisier the room. (At a small, noisy restaurant, the waiter may lower the lights "to bring down the sound.") Manhattan's Mesa Grill is one of the most frightening examples of noise-light affliction—it is a horribly trendy, uptown, upscale eatery specializing in southwestern food that offers every kind of upmarket gizmo and none of the peace that makes the southwest a sanctuary.

In the style of New York chic, a very discreet entrance (just a plaque on the door as the only evidence of a restaurant—a common snobbism) opens onto a cavernous and colourful room with a main-floor kitchen and two storeys of tables. The noise level and bustle are intense and invasive. The food is fabulous, but by the end of one dinner, I couldn't tell whether the rawness in my throat was from the thrill of the chilies or the hoarseness that comes of having to shout across the table. We had to go out after to have the conversation we had planned.

Although restaurants with high lights are uncomfortable, rooms with eerie lights are worse. I avoid places with lime-green lightshades and I never sit outside on the patio at Puffin's in Toronto because the blue neon makes everyone at the table look as if they have malaria.

As I get older, I like fast-food places less, because of the high lighting. They want you out fast and the overlit ambience designed for that purpose is not kind to beings older than ten. While it may take a while for the high-fat food to show on my body (a matter of hours, in my particular case—a Big Mac cleaves to my hips like cheap steel to a magnet) the light does fast violence to my face.

The brightness of the artificial light is exaggerated by the yellow walls and furniture favoured by decorators for some perversely sunny reason.

Equally damaging to my serenity is the sound that accompanies the light. Shouting children, weary parents shouting to the shouting children, and the kitchen staff calling to one another create a commotion inside my head that feels like a thousand Cuisinarts on high.

Sometimes restaurants also use a soundtrack to increase the volume, to set the mood or to provide a neutral noise that will fill acoustical holes in the room. For a time, elegant restaurants played either the Pachelbel Canon or Vivaldi's *Four Seasons*. In the eighties, I sat through two decades of *Four Seasons*.

I loathe background music in restaurants. It is always in conflict with conversation—the best part of any meal. Either the music is crummy and too loud, and you must strain to avoid it, or it is wonderful, in which case you strain to hear it. In either case, the reason you came to the restaurant—to talk and listen to another person—is compromised.

Noise is the fashion in trendy restaurants, a planned part of the atmosphere. Rooms are decorated to reflect and exaggerate it, rather than to absorb it. Hard-surfaced walls, floors and ceilings, which reflect noise, have replaced the carpeted floors and clothed tables that once muffled it. The music is frantic, the pace is deliberately intense, the lights are high, the volume is pumped.

This craze feeds social needs more than it does gastronomic. The climate of the times may have affected our need to gather together; social noise disperses gloom. Because this fashion took hold during the Gulf War and in the midst of the recession, it has been postulated that noisy restaurant rooms offer a refuge where people can huddle for reassurance.

But large, bright, sociable, noisy rooms are also an antidote to the anonymity of large cities because they create an atmosphere that gives you a feeling that you know one another, even if you don't. Everybody does know each other in a certain way: at 5:30 p.m. you have a lot in common—you have just come from work, you had trouble parking, it's your first glass of wine for the day, and now you are selecting what to eat from the same menu in a restaurant where you have both been before. In a big city, that passes for intimacy. These restaurants are North America's answer to the British pub.

In loud restaurants the lights must be on high. "You have to have high lights when there is noise," according to one restaurateur. "One is strange without the other. No one would laugh in the dark."

The noisiness is also an antidote for that most horrible of restaurants, the empty one. I hate the self-conscious feeling of quiet places: the lonely agony that makes you feel sorry for the restaurateur, the way you feel for an actor who has just humiliated himself on stage.

The ambience in a modern restaurant is a troika of noise, light and speed. Today, restaurant service must be fast. One restaurateur told me, "These days people won't wait through a three-hour meal. Activity is part of the fast-paced life of a city. People want bouncing noise and fast service."

At Auberge Gavroche, a small French dining room in Toronto that succumbed to the recession—and was also one of the many victims of the fashion for franticness—I once overheard people at the next table complain when the waiter told them that the tarte tatin—a glory of caramel, pastry and apples, prepared fresh to order—would take twenty-five minutes.

The waiter apologized to us for the fuss and whispered: "People hate to wait. It means they have to talk to each other." Why must fun be so fast? Whatever happened to camaraderie and conversation?

At Lotus, a small Toronto restaurant with superb food that is an evening's entertainment, people foolishly try to cram in dinner before a show. One regular boasted about his technique to ensure efficient dispatch of dinner. He would phone ahead to order the first course so he wouldn't have to wait once he arrived.

Is Diner à Deux Dead?

Noise, bright lights and fast service have cost us the quiet dining room where you could have the most nourishing of meals, the intimate dinner. I'm longing for the kind of restaurant we once called romantic: a candlelit corner in a small room, a lovingly-laid table, maybe even a violinist. Restaurants with strolling violinists may be hokey, but so is romance.

Of course food in romantic rooms is important. The menu should sound great and the food may even taste great, but, really, who's hungry? More vital is the waiter for whom your happiness matters more than his tip, the waiter you might make best man at your wedding. He should serve your meal in a quiet corner where the soft words taste as delicious as the morsels of food you share from each other's plates. These are the gestures that make the evenings that could stretch into morning: the evenings you don't want a dining room where you see anyone or anyone sees you. Your eyes are only for each other.

After three of Toronto's most romantic restaurants closed within a few years—Fenton's, Auberge Gavroche and Three Small Rooms—a caller wondered where he could propose to his girlfriend.

"There's a lot of romance under Toronto's steel and granite," he told me, lamenting the lack of places to express it.

He finally popped the question in the dining room on the fifty-fourth floor of an office building. "It wasn't a great room, but we had the world at our feet."

I get more calls from people looking for that kind of restaurant for a special dinner than for any other kind. When the caller asks for such a place, I think the one they probably have in mind is the restaurant in "The Young and the Restless"; it's the place where the women and the dining room are dressed alike—in brocade and chandeliers. I've never seen anyone eat in those scenes in the soap operas, no one even seems to order dinner. They just talk of love instead, and sometimes they dance.

199

People like dark and ornate restaurants for romance. I heard about someone whose marriage proposal came in the form of a diamond ring tucked among the garlic toast in a steak house. Another woman told me that her husband presented her with an anniversary gift in a fancy restaurant. A waiter entered bearing a silver dome, and when he lifted it, a bracelet was sparkling on a bed of lettuce. The woman was suitably impressed. "What a great restaurant!" she said. "I wonder what the other customers are getting?"

Japanese restaurants can rival even French for romance. Their tatami rooms offer rare opportunities for privacy, a quality absent from most of our trendy restaurants. Removing the shoes before entering is highly symbolic. The rice paper walls offer intimacy that is reinforced each time the waitress slides the partition closed after she serves your food, leaving the two of you inside, on the floor, knees touching. (Sake heated just a notch above body temperature helps too.)

The best restaurants for romance are so dimly lit that it's impossible to see anything but each other. And what you see is in a wash of candlelight. Years of watching people across the table from me has taught me that aging men must never sit under a pot light focused on the top of their heads, and women of a certain age should move the candle on the table off to the side because shadows from candlelight are more flattering when they are less direct.

I miss darkened restaurants in general. They help us preserve our illusions about each other and about the restaurant.

200

Returning to the Scene of the Prime

There used to be an inverse ratio of light to cost in restaurants: cheap restaurants had lots of light; expensive restaurants were dark. The higher the cost of the food, the lower the lights.

Since fashion has turned that concept on its ear, steak houses are the only restaurants left where the light is so dim you have a hope of concealing your baser activities. I once had a call from a transvestite seeking a nice restaurant that was dark enough so that he wouldn't be noticed. I couldn't think of any place to send him except a steak house, because they are often so shadowy you can see neither your plate nor your date. I haven't heard back from him, so I can only hope that his evening went fine.

The steak house—now there's a room with a past. Most modern steak houses give you the feeling that you went out for a smoke sometime during the seventies and when you came back twenty years later, nothing had changed. The lights are still low and what illumination there is, is shaded by counterfeit Tiffany lamps and absorbed by dark walls. It's as if the darkness is a shroud, leaving everything spookily untouched. The chairs are cushy and the waiters are in tuxedos. The people next to you are eating escargot bourguignon, which means that there are little flecks of dry parsley flakes in a pool of melted butter that holds small snails whose last address was a tin can.

Also, I miss the tools of the trade that were unique to rooms with a moo. Steak houses and hotel dining rooms are about the only ones left with their own special tools and trolleys. I never see shrimp sets anywhere else any more—foetal shrimp forks and dishes with ice in the middle and chrome edges for shrimp to hang despondently from.

Knives are always bigger in steak houses. Of course you need sharp strong knives to cut thick slabs, but you shouldn't need a machete. I still have a set from a steak house in the States that sold them as souvenirs. They are almost as long as the knives that were used for doing in the Sunday roast. With the passion for red meat now past, they languish together in the back of a kitchen drawer.

Steak house menus are always huge and usually take two hands to hold. Though there may be many pages, the actual list of things to eat can fit on one page—a few variations on steak, lobster and a token offer to non-meat eaters. (Steak houses never give you more than ten choices—including whether or not to hang up your coat.)

The Classy Joint

Steak houses are one of the few vestiges of the fancy restaurant. Ritzy places where the waiter calls the drinks beverages, and addresses you in the third person, as in "Would madame care for a beverage?" are hard to find in these days of casual noiseboxes.

Some elegant restaurants often seemed more like finishing schools where diners were put through their paces of etiquette and deportment—as if more was required from the diner than from the dined upon. Maybe that's why we all rushed to greet restaurants that turned up the lights and turned down the protocol.

The spiffy dining rooms of big hotels were often

used by the fancy classes to teach their children the etiquette of formal tables with their rows of fish forks and pâté knives and pudding spoons and a chorus line of goblets and glasses set there to show the value of an ordered life.

Big luxury hotels which often subsidize the dining room are about the only places left that can afford rooms with posh amenities like huge cushy chairs and waiters in tuxedos. These rooms function without regard to economic curves or social change, always at the ready in case the Queen Mum should drop by. Because they are usually staffed by European-trained waiters and maitre d's who cater to every wish, they can be a boon to those with failing faculties. Truffles in the Toronto Four Seasons Hotel keeps eyeglasses on hand for middle-aged customers who can't read the menu because they have forgotten their specs. Perhaps the hotel dining room will return to fashion as the population ages. Although they feel stuffy and stiff, usually with food to match, I look forward to spending my advancing years in them, because there is always a lobby outside with a sofa you can fall back in and have a nice, quiet burp after dinner.

The spiffiest room I ever ate in was Restaurant Jamin in Paris. It took three phone calls, three months before, to secure a table, but what a table it was! Made up like a bride's bed, the generous linen was crisp, flawless and fresh. There was a row of cutlery on each side of a cover plate. Above the knives (where the catsup bottle usually sits) a row of wine glasses stood waiting to be filled, each in turn, for each of the courses. The round table for four that was easily big enough for eight was shielded from other diners by a glass screen and—even better—by space.

203

It was set in a small formal chamber of rose and dark green silks.

I counted six servers in an area that held five tables. They were there to facilitate every wish. When I asked for directions to a telephone, one stopped what he was doing, led me to it and handed me a coin.

Actually, I was afraid to leave our hard-won table, but I felt smug as I passed a desk where I heard the owner speaking by phone with another hopeful: "I appreciate that you are calling from Washington, madame, but we simply have nothing available until January [three months hence]."

Jamin is still one of the hottest tickets for the committed gourmet who is willing to pay—as we did—five hundred dollars for a dinner for two.

I love the appointments in fancy restaurants, where wine glasses often are steamed over kettles, then polished just before they are used, to ensure they are very shiny and clean. (Take note of the stem and foot of the glass, which tell you how clean it is, and which are easily overlooked.) Waiters are trained to put the plate down just so and turn it, with the design facing forward symmetrically, so that the foods are in alignment in their proper quadrant. In some restaurants, there will be a person posted at the kitchen door with a wiping cloth to make sure that each plate is perfect before it leaves.

The best thing about old-fashioned fancy restaurants is that no table would be caught without a tablecoth. I think part of the reason that people like fancy restaurants for romance is that the fully dressed table is a metaphor for seduction. Like each of the lovers, it starts the evening carefully assembled, only to be gradually disassembled as the meal progresses: first the appetizers, then the meat. Then the dessert.

Fancy restaurants often have big dessert trolleys that are wheeled past as you eat. They always remind me of how your mother would leave the dessert on the counter to remind you of the reward for finishing the turnips.

Presentation is big in fancy restaurants. In elaborate hotel dining rooms, food is often hidden under silver domes. The waiters do a minuet with them, placing their white gloves on the handle, raising the cover slightly and rattling it in a sort of gastronomic drum roll, then raising them high. (This must be accompanied by "*voilà!*" or "ta da!" Where there are silver domes, there is fanfare.) The people around the table contribute to the show by laughing and clapping.

Old-fashioned luxury restaurants usually serve continental cuisine, a hybrid of styles designed to cover all the things we think classy places should have, like coquilles St Jacques and fettuccine Alfredo and cherries jubilee. The continent it refers to is Europe, but only the fancy part, not Poland.

In a fancy restaurant, the bill arrives in an embossed leatherette folder. You know the food is good by the size of the bill.

In the past, French food was the cuisine most synonymous with luxury and no matter what else a restaurant called itself, be it Salon de Steak or Chez L'Europe, if it wanted to be spiffy, it gave you something that sounded French. We can thank the fashion for bistros for extending the North American definition of French. North American bistros have a style all their own that includes lace curtains, floral wallpaper and mirrors. (I imagine a smart marketing decor service has it all figured out: "That'll be bistro, aisle three.")

I often prefer bistro food to the food in high-end French restaurants, but I do hate the chairs and the tables you have to endure to eat it. Both bistros and trattorias make you sit on kindergarten chairs as if we all have little boys' bums. There's no such thing as a good table in a bistro or trattoria. They're all the same, like the chairs—tiny.

Talking Tables

When people talk about getting a "good table," they usually mean location. The restaurateur often seats you to suit his needs rather than yours. He will fill the tables in the window so the restaurant will look busy from the outside; similarly he will fill the tables in the centre of the room before the more desirable tables on the periphery, because that way the room looks busier. Most people feel awkwardly vulnerable at centre tables, but rarely do people ask to be moved to a better one.

Where he seats you tells a lot about who he thinks you are and what he expects from you. A lone woman or two or more women eating together have traditionally been seated by the kitchen, cash register or washroom, because we are reputed to be poor tippers. If you are directed to the centre or to Siberia, do not sit down, because then you will have to ask to move. Until your ass is in the chair, you are not considered a committed customer and that alone should be motivation enough for the restaurateur to make you happy.

The conscientious diner will learn the numbers of the best tables in the restaurant. Table 3 may be the one by the window, the only quiet table in a clamorous restaurant, or the table with the best view of the movers and shakers in a trendy place. Knowing the number not only means you are more likely to get the table, but it will impress the headwaiter. He will treat you like a regular, which always means getting the best service.

The construction of the table may be felt only subliminally, but it is vital to the notion of "a good table." A table is psychologically very important, and its size, shape and positioning can affect your experiences in many unseen ways. The kinds of tables and chairs may be part of an unseen plan. Restaurateurs like their customers to feel comfortable enough to want to come and stay a while—at least as long as it takes to drink and eat and drink again—but they do not want them so comfortable that they just sit and talk and don't leave, so a new group can come and drink and eat and drink again.

Almost all our social transactions occur across a table. You want to see a friend, you negotiate a meal, and the importance of the meeting will be measured by the style of the meal and the table. Let's have coffee means a small table in a bright place and means the conversation can be casual; while dinner in a white-tablecloth restaurant with reservations sounds serious. (This could be big.)

A theory called "commensality" (from the Latin *mensa*, for table) argues that the common surface is vital to help people connect. The shared surface is a link; conversation would be completely different if people were sitting in two armchairs with a low coffee

207

table between them. The most important of our modern negotiations in western society—everything from romance to business—are conducted across tabletops.

The shape of the table can determine the interaction of the occupants: a round table suggests democracy; a long boardroom table with a place for only one person at the head of it denotes hierarchy; a couple seated side by side, facing together into the room, suggests intimacy and unity. (Maybe opportunity too: at one restaurant, known as a venue for illicit romance, the manager would seat special couples side by side "so they could hold hands—or whatever.")

The height of the table also offers some psychological protection, some screening. You feel safer behind a table than you do completely exposed.

A good restaurant has good talking tables. The surface must be big enough so you and your partner do not spend all your time negotiating where to put your knees: intimacy is fine when you are ready, but irritating when you are not.

A generous surface also means there is enough room for the dishes. Although this might seem like a minimal requirement in a restaurant, it is surprising how often tables are so tiny that you have to put the bread basket in your lap when the main course arrives. There is no place even to put your elbows. Ironically, tiny tables for bistro-trattorias appeared at the same time that people began to huddle in groups and at the moment platters got fashionably large— with the obvious result. At the restaurant in the Museum of Modern Art in New York they cut off the corners of the black, rubber-topped trays so that four can fit together on the table.

In big cities, where space is at a premium, restaurants seem to favour lines of tables against the wall. This means that two people sharing a meal will have distinctly different experiences: the person looking into the room is part of it; the luckless companion (usually the man) must pass the time facing the wall, which may be graced with an interesting poster or painting, but is more often hung with a mirror.

Often, in areas where rent is at a premium, tables are pushed so close together there is little distinction between your surface and that of the people next to you. This can be a boon or a bust depending on whether you want privacy. It makes conversation very stilted—or, if not, it should be. Catharsis is not appropriate at these close tables: I have learned astonishing things about people's lives at them. Not that I mind: being a critic can be used as a licence to stare at everyone in the restaurant, to watch what they are eating and how they are eating it. I always did that anyway, but now I like to think I do it for my art. For journalism.

Eavesdropping is also one of the perks of my trade. At North 44, in Toronto, a quirk of acoustics means that the private conversations in the upstairs bar can be heard at the table downstairs. It is wonderful to be able to eavesdrop so secretly.

Banquettes, like the cushy ones found in fancy restaurants, allow people to sit side by side. They give a cozy, safe feeling. I especially like them at breakfast in hotel dining rooms, because they feel like a continuation of bed. The only problem is that they are sometimes so cushy you sink into them and the tabletop gets too high. In fact, people who sit in restaurants a lot become very conscious of the height

209

of the tabletop. After a while, if you try to rest your arms or elbows on a table that is too high, you get an ache across the top of the back.

I wish booths had never gone out of style, and I love to frequent places like Tadich's Grill in San Francisco, which are so old that they still have them, or newer restaurants which have resurrected them, like the Senator in Toronto.

Booths are great when you're having a fight, and they're ideal for nursing mothers. (However, at MacGregor's in Kleinberg, Ontario, a notice on the wall says "Mothers: please nurse and change your babies in the privacy of our third-floor room.") But a booth is a pain when the kid in the next one hangs over, looking into yours.

The feel of a dining room also depends on what's hanging on the walls, mirrors especially. Mirrors are certainly popular in restaurants but are often badly used. They usually line a wall to make the restaurant look bigger, which keeps diners looking at the other diners. In some restaurants where half the chairs face the mirror, half the diners are looking out into the room and the other half are looking into a reflection. It means that the date whose attention you seek throughout dinner can't keep his eyes off himself.

A wise restaurateur will invest in a high-quality mirror that flatters his customers. I favour forgiving mirrors that restore the colour alcohol has drained from my face. I wish restaurants would use the same kinds of mirrors they had about ten years ago: I looked younger in them.

Restaurant designers George Yabu and Glenn Pushelberg favour restaurant mirrors enclosed in frames and widely spaced on the walls. Tilted slightly downward, they reflect the room, and make the reflecting glass a piece of moving art on the wall.

And then there are ceilings. Very few restaurants in the entire world have ceilings worth looking at. In fact, most are over-ugly because the acoustic tile is studded with machinery—smoke detectors, sound systems, sprinklers. It is like letting your underwear show. Do restaurateurs think no one ever looks up?

In my line of work I spend a lot of time in restaurants, and, by axiom, some of that time in that most important of restaurant rooms, the washroom. I think they have changed. The fashion for furnishing the washrooms in our own homes is spilling over into restaurants. Restaurateurs think they help sell the place.

"People remember a great restaurant washroom," says Pushelberg. His firm designed one of the most fabulous restaurant washrooms in the now defunct Oceans restaurant in Toronto. The room was fitted with dark, polished wood and low lights that glowed more than shone, giving it the cocooned feel of the Captain's quarters of a ship. The water spout was integrated into the mirror so that the water looked as though it was flowing from the mirror. Their design for the new restaurant Aqua, also in Toronto, has floor-to-ceiling windows with a great view, and titillating opaque glass on the cubicles.

I prefer restaurants that emphasize the restroom's function as a refuge, an oasis, a spot for renewal and reassurance. I feel nostalgic for old-fashioned fancy restaurants where the washroom was called the ladies' lounge, and had chaise longues for all the times women fainted.

My favourite restrooms are very clean, and show evidence that the restaurateur has considered its importance by adding little touches—fresh or dried flowers, nice-smelling soap, really clean non-paper towels with baskets to drop them into after you've wiped your hands. If I had a restaurant I would consider the cost of having a few soft real handtowels well worth it. It would be a small restaurant, of course.

Inexpensive, funky little restaurants with weird art on the walls can have the most imaginatively decorated washrooms. It doesn't need to cost much to create a pleasant spot, so it's hard to understand why so many restaurateurs treat it as an afterthought, like the ceiling.

Washrooms in some places are not just crowded and creepy, but you take your life in your hands going down rickety, uneven stairs to get to them. I have nearly lost my lunch during the frightening trek down dark basement alleyways.

Sometimes privacy is threatened by doors that swing into public corridors. Or by creeps. There was the horrible case of former rock star Chuck Berry, convicted of getting his warped kicks by video-taping women in restaurant washrooms.

Some restaurant washrooms use modern technology in imaginative ways. I enjoy the ones that are like entertainment centres, including the newest state-of-the-art versions with toilet seats that cover themselves automatically with plastic (as if your mother was behind the wall), toilets that flush automatically when someone stands in front of them, faucets that flow when someone runs a hand beneath them, and dryers that blow hot air when they sense the presence of a humanoid hand.

But all that fancy business can backfire. I was once a prisoner of technology and spent an unsettling amount of time trying to exit the washroom in La Fenice in Toronto. The room had been renovated to include clever door openers that needed an engineer to operate them—not a ham-fisted restaurant critic a bit buzzy on two glasses of Barolo.

Had I been in the men's washroom, I might have had some distraction. I'm told that some restaurants hang newspapers at eye level in front of the urinals. (Sports and business sections.) A Toronto pub has installed a chalkboard and chalk so that people can write non-defacing graffiti.

A health inspector once found graffiti at the base of a toilet. It quoted the tiny star of Fantasy Island: "Look boss, the plane, the plane." At Baci, a trattoria in Boca Raton, Florida, the pay phone is right next to the urinal in the men's room, so that one doesn't waste a minute. At Hy's Steak House in Toronto, a patron who complained to a waiter about the quality of the custard sauce later found himself standing side by side with him at the urinal, and regretted his vulnerability as the waiter then questioned him about his critique of the custard.

Some restaurants like to emphasize the importance they attach to their washrooms by placing a check-list on the wall. Mövenpick restaurants have employees check every fifteen minutes, and sign their names to attest to the room's acceptability.

Tables for changing babies' diapers are now common in both men's and women's washrooms—a sign of the times that a restaurant accommodates fathers too.

I would like to see a clear, universal sign to tell you where the washroom actually is. Some restaurants use cute or impressionistic drawings or euphemisms to denote the men's and ladies' and it's hard to figure them out, especially after a few glasses of bubbly. I have stumbled into the wrong gender washroom and, equally, been stumbled upon.

Washrooms, of course, are most challenging in those restaurants that revolve; they will not be where they were when you entered. The fact that many cities have kinetic restaurants, and that many people eat in them, is testimony to the importance put on the view—for some, it is food enough.

It had better be. Revolving restaurants are seldom known for the craft in their cookery. Plain common sense should suggest that it is unwise to eat in a room that turns faster than you can digest.

Rooms with a View

I prefer a steadier scene. At the Highlands Inn in the hills north of Carmel, California, I can hardly keep my mind on brunch for the view of the ocean, the seals and birds. All of Northern California is a mix of forest, sea and sun. And now this food. In this place. The large room is tiered, giving tables a maximum view of the ocean, the forest and the hills.

Orange juice is poured so freely and it is so thick, so rich that one glass nearly puts me in a coma. There are tables at the back of the room where flinty, raw oysters, beds of pink shrimp, and fresh crab are served—the big kind that grow in the western ocean, and give you a mouthful of sweet crabmeat. At the end of the lunch, huge waffles, with square canyons deep enough to hold a bathtub of syrup, are filled with fresh fruit, just warmed to body temperature to take the chill off it.

"I know what happened," I said as the waiter poured more thick, fresh orange juice in one glass and sharp white California wine in another, "the plane crashed and this is heaven."

At night, dinner starts early so you can watch the sun set, provided you can lift your gaze from the velvet corn soup, smooth except for the chunks of lobster that break its surface, and the cucumber spaghetti that slides down cool and neat, and more warmed berries—blueberries and raspberries—coddled in crème brûlée and capped with a ceiling of sweet burnt sugar.

In summer, many restaurants make use of patios—out of some misplaced notion that people actually like to eat outdoors. Food is moved from the fast lane into a parking lot: they take a strip of sidewalk and turn it into a restaurant. I hate eating outdoors. The sun gets in your eyes. Things fall into your food. Or you wind up fighting for every mouthful with a fearless wasp.

I believe that people like the way that it looks when people eat outdoors, but, unless you are perched on a cliff in Italy or Greece, eating on patios is terrible. I prefer to see the view from behind glass.

Whenever I see a patio with a beautiful view, I think: "Nice place for a room." If God had meant us to eat outside, he would not have given us those rooms in which we come together to eat.

Pie
in the
Sky

Owning a restaurant is a common fantasy. People who love to eat out sit over coffee dreaming that if they were in charge, they could do it better. Some see themselves as earth parent, feeding and soothing all who come through their doors. Others are drawn by the art of hospitality or of cooking. Still others wish to fill their lives with good food, all day, all night. They imagine themselves at the market, steadfastly searching for the perfect tomato, carefully tasting the dish that it transforms.

You can see the pleasure that comes from running a successful place on the face of a weary restaurateur at midnight, when the rush is over and his last few guests have settled into a pleasant gastronomic glow. But if you want to see how really nasty the business can get, you might glance at that same face at 6:00 p.m. on another night when the chef has called in sick or a bad review has brought a crush of cancellations and a call from the banker.

Here then, is the story of Hugh Garber as told by him—a man who, by any reckoning, has been lucky with his dreams. He headed a fashion house and designed dresses for stars. Then he invented a restaurant that specialized in big pies even before television's "Twin Peaks" made pie the dessert to die for. In between, as a hobby, he wrote jokes. One day, watching Joan Rivers on television, it occurred to him that some of his were funnier than some of hers. So he sold her about two hundred—for about ten dollars each. They included some of Rivers's favourite fat jokes about Elizabeth Taylor. You've probably heard them. Liz Taylor probably didn't think they were funny. Now, he won't repeat them, even when coaxed: he says he had to sign a release promising Rivers exclusive use of the jokes she bought.

Ten dollars is, itself, a joke to Garber now. For all the fantasies he fulfilled, he wound up with the one dream that's even bigger than owning a restaurant: in 1987 he won $3.4 million in a lottery.

Garber now spends his summers on a thirteen-acre apple orchard near Toronto and his winters in a house in Palm Beach County, Florida. He still can't believe his luck.

By the time he and I sat down to lunch in a trendy restaurant in downtown Toronto, he had abandoned all his earlier pursuits—the restaurant and fashion house had been sold, Joan Rivers was finding gags elsewhere. When he told me that he had gained weight since he sold the restaurant—his life is more sedentary and less aggravating—I did wonder if he now shares Liz Taylor's distaste for fat jokes.

The man whose life was once about pies ordered a sparse lunch: clear vegetable soup, a crisp house salad with cheese and turkey, bare of dressing. He asked that the salami be left out of the salad. Garber hesitated for a minute when the dessert card was presented, weighing the pros of abstinence against the cons of gratification, and when the scales tilted towards indulgence, he ordered the crème brûlée. A dessert lover like Garber may find restraint possible in the savoury first courses, but not at dessert. He savoured the custard as if it were manna from heaven and revealed the hunger that led him to pie love. With the edge of the spoon, he gently knocked on the caramelized sugar lid to make sure the crust was as firm and hard as culinary canon requires. Tapping a crack in the surface, he forced the tip of the spoon through it and then coated it with a fleck of custard, tasting carefully. God, it was perfect. "I love this," he sighed. "This is the best."

I had asked Garber to tell me about the fantasy of owning a restaurant compared to the reality of running it. He is well qualified to comment—especially now, when financial freedom gives him nearly unlimited choices. Garber is still fresh and funny; it is worth hearing the story in his own words.

J always thought about owning a restaurant when
    I was young, but I never seriously planned to—it
    was one of those things I could do, rather than
    I would do. I worked in a restaurant in Montreal
    owned by my brother in the early sixties, the
    Rib n' Reef. It was one of those names meant
    to remind people of surf and turf, the stuff
    everyone was eating.

I've always been addicted to food, but I'm not a gourmet. I'll admit I still like Velveeta cheese—there's no grilled cheese sandwich like one made with that. Same with peanut butter. I love it—but not the health food stuff. I can't keep a jar in the house. It never sees a piece of bread, I eat it with a spoon. In the States now, they have peanut butter made with honey roasted peanuts. That's why I live there.

When I was a starving student of fashion design in London, I worked in restaurants as an assistant potscrubber. Imagine, not even the head potscrubber. But I always watched the chef.

For years fashion was what I did, and I loved it for a long time. I worked at a fashion house in Rome which dressed the glamorous of that time like Cyd Charisse and Dinah Shore. When I worked in Montreal, Ivana Trump was one of my models. She was very professional. I liked her a lot. I saw her nude before Donald did. Later in Toronto, I opened Hugh Garber Fashions. Even though fashion was my business, people knew me for food. I cooked on TV shows, among them Margaret Trudeau's. She wanted me to teach her how to make gnocchi. She called them nookies.

At fashion shows, I would slip printed personal recipes into each shopping bag. Everyone was crazy for my spaghetti della estate. You toss hot spaghetti with fresh basil, balsamic vinegar, mozzarella and fresh tomatoes. The heat from the spaghetti melts the cheese.

219

My decision to open a restaurant came almost like a flash of light one Sunday morning. I was reading an article in *Interview* magazine quoting fashion designer Karl Lagerfeld. "This year," he said, "we will overdress in pastels." It revolted me. It was so excessive, so ridiculous. I kept flipping through the magazine and came across another article, this one on Peter Morton and his extremely successful Hard Rock Cafe. [Morton is now in Los Angeles at Morton's.]

Those two articles really collided for me, coming at that time. I started thinking again about my old dream of running a restaurant. The article on the Hard Rock Cafe made me want a playful, popular restaurant serving good American food.

I opened Hughie's [in Toronto] in 1984. It was a really nice place, a 240-seat restaurant specializing in hamburgers and pies. It cost $300,000 to put together. The rent was about $12,000 a month. We worked hard to raise that money. It was scary.

Most restaurants make money from selling alcohol. You don't sell a lot of wine with hamburgers: people buy more wine with fancier food. If I were doing the restaurant again, I would have burgers for lunch and dining for dinner. That way there'd be a higher cheque for dinner.

My original concept was a small, intimate restaurant. I thought of my place as a sort of upscale Joe Allen. Hughie's Casual American

Cuisine. In the theatre district. The walls would be dark green and there would be lots of brass. I never wanted to be gourmet—just the best burgers, the best fries.

Well, I found out that, with our kind of menu at our kind of rent, you can't have a small place because you just can't make enough.

I didn't use any consultants, nothing. I found out fast what a novice I was. The city wanted vents in the ceiling and, of course, we couldn't open without satisfying the city. But when you're dreaming about a restaurant, who thinks about vents?

It's funny in retrospect what we did think about. We worried endlessly about the distribution of the tables—how many tables for four, how many for two. But those worked themselves out. Sometimes it seems like nothing else did.

I loved having meatloaf and macaroni and cheese on the menu in my restaurant. We had turkey pot pie with big chunks of turkey in it. We made the meatloaf with ground beef and pork and basil and Parmesan, then we poured a tomato sauce over it. I figured people were sick of poached swordfish with blueberry coulis. I sure was.

I had this vision of how I wanted the food to be and that's how I did it. It was my restaurant—every recipe was mine, every sauce, every pie was one I'd made and liked. Before we put it on the menu, we'd hold these contests to find the best recipe: chili contests, Mexican pizza contests.

221

The menu was fun the way we did it, making everything from scratch to our tastes. But food and labour costs were very high. If I were doing it now, I'd be more cautious and it wouldn't be as much fun.

You have to be so careful about a menu. I had this great eggplant Parmesan. It sounds so good in your own kitchen; so everyone says, you gotta put that on the menu. So you do. Then you learn. Well, you know eggplant. You gotta slice it, salt it, and sweat it. When you make it for a restaurant, that's a lot of sweating eggplant. Those slices covered the whole kitchen, every counter space.

We made this fabulous Mexican pizza. The crust was a cornmeal dough that was made with *masa harina*, which is often hard to get. We made it by hand so it meant kneading, and letting it rise, popping it down, kneading, and letting it rise again. Then we put our own salsa on it. Then there was Monterey Jack cheese and red and green peppers. We sold it for $4.95 a slice. If I did it again, I would charge $99.95.

We also had sweet-potato fries long before they were trendy. Once people knew we had them, they expected them. So we'd buy the potatoes and make them, in season, when the potatoes might cost 30 cents a pound, or out of season, when they might cost $1.60 a pound. Now that I know how much has to go into each item to make it well, I always suspect a restaurant with huge menus.

I have strong ideas about hamburgers and that's why I wanted a restaurant that specialized in them. A real hamburger is made just from good, freshly ground meat seasoned with salt and pepper. It should be a hamburger, not a meatloaf filled up with breadcrumbs and eggs. And it has to be on a hamburger bun. Not an English muffin, not a bagel and not a kaiser roll either. That's not what nature intended. Of course, the hamburger bun can have sesame seeds on it, and the meat doesn't have to be beef. We had a lamburger served with mint sauce.

My favourite of all the pies we made was white chocolate mousse, which sold for about $3.95. It had a glaze of bittersweet chocolate lying over the mousse. Then there was a pile of whipped cream thick over that—just in case there weren't enough calories in the mousse! That pie is one of the things I want on my tray when they take me to the guillotine.

Before I opened the restaurant, when I dreamt about it, I thought about how my friends would come and because we were near the theatres, celebrities would come. But when your friends come in, you don't have time to talk to them. They stop coming, because they can see that they are taking your time. Then there are old friends and family who think you should be giving complimentary meals. Celebrities think like that too.

It's crazy: I don't go to see *Fiddler on the Roof* at the O'Keefe Centre for free. Why should some

223

star think he should eat at my place for free?
If everyone who thought he should eat free ate
free, you'd be closed in three months.

When I dreamt about my restaurant, I pictured
that people could come and sit and talk and stay
as long as they want. But to stay in business, I
had to have lots of turnover. It was deadly when
people came and sat forever over a cup of coffee.

I tried to cram in as many seats as possible
so I could keep the price of the hamburgers
down and still pay the rent. Also, I had to get
tough about reservations. For instance, at lunch,
I would only take reservations at noon and at
1:15 so I could get in two seatings over the lunch
hour. Singles were seated at the bar, so they
wouldn't take up a table that could seat more
people.

There were other things that I just didn't expect
and that you can't control. Things like the
computer going down over lunch weren't in my
dream. I hate it when things go wrong. And you
can't control most of them.

In my fantasies, I pictured myself in my place,
with control over every recipe. I'd know every
piece of equipment, as I do in my home kitchen—
friendly sort of stuff that helps you. But the huge
restaurant equipment terrified me—five fryers
bubbling hot fat; dishwashers billowing steam,
it's scary.

Then there are critics, who are just mean.
I've never been in any profession that didn't
involve critics. You work so hard, then someone

in two sentences can cause you to be closed
down if people are gullible enough to believe
everything they say. The best restaurant can
have a bad day, someone gets sick, a cook walks
out, anything. But there are more people who
take great pleasure in finding fault than in
looking for the good. You ask me if I have any
fantasies left? I'd like to cater a memorial dinner
for a couple of critics.

We owed the bank and the shareholders and
that's always at the back of your mind. The
money part. People think of how much money
you make because they see a cash register
ringing. I guess you could call it a living, but
unless you're prepared to work very hard for a
long time without taking much money out of
the business, you can't make much.

And there were a lot of shocks. The pastry
chef quit two days before the restaurant opened.
Can you imagine? Our menu had six pies and
a daily special and it meant that thirty or forty
pies were baked each day.

Staffing is always tough. At the height of the
restaurant we had fifty-two people. At any
time, about 8 to 10 per cent of them wouldn't
turn up. Before, when I dreamt about the
restaurant, I didn't think about staff phoning
in on a Saturday morning to say that a
grandmother was sick and they couldn't come
in. Then you'd hear they were on the beach.
Or waiters who were actors, cancelling at the
last minute because an audition suddenly

came up. A lot of waiters are actors. A lot.

It was hard, but I had to learn not to get too friendly with the staff. If you've had a staff member to your house, it's hard to reprimand or criticize because it's taken personally. It's too easy for the owner of a small single restaurant to get too friendly. It doesn't happen with chains. On the other hand, sometimes when you're friends, they'll give 200 per cent. It's a hard call.

We had a separate lottery pool in the restaurant that had run for about two years. When I won, I gave everybody who was in that pool one thousand dollars each. Three of them quit. It sure taught me a lesson about how friendly you get with staff.

On September 19, 1987, a Sunday morning, I had twenty dollars worth of tickets on the lottery. I didn't hear the numbers, so I called my mother. A television station announced my address along with the news of my winning. Of course, I had to get out of town. I took two friends to London and we rented a suite at the Park Lane for five hundred dollars a night. I went back to the Stock Pot restaurant where I'd worked in the sixties as a dishwasher. I told the people there I used to work at their restaurant. But it didn't really matter to them. None of them had even been born then.

After I won, I got to be a celebrity like the kind I wanted to come to my restaurant. Except that then everyone knew me as Hugh Garber who won the lottery, not the restaurant owner or the fashion designer.

As far as restaurants go, I'm fantasy burned out.
You know that old saying about being careful
about what you ask for because you may get it?

I have been back to my restaurant since I sold
it. It feels funny. After all my efforts to decorate
Hughie's according to my dream of how it should
look, it's a little funny to see it now with a
chrome banquet table at the back. I talked them
out of a revolving pastry case. But now the place
is theirs, not mine. I'll bet I'll walk in soon and
there will be murals of the Acropolis.

People have restaurants for different reasons.
I'll tell you this: if someone means to do it to
make a living, they need a consultant. So I
would tell someone like a lawyer who had a
dream to open a restaurant to hire one. I don't
know how much people who have a dream of a
restaurant really think that out. Everyone
wants to open an inn or restaurant. Actually,
I think what they really want to do is decorate
an inn, not run it. It was the same for me
before I actually did it. I guess I had a fantasy
about the restaurant the way people dream
about running an inn in Vermont. With
bluebirds singing.

My fantasy was just that, pure fantasy. It
had nothing to do with reality. Looking back on
the beginning of it all, it was fun. But it was
the lack of caution at the beginning that made it
that way. We just didn't know what to be afraid
of. Ignorance is bliss, I guess. Mind you, I still
have a fantasy to be in food. Maybe I'll do
desserts.

Remembrance of Things Pasta

*I*n the easy days Before Pasta, Italian food meant a plate of noodles with red sauce. But now the arugula generation has abandoned meatballs to eat sun-dried tomatoes as if they were pharmaceuticals and drink olive oil as if it were a beverage. Italian restaurants with homey red-checkered tablecloths have become ristorantes with cold marble tabletops; candles in Chianti bottles have given way to pinpoint light from hanging halogen lamps. Since the Italian food reformation, edicts require us to try amazing and delicious Italian dishes full of ingredients that even Italians could only dream of.

I'm dying for a plain plate of noodles with red sauce.

The long road to pasta fatigue began in the seventies, when our love affair with French food began to pall. French cuisine (as it was always called) had defined the pinnacle of quality food, its chefs were our saints and its restaurants, the *ne plus ultra*. With the fitness revolution and a style that favoured down-to-earth, democratic eating, French food felt over-worked, overstuffed and old-fashioned; the sauces too rich, the ingredients embarrassingly haughty. Lobster Newburg, with its butter, sherry and cream sauce, had had its day.

A brief flirtation with nouvelle cuisine hastened the end of the affair. Though its priggishness was intended to free classic French cookery from its heaviness by using ingredients of great simplicity, in practice, the pretentiousness made it arrogant, pricey and sparse. We called it kiwi cuisine and treated it as a gastronomic gag.

The nouvelle effort to lighten things up only made things worse, because the joke turned out to be at the expense of all French cuisine, which was seen as thoroughly aristocratic, snobbish and out of touch. The hearts of the generation who had cut their gourmet teeth on French food turned cold until the late eighties, when the bourgeois ways of bistro cookery thawed them.

As we cast about seeking another romance, our eyes fell on Italy. Love flowed through us like Barolo at a wedding. With its sunny colours and strong flavours, Italian food became a metaphor for passion and peasant earthiness. Throughout the eighties, movie scenes of lush family tables (*The Godfather* and *Moonstruck*) inflamed us more.

Italian food not only had the cachet of the French, but it attracted the customers. French restaurants languished as we fled to Italian eateries. We became so enthralled with all things Italian that we forgot our disdain of aristocratic cookery and embraced even fancy Italian food and spent a few exploratory nights with nuova cucina, Italy's answer to nouvelle cuisine. If it was Italian, it was okay by us. In the words of *New York* magazine's food critic, Mimi Sheraton, "Italian food has an easy, casual, modern elegance, like an Armani silk shirt. It could be enjoyed without the kind of tight-assed intellectualism that appreciating French food seemed to require. You could mix and match it without the formal arrangement of a French meal."

Italian restaurants were the cornerstone of the food explosion of the eighties. As other dining rooms fell like tenpins, they seemed to survive. We lionized Italian chefs and acclaimed the superiority of Italian wines. Today, chic Italian restaurants ply peasant dishes while peasant restaurants sell chic. Ristorantes and trattorias are as common as McDonald's, with names like Ciao or Grazie or Scoozi, each promising that the chef in the kitchen is from Italy. If that is true, we might well wonder who is left to cook for the folks back in the old country.

It is obvious that food fashion fatigue has been behind the hunger for peasant cookery that has overtaken us since the eighties. Its flavours are like a whiff of ammonia to palates jaded by esoterica. Vulgar flavours like garlic, onions, rich red wine, strong-smelling cheese are foods that kickstart the mouth motors and are a shock to a weary solar plexis. Of the Italian regions, Tuscany has captured our imaginations the most, basting the belly with big bowls of beans, reworking the jaws with crusty breads.

As well, the earthy foods of Tuscany have been politically correct, offering ingredients from the fields at relatively low prices (prices which get bigger and less peasant as the food gets more fashionable, but that's another story). Tuscan fibrous beans, breads and pastas fulfil nutritional edicts.

Not incidentally, Tuscan food tastes swell, and it was a relief to come back to mouthfuls of familiar tastes. The region that includes Florence and its hills, the source of so many of the world's visual treasures, is also the source of many of Italy's signature foods: Parmesan cheese, prosciutto ham and wines— Tuscany has the winding road known liquidly as the Chianti trail.

Italian cooking classes featuring Tuscan foods are among the most popular being offered. People everywhere pay fortunes to try the latest Italian flavours in North America in the winter and troop to Florence in the summer to take classes with Bugialli and Marcella Hazan, at a cost of a few thousand dollars a week. That's a lot of spaghetti.

As our Italian restaurant romance continued, our passions turned kinky. We wanted fancy ingredients and weird experimentation—the leather lingerie of gastronomy. An Italian restaurant in North York sold "spinach and ricotta cheese tortellini with beef, snow peas, red peppers, leeks and a fruit chutney." And "garlic and black pepper fusilli with sautéed chicken, roasted peppers, carrots, rosemary and gorgonzola." You could choke just ordering the stuff.

Now pizza dough is a vehicle for every ingredient and combination. Socially, it is very mobile, travelling easily between the handmade designer pizza that is worn in the best circles and the mass-produced corporate pizza that is swell at a ball game.

Pizza and pasta restaurants that have sprouted on every street corner became the fastest growing segment of the fast-food industry.

231

Pizza also has what passes for tradition in North America. It has been popular since the sixties, when the technology required to make it fast met with the American wish for a quick, slightly exotic food. In those early days, "fast" meant forty minutes. Now ovens that produce pizza in five minutes are common and the dish is no longer thought of as Italian—any more than spaghetti, once it became available in tins.

As we moved beyond the piquant pie, waves of Italian immigration to North America brought cooks and the produce for them to play with. Competition created energy; an explosion of restaurants followed. The food got better and our choices got broader. Once marginalized as "ethnic," Italian restaurants became mainstream. Italian food was no longer exotic: it was just what we ate.

Demand and culinary inventiveness made suppliers scrape every rock and shake every bush to bring us foods from all corners of Italy. Even an Italian would be baffled by the choices being offered: the variety of regions, terrains and interpretations means that the sophisticated dishes of northern cities might be as strange to a citizen of Naples as hominy grits are to a native of Kelowna.

Olive oil, sun-dried tomatoes and fresh basil have become staples of our everyday diet. We have invested them with heroic, health-giving qualities. Flavoured pastas have become popular and playful. Cooks outdo themselves, infusing pasta with beet juice rum and co-ordinating the colour or flavour of ravioli pasta with its filling: green pasta to go with spinach; red, green and white pockets of dough to mimic the colours of the Italian flag.

Most of the pasta has been fun, lots has been silly. Warm chocolate pasta with chocolate sauce and whipped cream is revolting and no fad will make it food. A man who figured out a way of incorporating mashed pumpkin into linguini was seriously described to me as a man of vision.

As with pizza, pasta is the denim of foods: it goes with everything. Like jeans dressed up with silk for a cocktail party or dressed down with a T-shirt for a movie, so goes pasta: dressed up with extra-virgin olive oil and sun-dried tomatoes for company and dressed down with tomato sauce for the family.

We became zealots about the preparation of pasta: it has to be *al dente*, not the soft, soothing macaroni and noodles of childhood. I still miss the feeling of long twirls of super-soft spaghetti snaking their way around the inside of my mouth. I can't get it that way except at home. The pasta I get in new-wave Italian restaurants is sometimes so *al dente* I can hear the crunch.

Although many of us had been through enough boxes of Kraft Dinner and cans of Libby's spaghetti in childhood to recognize a noodle from a nacho, we had no leg up on olive oil. Possessing only a weak grasp of the differences between corn oil and peanut, we were faced with a slippery selection of different lubricants from different countries.

Then there was the question of their virtue, as the comments about what made olive oil extra-virgin made the rounds at about the same time as the lightbulb jokes. "For all the extra money, what do I care what the olives were doing?" went one. (The term is actually a chemical definition, not an anatomical one.

It defines the acidity of the oil, the amount of oleanic acid, in a range from one to four.)

The trend of pouring a saucerful of green olive oil in a dish for dipping bread is one of the newest. A few gratings of sea salt and black pepper improve it even more. A pitcher or bottle of olive oil, usually with a few sprigs of some vegetation or a needle of chili, is served now in spiffy pizza restaurants. I have even been served a dish of olive oil for dipping raw chunks of fennel in at dessert time.

In Italy, where they don't share our phobia about fat, the olive oil may be poured liberally without your permission, the way black pepper is ground over everything here. In a small trattoria in Florence I shrieked aloud when I realized that the waiter had poured a full cup of olive oil into my soup. It was a pure green, the proud early harvest and it was served as a favour. He looked at me with the contempt that says "tourist."

I hope he thought I was an American. I drank the soup like the Italians around me—with a pleasure that comes from knowing something that may not be the best thing for you is the right thing to do. That's the reason we have emulated Italian food.

Parmesan cheese is grated on everything, in North America more than Italy, in amounts that mimic the way we once poured catsup. You can pass the gourmet exam with only two facts. The first is that Parmesan comes in every quality from dust to gold but the best is Parmiggiano Reggiano, a cow's milk cheese that is produced under strict regulations. It comes only from certain dairies in the area close to the city of Parma and only from April to November (the months when the cows feed on fresh grass); it can be sold only after it has been aged for two years.

The other fact is that Parmesan cheese is never grated on any dish containing fish, because fish is thought to have too delicate a constitution for the salty, fragrant flavours of this aged cheese. Allowing your waiter to do it marks you as a food nerd and he will punish you by selling you a flaming liqueur for dessert. (Italians think we're nerds anyway. Their name for us is *mangia-cake*, eaters of white bread or cake.)

We mark ourselves as well by adding dessert to an Italian meal. In Italy, there is a polite and gentle end to a meal, a course of fruit and perhaps some cheese. There are regions that quite rightly might extend that to include dipping hard biscotti into sweet wine called Vin Santo, which gets better and better as the wine is absorbed. But heavy cream cakes and puddings are seen as more suitable for a separate meal with coffee and conversation.

When it comes to Italian ristorantes in North America, the new wave of Italian restaurants is pretty old wave French at dessert time. They are massive, ponderous with chocolate, cake and cream. The menu headliner usually is tirimi su. In the past ten years, I have seldom been to an Italian restaurant where it has not been set in front of me, dusted with cocoa, decorated with cream, dragged through rivers of red raspberry sauce.

Tirimi su is like an English trifle, layers of cake and cream, with ladyfingers soaked in espresso serving as the cake and marscapone—a sweet cow's milk cheese turned triple cream (about 75 per cent butterfat)—as the cream. Unsurprisingly, the texture of marscapone is thick, like clotted cream, and the cheese may be encountered in other desserts, as a topping for fruit, or layered with other starches. Brown and white layered tirimi su anchors the dessert menus at Italian restaurants now, the way that cheesecake with cherries as shiny and red as the flashers on police cruisers anchored the steak house.

Tirimi su means "lift me up," but like many Italian dishes, its name provides no clue to the dish. We *mangia-cakes* need all the help we can get with Italian menus. When Italian restaurants suddenly became the eatery of the moment, a baffling list was thrust on a naïve public who were still trying to conquer the differences between Veronique and hollandaise. Italian menus are harder to understand than French because the language is metaphoric and chauvinistic. Some dishes, like tortellini, are named for parts of the female anatomy: according to legend, the little pasta twists were named by a visionary chef contemplating Venus's navel.

There are dishes that make slobbering references to sex as rascally Latins constantly seek new ways to make the obvious link between the two appetites. Pasta *alla puttanesca* is prepared "whore's style" because, according to food lore, its quick assembly of tomatoes, capers, garlic and anchovies took little time between engagements and, at the same time, gave off a heady aroma said to lure clients. "Arrabiata" means angry; saltimbocca is "jump in the mouth."

The real language of Italian food is flavour. With pasta, simple is best. Pretentious ristorantes could summon nectar from the gods and still not do as well as restaurants that serve a plate of spaghetti with a fresh tomato sauce and basil or olive oil and garlic.

I wonder if the people who used to cook Italian food are still working in secret somewhere, like Santa's elves in the cellars, while we're all asleep. In that wonderful place, I will find a waiter named Tony who wears a paunch and not a ponytail. He will serve me a plate of noodles, awash in red, by the light of a candle held in a Chianti bottle.

Leaving
the Garden
of Eating

A reader called: she was taking Special Someone out for his birthday and was seeking a great Italian restaurant. I told her of a terrific place near her and suggested they start with the carpaccio, a dish the chef prepares as if his hands were guided by the gods. He uses sirloin instead of the usual tenderloin for its superior flavour, I explained. Then he rubs the surface with crushed peppercorns and marinates the meat in balsamic vinegar and olive oil for a full four days. The time spent in that mixture turns the outside black and crusted, the inside red and sensual. The meat is very tender because the marinade has caused the membranes to succumb and release their hold. Then he slices it very thin—even without freezing it first, that's the kind of control the chef has—and lays a few brilliant slices on a bed of arugula, drizzles them with more of that gold-green olive oil and scatters some capers and shavings of sharp Parmesan cheese.

"I don't eat meat," she said.

So I sang to her of that restaurant's spaghettini with olive oil and garlic, a deceptively simple dish that tests the most capable kitchen because it needs intelligent balancing of the main ingredients: top-quality olive oil, fresh, strong garlic, freshly ground pepper and sometimes an edge of chili pepper.

"I don't like things with oil," she answered. "I want just, you know, something healthy."

Maybe she should dine in a drugstore. All this talk of healthy eating is putting me right off my food. We seem to talk all the time about what we can't eat and not nearly enough about what we can.

As the former author of a monthly nutrition column, I share the blame for our modern food terrorism—the often-irrational labelling of some foods as dangerous and the contempt for those who do not share ideas about how what we are eating is eating us.

There is always plenty of material. No matter how many alarming studies and statistics appear supporting the newest prohibition, you can bet that a new set of studies and statistics proving the opposite will soon turn up. There is rarely an official pardon for a "bad" food; however, another edible soon replaces it and the vilified morsel sneaks back onto our plates—a two-step of scolding and recanting danced in the food columns of our newspapers and magazines.

Now a death-defying eater, I have become a connoisseur of the genre and I treasure old food scares. Whatever happened to: red dye, eating salt while pregnant, the no-carbohydrate Atkins diet, MSG, saccharine? Remember when sugar was evil, implicated in mood swings and allergies?

These days, the doomsayers talk about "toxins." Nutritionist and author Rosie Schwartz issues a warning about toxin touters: "Often they are selling you purges. When you hear someone trying to sell something that rids the body of toxins, they want you to buy a product that gives you diarrhea. It is sanctioned bulimia."

As a coffee lover, I include failed coffee scares in my collection. Among the grimmer consequences the naysayers tried to pin on coffee are pancreatic cancer and cystic breast disease. But coffee has simply not turned out to be the villain it was reputed to be. Moderate consumption—up to three cups a day—is now considered acceptable.

Coffee has certain emotional advantages. Its status as an adult drink and as a stimulant makes it seem slightly titillating and naughty. Have you ever noticed that when people tell you they are trying to eat healthier, all they have cut down is their coffee consumption?

From the vantage point of today's carbohydrate lust, I remember fondly the times carbo consumption has been reviled. In 1958, in Britain, John Yudkin's book *The Slimming Business* warned against starchy foods; not long after, *Dr Atkins' Diet Revolution* had North Americans eating piles of sausages and denying themselves their daily bread.

Even the definition of what constitutes a good meal has changed. In the U.S. the four food groups have been shifted to a pyramid, with grains, fruits and vegetables spread across the base, while meats and fats take up the smaller space at the top. Canada illustrates its food rules with a rainbow, but the principle is essentially the same, with grains, fruits and vegetables occupying the largest arcs and dairy products, meats and fats the smallest.

Fat is the felon now and fat-gram counters sell in the same racks as carbohydrate counters once did. Red meat is the scarlet woman of gastronomy, shunned and reviled. The food phobics see the cheeseburger as the Satan of nutrition. It is a metaphor for evil: high fat, both dairy and animal, with extra grease on the onions and the carcinogenic charred meat, and a bun made from highly refined white flour and with catsup high in sugar. No wonder it is the preferred food of the western hemisphere. It is civil disobedience with flavour.

The notion of what's good for us swings, pendulum style, each movement initiated by the attitudes of the previous generation. In my babyhood, a good parent fed the richest possible milk to her children. My mother sought Jersey milk for its fat content; some poured whole cream down their children's compliant throats.

Today, parents are warned that cow's milk is bad. Perhaps someone has already begun a recovery movement for Abused Children of Cream-Feeding Parents.

Back in the days of cream-cramming, you knew you were a good parent if your kid's thighs filled her shorts when she sat down. It showed that the mother was motherly and the father rich.

Through the millennia, people have been concerned about having too little food. That is still true for much of the world's population. To be obsessed with the quality of food is a luxury for a small part of the population in a small part of the world. It is bitterly ironic that our fascination with foodstuffs is played against such a backdrop, but even that hasn't reduced the preoccupation. Perhaps we resolve the conflict through torturous exercise.

241

Through the last century, immigrants have shown the dichotomy most dramatically. I well remember my father's stories of his early years in Canada. To him having enough food was astonishing; having more than enough, beyond imagining.

For immigrants like my father, foods with protein, usually the most expensive, were worshipped as life sustaining and, therefore, families that could afford to enjoyed mountains of it at each meal. Immigrants and people born in affluent countries like Canada ate the same way: eggs for breakfast, salami sandwiches for lunch, roast for dinner. A meal without meat seemed like a booby prize. I think it is still hard for people who lived through those times to see meat as unhealthy.

Today, too much food hardly seems like much good fortune. To paraphrase an old Yiddish saying, too much good food is worse than too little bad food. The affluence of the industrialized world means that modern parents regulate their children's eating to spare them the curse of excess.

Although there is no question that healthy eating is better than unhealthy eating—whatever that may be—the next generation will have a good laugh when they examine the silliness now gripping us.

Some food manufacturers get their kicks from being contrary: a cola called Jolt promises a double hit of caffeine; a cream cake manufacturer declares that nothing about its cream cake is healthy; a cereal (promoted during the Bush administration) is guaranteed to contain no broccoli.

People who want both happiness and nutrition are taking the route of phoney food. They are buying products labelled fat-free and sugar-free, delighted to have fooled the devil. Turning the package over and reading the list of chemical additives used to suck out the fat and replace the flavour should wipe that smile right off their faces.

These ersatz foods fill the shelves of most North American supermarkets, but in Florida, the Capital of Facsimile Food, a population concerned with diet but too old to acclimatize to new, healthier foods is a target for food simulations. Supermarket aisles are filled with octogenarian cart jockeys collecting the likes of eggs without yolks, ice cream without cream, mozzarella cheese that's not cheese. (Have you ever tasted mozzarella cheese without fat? A T-shirt tastes better.)

Sugar is replaced by manipulated molecules, fat is engineered to travel through the food pipe without leaving any tracks. It makes me think of the replicas of the menu items in the windows of Japanese restaurants: they look very real, but looks are all you get. I wonder what happens when the chemicals hit the gut. The mouth sets up the taste. Here's a juicy hamburger, it says, and sends down tofu. What's this! says the stomach, indignantly.

Facsimile foodies will eat the ersatz goods only because they are low in calories. People will take a handful of diet chocolate as if it were a pill. Toronto nutritionist Rosie Schwartz watched as a bowlful of low-calorie jujubes was offered at a small party. The people on diets ate handfuls of them, but noted they weren't as good as the real thing. The people who weren't on diets didn't eat them at all because they weren't as good as the real thing. In the years of Metrecal milkshake diets, when the drink was supposed to be the meal, I gained weight because it tasted right only when accompanied by a hot dog and fried onions.

I believe that people often overeat because the food is so unsatisfying—there isn't enough texture, not enough taste, and there is the problem of gut betrayal. It makes you want more and more, when all you needed was something good in the first place.

Those of us who love food are trying to figure out how we can savour the best of what there is and, at the same time, take care of ourselves. That, in fact, is probably the main topic in the food professional's life these days, but finding the middle ground is difficult.

I accept the it's-good-for-you school of cuisine when the stuff is actually tasty. But many vegeateries promote the food according to its vitamins: "You'll love that kale. It's full of calcium." "Hey, honey, how would you like to go out for a nice romantic dinner of calcium tonight?" The manager in a macrobiotic restaurant once came up to me, a total stranger, and asked if I had any concerns about the effect of diet on yeast infections.

Those of us whose motto is "Better one swallow a month of a real chocolate milkshake than gallons of pretend, a great steak once a year rather than a mountain of tofu or other taupe-tasting food" had best look to Europe. There, centuries of apparent indulgence have not brought a higher rate of food-related illnesses.

My own research into this issue is based on staring. As I wait for my order in restaurants in Paris or Florence, I watch the locals to figure out how they eat it all and stay so thin. I observe a woman in Cibreo, a wonderful trattoria in Florence, and order exactly as she does: a risotto creamy with cheese, and a plate of veal. We eat in sync, she and I, every scrap, with bread and several glasses of wine. I know that by morning her admirable figure will not have altered by a molecule. I, on the other hand, will be wearing that dinner around my hips until the next century.

After dinner, the streets are full of Italians: for every bit they eat, they walk a mile. In fact, they walk to the restaurants and home from them. And it's not what they eat, but the way they eat it: the small portions, the drinks they choose to accompany the food, how long they hold the wine in their mouths, how long they stay at the table, as well as how long they walk afterwards.

The European emphasis is on the mouth—the taste and texture of food—while North Americans are concerned about filling the belly, which makes sense for a pioneering society that needed the calories. You don't build stockades on soufflé.

The phenomenon of how the French look the way they do, given that they eat the way they do, has been called The French Paradox and in recent years has received a great deal of media attention. In addition to numerous newspaper and magazine articles, it has been the subject of an hour-long "Sixty Minutes" investigation, which surely marks it as A Serious Issue. The French eat much more fat than we do, drink more, smoke more. Yet their rates of heart disease are much lower. We rage at the unfairness of it. In fact, thousands of us who rage at the unfairness of it do so every time we push away the frites.

Part of the answer comes from Dr Serge Renaud, director of the French National Institute for Health and Medical Research. He claims that alcohol is the key, especially in red wine, which cleanses the arterial walls. Red wine in moderation.

But other studies indicate that the French may be too quick to credit red wine. Some argue that although the French do eat fat-rich foods, they traditionally have eaten very little of them.

Now that the French are eating a diet more like a North American one (hamburgers and supermarket prefab foods), the higher cholesterol levels will show in due time. Even red wine won't save them.

However, not all food puritanism has been bad: the best thing to come out of it is the push for quality foods, an insistence that they carry flavour and texture. And the health food movement deserves credit for making us aware of vegetable quality. As a result, most restaurants now offer plates of vegetables only and creative chefs have used their talents to make these as satisfying as a steak dinner.

Today, the best place to find that kind of food is in restaurants devoted to cuisines that have always been vegetable based—for example, south Indian food, which is spicy and titillating, not prim or boring.

I have another food beef (lean, of course): the tendency to chat incessantly about the bodily functions that were once discussed privately (and, heaven be blessed, rarely). The subject was usually considered the property of the aged whose decrepitude gave them certain rights. Now, over plates of babaganouj, the young bore each other talking of blood pressure, or, over pizza, they compare pulse rates. There is open talk of carbohydrate metabolism.

Take fibre. Bowel motility has been all the buzz since scientist Denis Berkitt reported that the African gut was healthier than ours. So we began to compete for bulk with folks who had grown up having to eat gravel.

The food industry has become enthralled with our insides as we demand intestinal scrubbers. The trend became rudely known as the bowel movement and the health issue that once dared not speak its name now cannot be hushed.

"I love this stuff," my breakfast guest said, as she dug her spoon into a bowl of fibrous muesli at the new breakfast place where we met to talk about taxes. "It makes my stool float." Speakers lecture shamelessly on it. Tim Conway told Johnny Carson's international audience that North Americans were eating so much fibre that we would soon be passing wicker furniture.

And I'm finding that the obsession with one end seems to lead to increasing emphasis on the other, so that public hygiene has become part of the restaurant experience. Where we used to find people who washed off their cutlery in a restaurant a bit odd, we now gamely watch as they deal with the state of their cleanliness.

I am offended when I am handed a hot towel in a restaurant, as if I'm being reminded to wash my hands before dinner. Most people don't know how to use them and their embarrassment shows in the jokes they make about mistaking them for egg rolls, or the way they pretend to think finger bowls hold clear soup. They are rightly embarrassed by the sight of their fellow diners wiping their faces.

Some of the towels are so hot you have to throw them back and forth, like hand grenades. *Sunday Times* critic Craig Brown, however, has learned to love them: "When I first started going to Indian

247

restaurants, about 15 years ago, I don't think I had ever encountered a hot towel," he writes. "At first my approach to the hot towel was tentative and tinged with suspicion. I would unwrap it and flick some dust off my fingertips with it before returning it to its bag. But over the years a real fondness has developed between us, and I find myself wiping all but the most sensitive areas of my body with it, and generally treating it as a handy table alternative to a fitted shower unit."

I am finding germ phobia in restaurants more pronounced. Bread, once served in baskets, is now offered by tongs in individual pieces. The jelly beans or mints once casually crammed into open bowls near the cash register now either have to be recovered with the spoon provided or they come individually wrapped. (I have the world's largest collection of wrapped hard candies, taken from restaurants, ever since I heard of a study that found urine on restaurant jelly beans.)

Ironically, while people have been working themselves into a real frenzy about coffee, cheeseburgers and the like, they have not been paying enough attention to the genuinely serious issues. In January 1993, tainted hamburger meat at Jack in the Box food outlets in the United States caused E. coli poisonings, some fatal. The incident showed the real dangers of being too casual about our food supply.

But fatalities, while fortunately rare, are only a fraction of the real problem. Food poisonings are grossly under-reported because people don't seek medical attention and doctors don't always test to confirm the diagnosis. Health departments that

248

compile statistics won't consider a case of food poisoning until it has been corroborated by lab tests.

Dr David Waltner-Toews, a Canadian veterinary epidemiologist, says you should choose the food you put into your mouth as carefully as you choose your lovers. In his book *Food, Sex and Salmonella*, he calls food life's most intimate partner and argues that we should no more sit down to dinner without knowing where the food came from than we should have a fling with a stranger. Eating foods when you don't know how they were produced is like "engaging in sex with a blindfold," he says.

Waltner-Toews claims that two million Canadians suffer annually from food contamination. His book is rotten with excruciating stories of all kinds—for example, the Vancouver restaurants that served tainted chopped garlic and chanterelles—and he embellishes them with florid descriptions of regurgitations and hospitalizations. We shovel into our mouths the bacteria, pesticides and parasites that can cause anything from mild nausea to agonizing death as innocently "as children in Disneyland ride into the tunnel of love."

But a more functional attitude to health would mean more public awareness and action about the sources of our food. Now, most people ignore the fact that we lace animals with hormones and antibiotics, our fields with pesticides, and our waterways with poisons. We demand fresh fruits and vegetables at salad bars, so we allow them to be sprayed with sulphites, a chemical that keeps them fresh-looking but which can cause allergic reactions. We are threatened by radiation in our food that got there indirectly through nuclear leakage, or directly because we have

249

not insisted that our governments absolutely prohibit food radiation.

Waltner-Toews suggests ways to practise safe eating: meats must be cooked through; hot things have to be kept hot, cool things kept cool. Do not eat raw minced steak: singe the bacteria off the outside. Know the sources of your food. Do not wear blindfolds about additives and pesticides or radiation. Take responsibility for lobbying governments about regulating food sources.

But, beyond such common-sense precautions, each of us must measure the risks against our hungers. We who love sushi would no more stop eating it for fear of worms than we would abandon kissing for fear of germs. Caesar salad would be loathsome with a cooked egg. A world of deep-fried sushi and blackened salad seems too harsh. Those who live to eat can be reassured by Waltner-Toews's final instructions: "Wash your hands. Eat on."

Everyone who has ever had a bite of great carpaccio knows that health comes from happiness, not lettuce leaves.

The Cook, the Chef, the Busboy and His Lover

Saturday night offers the half-dozen hours when we are determined to get a kick out of life. At restaurants it is different from any other night, including Friday. On Saturday night, customers and staff alike are hyped to the max, determined to make this the anchor for the week.

At nine o'clock, the restaurant is humming and all the cogs should be working in smooth harmony. But they never are. That is because many factors add to the friction. Long, pressured hours may encourage kitchen staff to grab conveniently nearby cleavers and attempt to filet each other in response to crises— when, for example, they have run out of radicchio or the third person has sent back the soup. That's when the place hums with staff blaming the other. The chef sent it too cold. The waiter let it sit too long. The busboy stacked the bowls near the open window and now they're too cold for the soup.

But what turns disharmony into solidarity is that all restaurant staff are united against the common enemy: the awful customer. Trading stories about the worst of us tightens the bonds between waiters, busboys, chefs and owners.

"Yuppies are the worst to serve. They spend too much time trying to know or acting like they know more than they do. Also to show off what they know, they insist every dish be special—like Meg Ryan in Nora Ephron's movie *When Harry Met Sally*—they want the salad, but with the dressing only drizzled; the steak, but only half of it cooked, etc. Everything has to be unique and tailored for their egos because they have to show they know more than the staff about how it should be. It's hell on a waiter because it gets to be a kind of one-upmanship game where you have to let them think they win. And, practically speaking, they are hell on sales because they don't drink much. And they always want to divvy up the bill, calculating each penny."

A seasoned waitress finds that she is harassed more by customers than by fellow staff members: "I hate it when a customer flirts with me. What does he think? That he's bought me and I have to take it? When he does, I get very, very professional, very perfunctory. I may say to his wife, 'Do you let him do this all the time? Is he like this at home?' I try to be kind to her, poor woman."

They love to one-up the creeps: "You play status games all the time just to keep your ego in check. You can have your own control by how slowly or quickly you give information. If it's four guys half-crocked, who are being bossy and obnoxious, I go through the specials very slowly, just to let them know I own my space. I won't rush to get them what they want until I have some respect from them."

Sometimes it isn't anger but lust that fogs up the kitchen. Warm, close quarters and a profession that must be in tune with the physical senses may lead to situations where not all that's cooking is on the stove. The results can be quite drastic. In one place I know of, the wife left, not only with the cook but with the recipe for the restaurant's famous butter tarts.

The business is rife with rumours—about the people, the food, who is stealing, who is drinking. Dishing the dirt is part of the everyday business of dishing the dinners. Mean-mouthed co-workers have been known to try to kill each other with sharp tongues.

The dining room has a maitre d', waiters and busboys. Our sense of helplessness comes from the fact that most of us are oblivious to the hierarchy in restaurants and don't even know which one to ask for whatever we need. Seek help from a busboy and, no matter what you ask, you'll get a clean fork. If you ask a waiter for a clean fork, you will be referred to the busboy and by the time your meal comes, it will be so cold you can eat it with your hands.

By name and by practice, the chef is the chief of the kitchen. He decides the flavour of the restaurant, buys the food, chooses the menu, cooks or supervises whatever cooking he doesn't do.

The sous-chef, like any vice-president, works directly under the chef. He may have his own set of duties, making the sauce or salads. He, in turn, helps supervise the line cooks who cut the carrots and carve the potatoes. The number of line cooks will vary according to the size of the restaurant: a small dining room, say with thirty seats, will have one line cook; an important restaurant will have more: Restaurant

253

Jamin in Paris has a staff of seventeen in the kitchen to serve forty people in the dining room.

The waiter must treat a chef with respect because no one can screw up the waiter more than the chef. He can slow down his orders, send things out cold and, in short, get the waiter into hot water with the customer. Since the waiter is the person the customer deals with, he is the one who will get the anger and suffer the poor tip.

A celebrity agent in Los Angeles plans to package chefs like rock stars. The clients of Alive Culinary Resources, a subsidiary of a twenty-seven-year-old entertainment management company, are promised fame, status, more money, and more lucrative endorsements. Celebrity sells, says agent Shep Gordon. "Food is software for the body. And these days, all software, like CDs, athletic equipment and cosmetics, is celebrity driven. So, why not food?"

Here's why. The object of affection in a restaurant should be the customer, not the chef. Restaurants are places of pleasure, not of worship. Comfort in a restaurant is vital and it is destroyed when there is affectation about the chef's stardom or his untranslatable menu. When the purpose of the evening is to escape from the tensions of the jungle, such restaurants merely add to it.

Real chefs don't eat fame.

I'm just surprised that it took hungry agents this long to grasp the new business opportunity, though I suppose it was a logical consequence of the craze of the eighties, when gastrohype sprinkled stardust everywhere and chefs were swept into celebrity without the services of an agent. Paul Bocuse appeared on the cover of *Time*, Roger Verge's star rose even higher after the TV show "Lifestyles of the Rich and Famous" nominated his Moulin de Mougins in southern France as the most romantic restaurant in the world. Michel Gérard, the promoter of cuisine minceur—the precursor to nouvelle cuisine and the most joked-about cookery ever—brought out a line of corporate massproduced food. Famous French chefs went on tour through North America, like nomads, selling dinners at $150 a person.

Foodies who had never met a famous chef or eaten at a famous chef's restaurant referred to chefs Alice Waters, Jeremiah Tower and Wolfgang Puck by their first names. The stardust sparkled outside the star centres. In Vancouver and Toronto, anyone who has ever hungered for consommé of pine knows the Canadiana of German-born Michael Stadtlander. Names of the stars and the restaurants they made famous by their presence were little bits of social treasure, and foodies traded them like baseball cards. Anyone who didn't instantly recognize the names was presumed to have a palate of cork.

Some chefs have the temperament for stardom: Toronto's Gaston Schwalb, determined to minimize his contact with the tax department, named himself the high priest of cooking and designated his restaurant a temple of gastronomy. (Revenue Canada did not see it as a house of worship.) Another expresses his disdain for restaurant critics by ostentatiously wrapping his garbage in their reviews.

Restaurant owners have become ambivalent about star chefs. On one hand, a name chef guarantees a clientele of food groupies. On the other, if the success of a restaurant rests on a star, everything can fall with him too. As much as a chef's whims and personality increase the restaurant's creativity and energy, the business is left vulnerable to them. A celebrity chef who quits over artistic differences costs the restaurant its cachet and its cash.

One restaurateur prefers reliable cooks who are replaceable. His latest choice may not set the world on fire with his flair for frittata, but he can be counted on. The restaurateur says, "This is a business, not an art form." (Predictably, his establishment sells food that is capable, reliable and boring.)

Restauranting, after all, is a business that depends on an art form. Concern by chefs about the colour of carrots may seem frivolous to the restaurateur more interested in the colour of the ink on his balance sheet, but it is anything but frivolous to a creative chef intent on finding the ingredients that will carry flavour furthest.

Real chefs need to worry about minutiae because they care intensely about the tastes and textures they are creating. You could no more ask a real chef to modify his ingredients than you could have told van Gogh to make his sunflowers less flashy. Both are artists, and for the chef his plate is his canvas. But, unlike artists, most chefs usually have to work in or near big urban centres, in order to assure themselves of the clientele needed to support their long hours. This is more true in North America where customers are not yet in the habit of driving out of the way for a meal as they do routinely and happily in France and Italy.

Toronto's excellent Susur Lee prefers to run his own place; it means he goes to the market in the morning, figures out what to serve, then flavours it until it suits his palate. His soups, little piles of vegetables prepared with the Eurasian playfulness that characterizes his hand, are riveting. He once tried working for someone else because he got tired of balancing the books. The marriage lasted two weeks, ending when a kitchen flunky innocently suggested that the restaurant could sell more wine if the food was spicier. That was the last straw.

Most restaurateurs make their deals with suppliers and rely on what they are sent. Real chefs, like Lee, often insist on doing the shopping themselves, sometimes not settling on the day's specials, or the entire menu, until market stalls and counters have been raked for the freshest and the best.

Real chefs are fussy about how foodstuffs are manipulated. I once worked in a restaurant under a caring chef. It was a hot summer, in a fabulous restaurant near Montreal, Au Tournant de la Rivière. It was 1981, the time of fashionable foods.

Visiting chefs from Europe came to sup; local journalists proudly reported the foreigners' glowing reactions to the caring food of chef Jacques Robert.

My job in the kitchen, assistant to the assistants, was the lowliest, just one notch above the dishwasher whose status was so low he was allowed to smoke (he didn't touch the food).

My skills, adequate for a hopeful home kitchen, were clumsy in a professional one. I could not, for example, carve potatoes the way Robert demanded. He required that they be sculpted in perfect torpedoes. As he explained, with a patience I could sense he didn't feel, symmetry was as urgent as flavour. Symmetry meant consistency and consistency meant he could control texture; unevenness, on the other hand, made it impossible to ensure that each piece was the same—one potato torpedo might have been as soft as a jujube, while another as hard as a bullet.

Imagine the mouthfeel of such a mouthful. Later, as a restaurant critic, I would fault such an erratic jumble. (Potato carving is frequently an issue with serious cooks. In 1927, Madame Saint Ange, in a cookbook that carried her name, insisted that potatoes for a navarin be cut into the shape of "an elongated pigeon egg." Otherwise, the potato's sharp edges will disintegrate during cooking and thicken the sauce.)

Robert's food was so thoughtfully put together and so carefully thought out I couldn't understand why he would be so hurt when a thick-palated customer sent back some lamb because it wasn't cooked to his liking.

But, as a kitchen worker, my only recourse was to eat my mistakes before they were discovered. Excessively fond of Robert's sweetbread pâté, roasted sweetbreads puréed with cognac and sweet butter, I made a lot of mistakes when I dished out that appetizer, all accidents of course. I made so many mistakes that I might have gained ten pounds that summer if it weren't for the long hours, hard work and hot kitchen.

Too many chefs abandon such cares to technology and thus don't deserve their titles. There are machines that turn out uniform potatoes and perfectly cooked lamb chops, but they lack heart. In fact, one way to tell if the food on your plate comes from a package is to note how uniform it is: nature doesn't make French fries all the same; a handmade pie does not have even fluting all around its circumference.

The food in too many restaurants is made in central factories and shipped, portion-controlled and frozen, even to luxury restaurants, where it is thawed and microwaved. One ad for a company that does that tried to sell restaurateurs on the advantages of its system over those of having a chef: above a picture of a scrubbed young face, it said, "If you can teach him to boil water, you can teach him to cook." Managers of the microwave ought not to be called chefs, but food jockeys: they only play other people's songs. And you would no more go to a restaurant to eat that kind of food than you would go to a concert hall to hear a disc.

The recession put an end to the silly excesses of price and mindless chef worship that had become so obnoxious in the lavish eighties. But the downside is that the wonderful creativity, first evident in the seventies, was squelched. Since the economic deluge, many exceptional chefs lost their venues. Cost has become king in the place where concern for pennies rarely encourages experimentation. So eateries have turned to cheaper, formula foods and we are experiencing too little of the best part of star chefdom: playful experimentation and just good cooking.

This is not to say that every issue from a talented chef is worth eating. Diners take a risk with creativity, too. Constant experimentation means that few dishes are modified and improved.

I have enjoyed fabulous things from the stoves of Michael Stadtlander: a lamb consommé with amazing clarity of flavour and colour; some ravioli flaps of pasta with soft turnip purée and radish sprouts. But I also had to pay by being served monkfish with an abrasive yogurt and mustard sauce. Stadtlander meals are

259

always theatrical: He often serves foods on such pieces of Canadiana as rocks and twigs. Some displays tell a story. Once I got a quail served with a large duck heart, the two skewered together with a long piece of lemon grass, as if they had died in an embrace.

I have tasted some awful mistakes, most memorably a shocking bass wrapped in lettuce and served in a red wine sauce in a place in the Laurentians outside Montreal. In London, at the understated dining room of the otherwise fabulous Alistair Little, I loathed the John Dory fish, which seemed overwrought and undercooked; and I choked on a very dull plate of black beans and empty-hearted empanadas at Mark Miller's famed Coyote Cafe in Santa Fe. Yet, I still dream about Miller's southwestern cassoulet, a knockoff of the Provençal dish of beans and goose. At the Coyote Cafe, it is a fabulous collection of several different kinds of beans, spicy sausage and lamb chops as tender as a mother's love.

And I'll never love another crab sandwich like that created by Jeremiah Tower at San Francisco's 690. I order a soft-shell crab sandwich and receive two flat slices of wonderful bread, with a whole soft shell crab, shell intact, laid between them. The legs hang out the sides, as if the crab is trying to escape from the bread prison. I take a bite through the casing and the body and the legs crawl up my cheek. Such a delicious tickle.

At Montrachet in Manhattan, chef Debra Ponzek turns out foie gras, lightly grilled, so that the butter is brown and soft with the fabulous juices of the liver, and she sets that softness against the tartness of sour cherries.

It is no longer true that the best chefs are in

France, and in fact, that has been a cliché for so long that people are still amazed to get a bad meal in that overblown country. French restaurants, like those in other countries, have been vulnerable to technology and mass-produced ideas; their fall seems harder because of the heights from which they toppled.

But commitment to fabulousness is still in some bones and when a meal is good in France, there can be nothing better. The best chef's meal I have ever had was at the table of the much celebrated Joel Robuchon in Paris, a non-publicity-seeking chef who has had fame thrust upon him.

His signature dish is a three-layer appetizer of caviar, aspic and creamed cauliflower that is widely admired for its contrasts and contradictions: except for the caviar, the dish is created from mundane ingredients. And their marriage is odd: you wonder what led him to challenge the delicacy of expensive caviar with creamed cauliflower. But the effect is sublime. How does he achieve it? The cauliflower purée is like soft snow, the aspic like savoury lubricant. It is fabulous. The main course was a breast of pigeon, presumably of a better class than those that occupy the ledges of civic centres. The ruby-coloured meat was stuffed with foie gras and wrapped in cabbage, then belted with smoked lard and served over a potato purée that was one part potato and three parts butter. I wonder how he convinced those potatoes to accommodate all that butter? I think French food is so good because French cooks realize that butter is a flavour, not a fat.

Chefs sure have changed. We always associated cooking excellence with age and with formal European

261

training. Chefs were grizzled, grey wise men with experience and European accents.

In the seventies, chefs suddenly got young—many, like Michael Stadtlander and Jamie Kennedy were young lions in their twenties. Werner Bassen was barely twenty-three when he started cooking at Fenton's in Toronto, the still-lamented Toronto restaurant that introduced celebrity chefdom in the seventies.

At the same time that Chef Boyardee and his ilk began to share the limelight with young and serious chefs, formal training and fancy certificates from hotel schools stopped counting. What mattered was what turned up on the plate. Some of the newest and youngest had learned the rudiments of carving and accounting at community colleges. They learned the rest by book, by trial, by talking to each other. The main requirements were an earnest love of food, a keen sense of experimentation, and the talent to translate them to the plate. Sure, traditional chefs had those qualities, but they were bound by traditions that needed to be challenged. The younger generation could question why red went with meat, white with fish. And they did.

It took longer for women chefs to join the party, but by the eighties, they had arrived. Traditionally, women have had lower status in the kitchen, based on the French model. They were thought to be too weak to carry the heavy stock pots or endure the long hours and foul language that were as basic to the professional kitchen as a wire whisk. Now Ghislaine Arabian, the highest-rated woman in France, boasts two stars from Guide Michelin and a score of eighteen out of twenty points on Gault Millau's rating scale.

Women chefs worked unheralded for decades. In North America, the movement towards public acclaim began with Alice Waters, the owner and chief chef of the trend-setting Chez Panisse in Berkeley, California, which opened in 1971. At the James Beard awards in New York in 1992 (the Academy Awards of chefdom), Waters was named chef of the year and her establishment restaurant of the year. On that occasion, Maricel Presilla, professor of medieval history at Rutgers University said: "Men are very phallic in the way they present food; they're into pyramid shapes. Women's presentations are flatter and more organic; their garnishes are more subtle. We are nurturers; we want to soothe, to be mediators between nature and culture. Women's food is less threatening. Men, the hunters, are into beefy stuff. Women cook more vegetables."

Chefs may work independently, but new ideas have an energy of their own: they float through the air telepathically. Wolfgang Puck's smoked salmon and sour cream pizza topped with caviar is legend now. It was invented when the restaurant ran out of bread, and some pizza dough was served instead; the thin-crusted pizza became Puck's signature. And chefs everywhere picked up on the fashion. Lydia Shire at Biba in Boston produces a fabulous potato and smoked salmon pizza. Her tender, crisp crust is overlaid with ricotta cheese, and sliced sweet onions, then with thin slices of red-jacketed potatoes. A glop of sour cream runs rivulets around the potato slices, which are topped with smoked salmon. Baked together, the ricotta melts into the onions, the potatoes soften against the crispness of the pizza, the sour cream soothes while the smoked salmon titillates. God, it's good. And it is the only pizza I have eaten that is actually worth its embarrassing price of twelve dollars.

Sometimes, chefs have had celebrity thrust upon them by food writers, and find the time they have to spend in interviews and being lionized a nuisance. But the real chefs, the ones who turn out the kinds of dishes that other chefs emulate, spend most of their time behind the scenes, out of the limelight—in their kitchens or at the markets, agonizing over the colour and flavour of carrots. They don't have time to be celebrities. Real chefs don't preen, they cook.

Olive
Affair to
Remember

 he new breed of chefs are abandoning the limitations of classic rules of cuisine. They are finding ways to merge their own cultures with the place they live in and the best ingredients and techniques available to them. These women and men are codifying the best of the food revolution and producing the most exhilarating tastes and textures available to us today.

Toronto's Susur Lee is turning out exciting food that combines his Chinese background with European techniques and Canadian ingredients. London's Sally Clarke, an Englishwoman who spent several years in California, now has a terrific restaurant that carries her name, where she weaves California flavours into the British food she was raised on.

Todd English is an excellent example of the new breed, typical in that his talent is directed more by his background and passion than by formal training. After years of stirring the five classic "mother" sauces

265

at the well-regarded Culinary Institute of America in New York, it is his own mother's red tomato sauce he remembers and hungers for. His cooking is full of such bright strong flavours.

His hunger for foods that people really ate around nourishing family tables and the efforts to make familiar, family foods shine in the professional kitchen are common themes of modern chefs.

English was born in America, but his ancestry is Italian: New World blood enriched with olive oil. Such cultural interplay has created much of the interesting cuisine today—the chef's personality and traditions modified by and modifying local ingredients.

He doesn't look much like the traditional chef: he actually is tall, dark and handsome in a chiselled sort of way—a movie star look with a movie star name, like Cary Grant, I thought. But when he talks of Tuscan food, you are struck most by gastronomic passion. His phrases have a sense of wonder, and you get carried away by the bright eyes, the emphatic sentences as he describes an exceptional taste, or urges more food on you.

I met him by accident in a casual restaurant in Florence, Italy, when he and a wine producer were sharing the table next to us. He knew that restaurant's menu well. Have the bread soup, then the pudding, he said, his devotion obvious. You gotta try this and this, he said. We did and he was right—perfectly right about everything.

Even so, a year later, when I got to his restaurant in Charleston, Massachusetts, I was less curious to try his food than I was to see the restaurant of the man I had met in Italy, who had just won a national James Beard prize. On leave from my job, afflicted by the burnout that catches up with food followers of every stripe, the thought of a big meal was about as thrilling as a fall from a jet plane.

On that blazing hot June evening there were three dozen people ahead of us in line and experienced customers were assuring those lined up for the first time that the wait was worth it.

Was it ever. That day, English had stuffed large flaps of ravioli with squished squash, drizzled them with sweet clarified butter and freckled them with grindings of fresh nutmeg. Another appetizer was a wide slab of soft yellow custard made from Parmesan cheese resting in a green pool of puréed fresh spring peas.

His signature starter was a tart of olives and goat cheese, which was almost as good as one of asparagus and Fontina cheese, which provocatively was shot through with fresh lemon.

The main dishes, in daunting portions, were a fireworks of taste: sea salt, olive oil, garlic, fresh rosemary, brawny cheese.

I'm seldom grateful to have my hunger rekindled, but I was that night. When flavours "wow" in the mouth as they did, you want to know more about the person who made that happen. So I later called English at his home near the restaurant to ask what brought him and Tuscan food together. (Our long-distance phone conversation was often interrupted by tugs from his small son, Oliver.)

D espite my name, I am Italian, on my mother's side; her name was Vegara. The family is from Calabria and we once owned olive orchards and made olive oil. My grandfather was a broker and

267

sold olive oil to the villages. He met my grandmother at her family's olive orchard; she came to the U.S. about 1912.

At home, we ate mostly American food, the same food everyone else ate. We called ourselves macaroni-Americans. But at my grandmother's, we ate Italian. She would fry bread in olive oil and spread cooked crushed tomatoes on it. That was my first crostini. And I could never go jump on her bed because there was always pasta drying on it.

In her kitchen, there was always a lasagna with tomato, mozzarella or light, fluffy gnocchi made with ricotta. Thanksgiving never went by without lasagna. We had turkey too, of course. I guess we had to—we were American. But by the time we got to it, who cared?

When I was growing up, Italian was never spoken in our house. There was an effort to be American, not Italian. We ate a lot of American-style food like meatloaf while we lived in Atlanta and I remember creamed corn, fabulous fried chicken, pork chops, green beans overcooked in bacon grease that were unbelievable, when I think of them.

But I remember there was this sauce that my mother used to make: Batina's Red Sauce, we called it. It was a basic tomato sauce; sometimes she used fresh tomatoes, but often she used tomatoes she'd canned herself in the fall, and sometimes she'd use tinned. You know tinned plum tomatoes can be much better than the ones in the supermarket because they let them ripen first on the vine for the colour.

Tomatoes have to be the most abused of fruits. But the good thing about them is that I really look forward to getting a fabulous tomato at the end of August. I mean I think about it for a long time. It's good when it's like that with fresh food, when you can anticipate it because it's only good at a certain time. It can't be like that any more with zucchini, can it? Nowadays they grow it all year round and it tastes about the same all year round. Zucchini means nothing to me any more.

Batina would add different kinds of meat to her sauce. They were mostly cheap cuts of beef and pork, but sometimes veal and sausage. She'd let it stew for about a day and a half: it was always simmering on the stove. I can still smell it. Unbelievably good.

When I was training at the Institute [the Culinary Institute of America], they taught us what they called the five mother sauces: tomato, espagnol, hollandaise, béchamel and velouté. I remembered *my* mother's red sauce. When I tasted those sauces at the Institute I thought of Batina's Red Sauce and I thought, What's the matter with them? Now, the only sauce I still use that I learned there is the béchamel. But I put lots more nutmeg in it. That's a lovely sauce, béchamel. It's very light if you do it right, much lighter than cream.

My uncle owned a bakery in the Bronx where he did sort of classical French-Austrian cooking, strudels and pastries. I remember looking up at the table when I was small and seeing skyscrapers of butter. But on holidays he would make us polenta and cornmeal cookies.

Even though food like that excited me, I never would have thought that I would grow up to do this. I loved sports and I thought well, I'd do that or go into business. I never thought of food as a business—I guess I still don't. Food is just what you do. I worked in a Mexican and a French restaurant when I was in college and I loved it. I love the energy of a restaurant.

I love our restaurant. When we designed it, we looked for the hues of olives. The floor is stained olive green-brown. The other colours are eggplant, tomato and okra. We use themes of olive throughout. We call it olivacious.

The first time I landed in a restaurant in Tuscany, it was a style that hit home to me. The cooking seemed so honest. They have terrific ingredients in the beans, the oil and the prosciutto, and they use them properly. Ingredients like those, and a few centuries to try them out with one another, and you can see why Tuscan food is so good. The flavours are true. No one there would take a loin of lamb and try to make it taste like venison. I don't like fancy cuts and I thanked God when nouvelle cuisine ended. I like a plate to look like a plate and that's how they look in Tuscany.

Tuscan food uses beans—my favourite food in any shape or form. It's also extremely nutritious with protein and lots of vitamin B. We use bean dishes a lot in North America now, but they still don't taste the same as in Tuscany. I think that's because, there, they use the beans when they're fresher. The beans are dried, not petrified like they are here, so they are meatier. But it doesn't matter that much. What you do to them counts a lot.

For instance, at home I make a fabulous bean purée out of Romano beans that I've soaked overnight. We cook up a few white vegetables— onions, garlic and celery, a little rosemary with maybe a little bit of carrot for sweetness—in olive oil, just until they soften. Then I add the drained soaked beans, a bone from prosciutto or a chunk of fat from the prosciutto—but the bone's better. Add some water to cover and cook until the beans start to break down. I stir them and stir them until they are a thick purée. Then I whip some olive oil into the purée until it is like mayonnaise. Flavour with salt and pepper, then pour it onto a plate, scoop it up with chewy, crusty bread of sparse density—the kind with lots of big beautiful holes so the beans get into those crevices and you use the bread as a spoon. We make a meal of it with a chunk of Parmesan cheese, a salad and red wine.

I guess Tuscany is like most places: the best food is in homes; the best cooks are the women who have been experimenting and perfecting family dishes for years. When I go to Tuscany, I try to follow old people to their kitchens to see what they're making. I met this woman, Nadia, and she showed me this dish she made with Parmesan cheese and fresh peas. It's the Parmesan custard that I serve in my restaurant now. Nadia's dish was based on an Etruscan recipe that worked its way through the centuries and was brought to France by Catherine de Medici. I was inspired by Nadia and I played with the ingredients until I got it to taste as much like hers as I could. Of course, I was here and she was there.

Tuscans are very frugal with food, and their dishes based on leftovers are about the best there are. Bread is used the next day in soup, or in a salad served with roast meat. Have you ever had pasta with toasted breadcrumbs? You toast them in a frying pan with chopped anchovies and garlic. Toss them with spaghetti. Put some chopped ripe tomatoes on top. There's a fabulous contrast in textures in that.

Tuscany has all these incredible local ingredients. The cheeses, the wines, that Florentine steak. And the olive oil.

I would marry olive oil if I could. Is there any other kind? It's actually like wine, with its own character and also in its production. It's called a fruit because it has a seed, like a grape. It's a fruit we pick from a tree and press for its oil. Depending on when you pick the olive, it is different: pick it early, it's green and fruity; later it gets more peppery and takes on a different, lighter colour. In Italy, anyone who has vineyards has olive trees.

My friends tell me that I'm in a rut because I'm so crazy about olives. My wife's name is Olivia; my son's name is Oliver. I know it seems like a joke, but I am fascinated with them.

I love the beautiful hues of olives, their
subtle, earth colours. A lot of great painters
use the colours of olives in their work. The
trees are special with those silvery, luscious
leaves.The trunks and branches are gnarled,
old—they can be seventy-five to a hundred years
old. To me, they look antiquated and they look
wise. There's a picture of one in a cookbook of
mine. Sometimes I just sit and look at it for a
long time. Sometimes it almost brings tears.
No kidding.

I leave the business of a restaurant to my wife.
I know you have to keep the doors open, but
I can't get too hung up about it. The second
I find myself worrying about the cost factors,
I know I'm in the wrong direction. If I just let
myself cook, I know people will come and they'll
pay what's fair. That's my bottom line.
    I cook the food of Tuscany because I just love
the ingredients, but I don't try to represent the
cuisine here. It will never be the same food that
you eat there. You just can't have the same
thing. I mean, for example how are you going
to cook pasta in Tuscan water here? How can
seafood taste the same when it's out of a
different sea?
    I don't believe cuisines are transferable.
I argue this all the time with Julia Child, the
queen of the transferred cuisine, who made
her career out of teaching French food to this
continent. There's so much more to eating than
the palate sensation. There's the company you
eat with, the atmosphere in the room. In Italy

273

they live to eat, and though that's changing here, people in North America just don't think like that. You can't possibly duplicate that ceremonious ritual of Italy in a country that still eats to live.

I'm not a 100 per cent Italian. I can't take the American out of me and I don't want to. I think that it's good that Italian food there is different than Italian food here. The bad news is that it's changing there too. I have seen Knorr Swiss soup mix in Tuscan kitchens. There are McDonald's all over Europe, even in Tuscany.

For me to deny my American heritage would be like the way we once denied our Italian. And I really like the combination. When you make a good macaroni with Wisconsin Cheddar, you can't beat it; it's fabulous.

In North America, we're still in the educational process about food. And people will learn what is really good as they taste it. There has been this style of chain Italian restaurant which gives people a lot of dishes where the cheese stretches from the plate to the mouth. It's amazing what people will let their palates endure. Mind you, sometimes I think those places can help. They can introduce someone to paparadelle or to polenta. Then when they taste the really good stuff, they've really learned something.

For example, people come to my restaurant on Saturday nights and they always want veal and pasta because those two things mean Italian restaurant to them. So they get veal. I give them a shoulder, braised until the meat is fork

tender, with fresh fennel, porcini mushrooms
and olive oil. I put big chunks of fresh basil in
it. Then I serve it over homemade paparadelle—
you know, those big, soft, wide noodles. I make
the paparadelle myself and cut them big and
wide and boil them, just until they start to get
soft. You can pick up a lot of that delicious
garlicky brown veal sauce on the surface of those
noodles—even on just one forkful. Even with a
piece of that tender meat. So I give them the
veal and pasta that they asked for. But what
veal! What pasta!

Trimming of the Shrew

*T*he shrew is a voracious little mammal who must eat continuously, sometimes daily consuming three times her weight in food. Shrews are not fat. They eat all the time without ever worrying about their weight. Sounds like heaven to me. So I smile to myself when angry restaurateurs call a restaurant critic a shrew.

I only wish.

People who agonize over eating in restaurants because they fear curiosity will lead them into temptation and out of control wonder how critics—who *have* to eat out and *have* to try everything—manage to survive at smaller-than-blimp size. How can a professional eater refuse to test the pasta? the cheesecake? Isn't it mandatory for a critic to have at least a sip of the wine, a slurp of the brûlée? In one cruel episode of the popular comic strip "Blondie," Dagwood Bumstead remarks, when speaking about a restaurant critic to Blondie, "Pretty soon she's going to need her own zip code."

So it may surprise you to know that, like the shrew, many restaurant critics aren't fat. In fact, some are even svelte. When Ruth Reichl was appointed restaurant critic of *The New York Times* in June 1993—one of the most consuming jobs in eaterdom— she was described to me by an envious colleague as "a bone." She inherited the job from the slender Bryan Miller, who found the job required that he eat out seven days a week.

Another example is Edward Guiliano, who reviews restaurants worldwide for various guides and magazines. His work week may include a meal in Paris one night and a dinner in New Orleans the next, but after all these years he still slips easily into those tight airplane seats.

Restaurant critics are constantly asked how they keep their weight down—it is always the first question asked, even of those who are real porkers. "It's the dullest question in the world," complains Los Angeles critic Merrill Schindler. "People always think we're fat, effete slobs with little goatees, like opera critics." Schindler isn't fat either. He says his main trick is to avoid the wine. "You can drink calories faster than you can eat them."

Other critics, bored by the question, give boring answers. They usually say: "Well, I just eat the good things and only taste the bad," or "I watch it between meals."

Like hell. I have broken enough bread with other restaurant critics to know that they don't "just taste." At meals I have shared with professional eaters, I have watched them clean their plates, drain the wine, polish off the dessert and leave the restaurant eating the mint that came with the bill.

277

Sharp-eyed readers will notice that three out of the four critics I named are men, a mutant breed of eater who drops five pounds by such rigorous self denial as leaving the crusts off the bread.

Women do not have such luxury. We lose weight by the gram, a week at a time. After the age of ten, our bodies become fat-making machines and a "taste" clings to the thorax like barnacles to a ship. To me, a few "tastes," back to back, mean that the next time I get into the bathtub, all the water will get out.

Keeping my weight down has always been a torment for me, long before my chosen profession increased the conflict. I learned early the difference between what a taste means to a man and to a woman. When I was in university, two women friends and I had a diet race with a young man to see who could lose ten pounds fastest. He won. Not only did he have a head start because his gender made him lose it faster, but his gender made him craftier: just before the weigh-in he donated a pint of blood to the Red Cross.

Restaurant critics can't employ the extravagant weight-loss tactics usually associated with jockeys and fashion models, who are free to live on three blueberries and a piece of sushi, should they choose. A professional takes no holiday. We keep in form by eating on our days off, rather like the long-distance runner who power walks between marathons.

The danger for critics comes not from an overwrought sense of responsibility but from an acute appetite. For most of us, our motto is "I'd rather eat." Few will miss an opportunity to do so, if there is any hope that the food will be enticing. And when it isn't, we keep on trying.

Food love can be blind. Most of the critics I talk to refuse to blame eating out for weight problems. It isn't eating in restaurants that makes you fat, they say, it's life. "It's not the fault of restaurants if you get up at midnight and eat spaghetti out of the fridge," says Los Angeles critic Colleen Dunn Bates. She argues that eating in restaurants is a good weight management technique because "the portions are controlled, the meals are balanced and it's hard to take seconds as easily as it is at home."

Professional eaters are also vulnerable to the same social pressures as everyone else. Food is connected with nearly every other activity worth doing: it is how we connect with each other. We arrange business over lunch, gossip over tea, romance over dinner or a drink. And we punctuate all occasions by eating. We won. Let's eat. We lost. Let's eat more. Any effort to subtract food from a transaction will fail: what's a game of bridge unless it's followed by coffee and cake? If that sounds neurotic, it's a common madness.

I have constantly sought counsel during my career. The helpful hints never helped. "Well, have just a taste," said one of the many nutritionists on whose shoulders I have wept. How could she understand the tease of just a taste of risotto after it has been stirred, long and slow, with butter and so much softly melted cheese that each rice kernel is the caloric equivalent of a Mars Bar? A bite? A forkful? Are you kidding?

I go to a restaurant promising chastity and yielding to gluttony—within minutes I am in the thrall of the seventh sin—knee deep in olive oil, up to my elbows in tortellini, a pushover, a pasta slut.

I once went to a diet doctor who advised me to break up my eating into smaller, frequent meals. She wrote a list of what I could have and divided it into six feedings. (She wrote it just like that, in big letters at the top of the page: "Six Feedings.") When my boss saw the list on my desk he asked, "Who did you go to this time, a vet?"

One professional eater of my acquaintance takes attractive men to good restaurants because she is too enamoured to stuff her face in their company. It hasn't worked for me. Few men I know can compete with a well-turned tortellini.

Another doctor instructed: "Learn to love leaves." Trying to be co-operative, I told him I like crunchy greens, especially when stirred into risotto. And since health is a priority with me, I try to eat it often.

Career dieters have hints. An acidic drink like grapefruit juice will reduce your appetite, offers one. Another, claiming the Pritikin diet as his source, suggests that the amount of salad dressing can be reduced by dipping the fork first into the dressing, then spearing the lettuce. Never dip the vegetable into the dressing. Another described bagel scooping: the soft interior of the bagel is removed, leaving just the crust. The ruse fools the appetite into thinking that the bagel is intact.

Do not let embarrassment prevent you from employing any of these tactics in a restaurant. In the words of one career eater, "You can't save your face and your ass at the same time."

I have found advice from other critics especially useful because they know where I'm coming from— and where we're all heading if we don't get it together.

The truth is that we keep weight down in the same way as everyone else: with agony, with effort and often without success. We fight to balance our appetites, our consciences and our careers. And each of us has her own special method.

Author Patricia Wells, who reviews Paris restaurants for the *International Herald Tribune*, has used "The Paris Restaurant Diet," which, she claims, allows you to have anything you want at breakfast, including cake or ice cream. The other meals are limited to Champagne, fat-trimmed meats and fish, and an occasional carbohydrate. All fried and breaded foods are forbidden.

New York magazine critic Gael Greene, who is obviously made of sterner stuff, has seen the lite and is determined to stick to it in restaurants. In an article describing eateries that serve low-fat food, she revealed that she has had to give up caloric recklessness because she loves life even more than food itself.

Greene suggests you try to get a restaurant to change its stripes and respect the need for low-fat food. New York is a good place to try, although frankly I find it difficult to steer clear of New York's most delicious dangers, like the sour cream at The Russian Tea Room or the blueberry pancakes at Vesulka or especially the skyscraper meat sandwiches at the Celebrity Deli. Those aren't the kinds of places where you want to toy with the menu. Tell the gruff waiter in an apron in a New York deli that you want him to tailor the food to your diet and you risk your health in a way that nutritionists have never considered.

Maybe Greene has better luck than I do. I find restaurateurs notoriously unsympathetic to concerns about weight control. They sneer at us in the kitchen and ask each other why customers come out to eat if they are on a diet. They may even see the dieting customer as a special challenge. Montreal waiter Angus Duff says, "You're in a French restaurant. The food is spectacular. If we accommodate the diet, it will affect the experience. So what I say to them is, 'Let me put together a special menu.' That way the sin is on my head. These people don't really want to deprive themselves. They're itching for a way out of that diet."

A critic must counteract such offence tactics. Strongest among them is defensive eating. We take an example from Jane Fonda who, when offered a plate of food at a banquet in Toronto before the 1992 World Series, answered "I ate before I came. Doesn't everyone?"

Defensive eating: Careful critics know the work starts before you go to the restaurant. They don't wait until they're gnawing the edges of the notebook and are hopelessly vulnerable to the menu's sales pitch. The trick is to shore up your hunger: eat little before you eat big. If dinner is at seven, have a bit of low-fat cheese at six. Before a late lunch, try a cookie or some yogurt. (But be warned, this method has its own risks: a bran muffin and tea at four can too easily lead to a cheese sandwich at six. By then you are well beyond dinner at eight.)

Order course by course: Ordering everything at the beginning of the meal, when you are hungriest and vulnerable to the sales pitch, means you are likely to overorder. And once the plate is on the table, it is impossible to resist. Allow about twenty minutes before you order the next course to take advantage of physiology. In twenty minutes the brain will have received a message from the stomach that food has arrived and hunger is being satisfied. The course-by-course method irritates chefs and waiters who like to know the scope of your entire meal, so they can pace the kitchen. Apologize.

Plate removal: Ask the waiter to remove the plate while there is still some food on it. If the plate stays, you will eat, slowly perhaps, guiltily for sure, but you will eat.

Food refusal: Find the courage to banish free food that you haven't ordered. Ask to have the bread basket removed; send the free pâté packing. A plate of olive oil is becoming common on the tables of Italian restaurants to replace butter for the bread. Make it go away before you start. In an Italian restaurant near my home, they put out a free bowl of hot peppers in olive oil with the bread basket as soon as they have captured the order. It is usually half-gone before the waiter turns his back.

Watch out for seduction techniques: Dessert is such a high-profit item that some restaurants offer "just a taste" to get you going. When I fell for that offer at L'Europe in Delray, Florida, because I wanted "just a taste" of chocolate mud pie, I was soon submerged. One free taste of real moist chocolate and you will mortgage the house to satisfy the hunger.

Give it away: Los Angeles critic Meredith Brody says she's comfortable just as she is: "I'm a high-fat kinda gal," she says, pinching "this delicious layer of butter-fat under my skin." But, when I shared a meal with her, I noticed that Brody, in fact, eats only a portion of what she is served and asks that the rest be packed for take-out. Of course, this method works only if you give the food away immediately and do not, as you assured the waiter, take it home. For food harlots, leftovers are no safer in the fridge than on your plate at the restaurant. Brody usually gives the food to the many homeless on L.A.'s streets. "This is terribly spicy," she cautioned the man who received the lion's share of her enchiladas with green chili salsa from Le Mexicanos that night.

Medical defence: The best strategy is to use medical terms, the more obscure the better. Describe your allergies, your heart condition, your tricky kidney. Medical fragilities strike fear into the hardest heart—less because of compassion for you, and more because of the terror of imagining what will happen to business if your symptoms erupt at the table. All restaurateurs have nightmares about ambulances screeching up to the door and too few have insurance to cover them if it happens. Tell the owner that a drop of butter on the fish will make you heave and you can be sure that he will supervise the cooking personally.

Learn to love the eats of the East: It is safest to develop a deep attachment to those cuisines where the food is lean by nature. The Japanese have perfected the flavours of lean protein, clear soups and lots of rice. Writing in *Vogue* magazine, Jeffrey Steinberg, who admits to having a lifelong struggle with weight, notes that after a month in Japan, eating all he wanted, he had lost five pounds.

Other Asian cuisines, including Chinese, Thai and Vietnamese, can be as delicious, and low in calories. They feature small bits of meat, because meat was rare and expensive back home; quick cooking, because fuel was costly; lots of vegetables, because they were more available. Heap it over rice. Perfect. In fact, the number of restaurant critics who choose Asian food as their specialty is on the increase.

But be wary. Chinese noodle soups are terrific, as are stir-fries and steamed dishes. But dim sum may be battered and fried, and those little sweet-and-sour pork balls have the fat equivalent of a stick of butter.

I felt safe with East Indian food, until I started to cook it and realized how much of the deadly ghee goes into it. Ghee is a butter bomb. It is made by melting butter, pouring off the milk solids (the skinny part), leaving only the concentrated, clarified fat. Curries start with ghee. Oh I tell you, it's a minefield out there.

Bring along a good eater: A critic must have access to several meals so she can judge a variety of the chef's efforts. But she cannot just taste, then leave a full plate because that will alert the chef, who may want to know what's wrong. That compromises the anonymity that is essential to critics. Better to bring along a someone, or several someones, who can share the copious amounts of food you must order to properly sample the menu. The general principle here is to eat a few bites off your own plate, then rotate the plates around the table so each person samples each dish. The critic makes sure that the plate that spends the longest time at her place has the lowest caloric

285

content. Let the others do the noodles Alfredo, the critic gets the steamed bass.

A critic has to choose carefully when looking for a sidekick. It has to be someone for whom eating out is an adventure and who has no hesitation about clearing first her plate, then yours. She will also be delighted to order the heaviest meals and consume the lion's share before you can even get your fork near her portion. My favourite eater brings along a plastic bag and deftly slips the excesses into it. Barf bags from airplanes make good containers for this purpose—they are well lined and easy to fold over and dump.

The main character in the mysteries by Michael Bond is a restaurant critic who divides his dinner with his dog. The canine gets most of the calories under the table (and the critic keeps his waistline). A fantasy, I'm afraid. Only in fiction and in France are dogs permitted into restaurants.

Choose with caution: Professional eaters know how to pick their way around menus of any stripe. In a French restaurant, we shy away from assembled and layered dishes. Classic French cooking and the currently fashionable bistro cooking means many piles of food, each the result of its own high-fat preparation. Keep it simple. Stay away from French onion soup, or anything that says *au gratin* because it brings butter and cheese on top. Have meats *au jus*, or nouvelle recipes where sauces are based on vegetable purées and reductions of low-fat foods. (Nouvelle cuisine may be passé everywhere else, but its principles remain the staple of restaurants that want to offer diet-conscious customers something less humiliating, and tastier, than pressed cottage cheese.)

Beware of hidden ingredients: If you have bought the currently fashionable line about how pasta is good for diets, you must be on guard in Italian restaurants. The dieticians mean nude pasta. In Italian restaurants you are more likely to see a nude chef. Italian cooks tend to take your aunt's approach, which is "My food won't make you fat" and then freely pour the olive oil. Remember this rule: if it tastes too good, it is. Have tomato-based pastas and meat dishes: marinara, marsala, limone or primavera, a vegetable pasta as long as it's not bound with a cream sauce. Order the appetizer portion for the main course and have soup first. Do as the Italians do: no cream and cake desserts, just fruit.

Be equally wary in Mexican restaurants because the food is deceptive, taking on fat without changing colour. Mexican dishes are often fried in lard; refried beans may look chaste, but they are deadly. Tortillas may be fried in lard or baked. Eggplant seems innocuous, but it sucks up oil like a blotter does ink.

The sad truth is that the best foods in any cuisine simply disguise the fat. The revolution against fat has never faced up to the fact that the fat often carries the flavour. Prime beef is called that when the marbling suggests there is enough fat to make the dry meat juicy and beefy tasting. Croissants are made by stretching a piece of dough and lacing it with butter—a layer of dough, a layer of butter. To your palate, a croissant is a delicious roll, especially when served hot in your favourite restaurant. To your hips, the croissant is really just a conveyor for butter.

Constant temptation; constant self-denial: Everyone knows that an extra taste twice a day, an extra cleaned plate twice a week, can mean a pound of fat a year. For someone who has sentenced herself to a career in eating, it can also mean a job that sounds terrific but is a perpetual torment, in which she is doomed to continuous rounds of nutritionists and dieting. Just a taste? It is to laugh.

I once spent forty dollars on a procedure that determined the ratio of body fat to muscle and bone mass. A masochistic exercise: it doesn't take a rocket scientist to figure out that the body fat ratio of a restaurant critic will be higher than average.

And it was. I lay down on the examining table, while the lean young man who makes a career out of measuring body fat attached round rubber discs, with wires, onto my legs. (I wondered if I were about to be executed without even a last meal.) I held very still while he pressed a button which zapped an electric current through my body from ankle to neck.

He calculated furiously, then presented me with my money's worth: a sheet of paper with graphs and squiggles and the news that my ratio of fat to lean was too high. His advice was to change the ratio through diet and exercise. A breakthrough.

I suppose you could spend thousands of dollars getting the same information packaged in different ways, in an effort to avoid swallowing the bitter pill, but all regimens are based on self-denial. If you eat less than you want and exercise more than you want, you will lose fat (but not necessarily weight). And if you had been doing that all along, the fat wouldn't have found you in the first place. Which is how shrew(d) restaurant critics keep their weight down.

That will be forty dollars, please.

A Slash in the Pan

The restaurant was pretty and the night was soft. But the soup was cold and the salad was warm. The waiter was rude and the bill was high.

But I didn't get angry.

We restaurant critics have a saying: Don't get mad, get published.

The job of a restaurant critic is to eat out at someone else's expense so we can be unbiased crusaders for gastronomic justice. We must expose pretension, unfair pricing, bad food and sneering hospitality. We are always working towards the magic moment when we can say: "This is a great place. Go there."

In the meantime, we earn our daily bread by poking our forks into a thousand meals in the hope that one will bring ecstacy. And it is out of duty and a desire to be fair—not from hunger—that we return to dining rooms that have been the scenes of crimes against gastronomy too vile to describe. Contrary to common belief, restaurant critics are not paid to have fun.

I wrote my first restaurant review for the *Winnipeg Free Press* in 1972, and since then I have found that when I tell people what I do, an odd look of contempt crosses their faces, perhaps because they see the job as celebrating excesses. Then they brighten when it occurs to them that I may have some knowledge of a secret restaurant, a favourite place that I keep close to my chest.

Forget it—there aren't any. Your therapist may know about a restaurant, but she is free to keep it all to herself; your dentist may recommend one, but he might have bought a share in it for tax purposes. As a food critic, your job—and it is a job—is to write about your dining experiences for the edification and use of your publication's readers. Keeping secrets is not a recommended way of keeping the job or of keeping your editor off your back.

Is it the most wonderful job in the world? Yes, a thousand times, yes. Despite belly burn-out, frothing chefs, cruel deadlines, a critic gets to work in appealing circumstances—restaurants—on your own schedule—as long nights are part of that schedule—and you can take your friends to work. And you get paid for this. A survey done by Edward Behr for his newsletter *The Art of Eating* reports that staff critics for big city newspapers in the United States may be paid $85,000 to $100,000 yearly (the critics paid those exalted sums can probably afford to hire someone to eat for them). More commonly, the critic works on a free-lance basis for much less, and is paid by the review.

It is part of the critic's job to help people sift through the vast range of choices of restaurants, point them to good ones and away from bad. This is an important service in a large city, where the choices are overwhelming.

To sort them out, a critic's experience must be broad and her interest in food genuine and intense. An editor once described to me what she looks for in a restaurant critic: "I like people who run off at the mouth about food. You ask them what they ate and there's a stream of words about tastes and textures that are specific and graphic. Also, their knowledge needs to be international. They need to have a global view. It isn't enough to know just about French and Italian. These days food is a combination of Japanese-Italian, French-Chinese."

The critic may be a good cook or chef, but that particular talent is beside the point. You don't have to be a painter to write about Rembrandt.

Just as critics wish that chefs were more careful and restaurateurs were more wise with hospitality and generous with quality, chefs and restaurateurs may wish the same from the critic. A good critic has many obligations.

She should recognize the difficulties of running a restaurant—the lamb chops didn't arrive, the supplier stole the Scotch, the chef called in sick for the second time this week, the headwaiter hates the busboy—and then forget them. She must have the guts to taste democratically, without concern for the pedigree of the chef or the reputation of the place. He may be a wonderfully kind person, the owner may be a prince of a guy, but if the food doesn't taste good, that has to be said.

A prudent critic will refrain from socializing with chefs and restaurateurs because the relationship may compromise her objectivity (their stories of grief and hard work would soften the heart of a finance minister and weaken a critic's will).

Similarly, a critic must not put herself in a position where she is obliged to a chef or a restaurateur. To ask a favour of a restaurateur means that he can ask one back. I am often asked by friends or relatives to call a restaurant for a good table or to secure special service for a special occasion. I can't.

To be fair to both the restaurateur and the reader, a critic ought to visit a restaurant often enough to get a feel for its consistency. Many critics, restricted by budget or by inertia, only go once, but especially before condemning a place, it is only fair to return to see if the terrible food is still terrible. It nearly always is. Except for the once it isn't. Every critic has had the experience of testing a terrible restaurant several times and on the fourth visit, something magic happens and it is wonderful.

There is a myth that critics love lousy restaurants because they make good copy. Not true. While the writer in you may want to get off some clever lines at the restaurant's expense, the heavy hand of fairness (and of the newspaper's legal department) make you err, if anything, on the kind side.

Rave reviews are a cinch to write: you are driven by the basic human need to spread the good news. But the tough ones are for those innumerable restaurants awash in mediocrity. While I can hardly wait to describe a fabulous find or vent my spleen about a bad one, 90 per cent of the restaurants I visit are neither. They are just okay and "just okay" is no more thrilling to write about than it is to eat.

Any restaurant critic needs two things from her publisher: a good expense account and a loyal backup.

It is impossible to fight both restaurateurs and your boss. He must also firmly keep the ad department away from you. Whether the column draws advertising or threats to withdraw advertising, ad revenues must be of no concern to the critic.

Some newspapers and magazines have whole sections of restaurant advertisements disguised as reviews. They are usually marked as advertisements but so discreetly that the reader must be alert. Sometimes a reader can spot a biased positive review by its proximity to an ad for that restaurant.

Although I have been threatened with lawsuits, I have never been successfully sued. A critic must be very careful with facts. Opinions can be expressed freely, as they should be, so I can say that the steak tastes like rubber. But carelessness with facts is dangerous: if I say the steak *is* rubber, an angry restaurateur can force me into court to prove it.

Anonymity is a unique essential of being a restaurant critic: book and movie reviewers hardly need be unknown because the work they judge can't be skewed to please them. A restaurant meal, on the other hand, can be prepared and served differently if the owner or chef knows a critic is scrutinizing.

I don't make reservations under my own name, and I am always looking for other monikers. I can't just pick something out of the phone book—I tried, and wound up, standing in the entranceway, trying to remember my name. I prefer to rotate a list of names and am partial to those on Mr Blackburn's annual worst-dressed catalogue (although Goldie Hawn appears rather too regularly to be useful to me).

My credit cards are in various names, none of which are my by-line. Although the meal will be finished by the time I pay, the waiter would remember me and, given that waiters move from job to job, might show up two weeks later in another establishment I'm going to review.

In the line of duty I have employed a number of disguises—wigs, glasses and variations on make-up. The producer of an investigative television show once told me that the best disguise was to be a middle-aged woman because "people seem to look right past them." I find this an easier disguise as the years creep on.

I don't much like wearing wigs to restaurants. They are itchy and awkward, and I often remove it as soon as I leave the restaurant. Once I left it in a cab and was forced to phone the company and describe the headless hair in the back seat of taxi 320.

Despite our best efforts at disguise, restaurateurs often claim to have spotted us, even on nights the critic is in bed with the flu. When my cover is blown, it's often because another diner recognizes me. Restaurateurs and chefs spend so much time with their heads in a stockpot or in the accounting books, they barely remember what their kids look like, let alone me.

There are critics who argue that it makes little difference if they are spotted. "Anonymity is not of much importance," Andre Gayot, head of the Gault Millau guides, told me. "When you make a reservation at 5:00 p.m. for 9:00 p.m., do you think that they will revise the menu for you?"

True, the food, decor or wine list cannot be instantly changed but my suspicions are aroused if my portion is heartier, the shavings of truffle a bit higher or if waiters start fluttering around our table and ignoring others or if suddenly the waiter changes mid-meal. I find the loss of privacy a pain and I find the embarrassment of being spotted more onerous than the difficulty of determining whether the food has been doctored. Once I was spotted at a Toronto restaurant by the owner, who sent over a bottle of wine and then proceeded to explain each dish. "The spaghetti is too dry," he said, adding a few drops of olive oil. I was terribly annoyed that I had to go back—this time in disguise (that damn itchy wig)—before I could write the review.

Still, anonymity ensures that none of this happens and I hold that a critic is best served by it. I try to be quiet and inconspicuous. If someone is making a scene in a restaurant, you can bet it isn't me. I save my fury for the word processor. I even interview restaurateurs by phone and never go to restaurant openings or special events.

Making notes is a challenge when you are trying to be discreet. The difficulty is greatest at dinner, since lunch is often for business and diners may take notes through that meal. Some restaurants provide pencils and paper tablecloths just for that purpose, though one must be careful not to get into the habit. Drawing on the damask at Chez Pricey is a dead giveaway. At dinner, I once carried a tape recorder in my bra with wires leading from it to a tiny microphone pinned to the interior of my lapel, but I abandoned it when the maitre d' looked at me oddly as I was whispering into my buttonhole.

If you can steal a menu, all this subterfuge may be unnecessary. The list of dishes, ingredients and prices serves as a quick reference and reminder of the meal when you have to assemble the review. A critic's palate dulled by the extra glass of wine taken to blunt the flavour of a poor soup may not remember that the roast beef in the course that followed was deglazed with kumquats.

Why not just ask for the menu? Well, you can't, because it may draw attention to you. And if you are refused, the staff will watch you like a hawk expecting you to steal it, which is of course what you have to then do, so you might as well plan to steal it from the start. I often take newspapers into restaurants because I find that they are good to pass the time when the table-mate is late, or for company when I eat alone, and they make ideal carriers, especially for those outsized fancy menus. Magazines can be good too, but the relatively small formats of *Maclean's* and *Time* magazines are obviously less useful than *Life* or *Interview*.

The best menu thief I ever encountered was a former federal cabinet minister. Tom MacMillan had joined the Designated Eater and me for dinner and chivalrously responding to my concern about the very large, hard-covered menu, offered to pinch it on my behalf. His skill, perhaps honed by years in political life, was noteworthy. He simply slipped the menu under the white tablecloth where it lay flat and unobtrusive throughout dinner: the waiter served three courses—soup, lamb chops and crème caramel on top of it. At the end, the bill paid, Macmillan retrieved his coat, sat down at the table, slipped the menu inside his coat, and quietly left the restaurant. He handed it to me in a darkened doorway.

When I cannot get a politican to steal menus for me, I find a well-trained Designated Eater to be almost as good. The D.E., as I've come to abbreviate the term over the years, is invaluable. Not only will he or she steal the menu, but he or she will take the overload of food, ask probing questions of the waiter and thus help preserve the critic's anonymity and waistline.

Designated Eaters must do nothing to attract attention to our table. They cannot call *"garçon"* across the room, return everything to the kitchen to show how tough they are, or stump out cigarettes in the salad. They must not whisper to the waiter, "You better be careful if you know what's good for you" and they cannot call me at 6:00 p.m. to cancel.

Many Designated Eaters find that the glow comes off when they are assigned to try the creamed okra at the new Ethiopian Grill down the road, rather than the free frites at the spiffy new bistro. I am a fascist about what they order. They may have been dreaming for months about the carpaccio, but if minestrone is what I need to know about, minestrone is what they eat. Yes, in the line of duty, I have even forced spinach on children. If I am sharing a table with several people, I usually order last, waiting to see what each has ordered. I try to order three courses—appetizer, main course and dessert. If the D.E. does not fall into line, I may prod him: "The carpaccio of swordfish beurre blanc sounds so much more interesting than the porterhouse, don't you think?" The meal may be their night out, but it's my work. They want to linger over coffee. I itch to get back to my desk and make notes. Deadlines make deadly desserts.

What is a good restaurant? A good restaurant does what it promises. If it is food fondled by a star chef in a fancy room for high prices, the soup must sing and the service must soothe. If it is a highway diner promising old-fashioned milkshakes, that milkshake should be thick and taste of fresh ice cream, ice-cold milk and real flavourings. A diner that serves a milkshake that was extruded in a mushy squirt from a machine (or a lunch counter that serves a clubhouse sandwich made from that slimy packaged turkey) needs someone to say the emperor has no clothes and the cook has no taste. That's what a critic does.

We got into this line of work because quality food is precious to us. What wakes us up is neither the new vegetable nor the artistry of a flamboyant chef in the throes of inspiration. The day is made when something works, when the dreams of a creative chef come true on the plate. Equally, we become infuriated at carelessness, heartsick in the face of incompetence. We are working at every meal; we can't pass a doughnut shop without wondering if they are making good doughnuts. We can't enjoy the luxury of saying, "The food is mediocre, but what the hell, I've got a great date."

Contrary to the picture of the snobby restaurant critic as an aesthete, most of us aren't after "gourmet." I loathe the word, which has been abused and rendered meaningless by commercial exploitation. "Gourmet" ingredients and esoteric language are undemocratic and make people feel they aren't equipped to judge for themselves. I have never had much sympathy for the affectations of my trade: foodstuffs rolled about in the mouth, flavours ostentatiously savoured, pompous pronouncements from snobs. Show me a food connoisseur who rests each morsel on the tongue as if its essence were of the angels, and I'll show you a pretentious jerk.

Wine tastings can be particularly ridiculous. My favourite review of a wine came when a woman asked her date for his opinion of the premiere cru. "It's making me horny as hell," he said. "Let's go home."

People think we expect good food to be fancy when, in fact, critics as a group are so overexposed to exotica it becomes boring. Personally, I like food that fills the mouth with wonderful textures and strong flavours. I care about the taste more than the style. The excitement is for the food, not the foodmaker. We are a jaded lot and presented with fricassee of lark's tongues can only say, "So what else is new?" Whether the food is rare, expensive, exclusive, excessive or hard to prepare is meaningless. We ask only one question: how does it taste? Speaking for all of us, I would rather have a good bowl of oatmeal from the cook who lives next door than a silly-sauced breast of seagull served by a celebrity chef.

Merrill Schindler, restaurant critic for Talk Radio KABC in Los Angeles, did a survey of that city's restaurant critics to ask them which of the city's foods they would crawl across town on their knees to eat. Nearly all of the answers were down-to-earth foods—hamburgers, fries, the best bowl of minestrone, the grandest Caesar salad.

The power of a critic may be overestimated. While it is true that if a restaurant has not been discovered and can't afford to promote itself, a critic can bring it to the public's attention, a bad restaurant doesn't shut down because a critic hates the place—it shuts down because the public hates the place.

People often want a critic to keep the best little neighbourhood restaurants a secret. They fear that their favourite small places will become overcrowded, that they will not be able to get a table or that the restaurateur, overwhelmed by the crowds, will allow the quality to slip.

I've discussed these possible dangers resulting from publicity with the owners of small restaurants, asking them if they wished to be subjected to the demanding hordes of hungry people. Their answer inevitably is: "Subject me. Please." But it's up to the restaurant from there. There are plenty of restaurants which fly high for a month on a good review, then crash when the crowds move on to the next discovery.

Restaurateurs who have been dumped on are often cynical of the critic's motives and few are shy about letting you know. They commonly believe that a competitor has hired you to be cruel, or that a senior editor has ordered you to write viciously about them. Should you compliment a competitor, they will say it is because you are sleeping with the chef. If you write a bad review, they say it's because you're not. Someone is always taking a shot at a restaurant critic. I like to think of us as the goalies of gastronomy.

A thick skin is basic working clothes. I have found my job—and my life—much easier since I stopped worrying that people would call me a bitch. It is an unfortunate reality that often a critic is called most honest when she slams a restaurant. Good critics always tell it like they see it, bad or good. It is as unethical to be deliberately harsh as it is to praise an undeserving place. Honesty must be the critic's stock in trade.

It is a job of excesses, a difficult one to rationalize in light of global and personal woes. I don't like the job much on the days I have spent on the phone with a chef's sobbing wife, or a threatening lawyer. Eating a perfectly lousy dinner in a virtually empty restaurant, with the pitiful owner watching every forkful and then having to go back again for another terrible meal is something this side of torture. Some days I wonder if there's an opening in the sports department.

Most of us are vulnerable to sob stories from chefs and restaurateurs. One called after a negative review to say he had been working so hard lately that he saw his four-year-old daughter only when she was sleeping. Succumbing to such tales of woe does no service to the reader. The chef's fatherly instincts get a ten; his pasta fazooli still gets a four.

Once, the owner of an awful restaurant called and tried what he must have assumed was a very subtle ploy to make me feel guilty: he thanked me for taking the time to come to his restaurant and assess it. "It's only through honest criticism that we can improve," he said lickingly. And then: "Of course, you couldn't have known that the sous-chef had been getting death threats. The latest was written on her mirror in lipstick." He said that the review had only added to her grief and she took refuge in the home of the chef. "He was in a position to really understand. The last time he had a bad review, he made a suicide attempt, so, of course, we were very worried about him too. But that shouldn't concern you. You have a job to do." You bet.

I try to ignore the letters that are written all in capital letters, and I have a special file for those that start "I know where you live." A restaurateur writes to my editor: "You have issued her with a license to kill." A woman expresses her disapproval of my table manners: "You should know better than to dip your fork into the salad dressing meant for the table. It's disgusting."

When I described a restaurant's food as limpid, its service as flat and its hospitality as frosty, the owner's cousin called my editor, who in turn called me. "I wouldn't turn on the ignition in your car," he warned.

In Toronto, chef Gaston Schwalb is noted for his outspoken views on anything connected with food (he once called nouvelle cuisine "gastronomic masturbation") and on many other topics (he briefly ran for mayor). When he received a nasty review in 1980, he put a sign outside his restaurant saying "No dogs or critics allowed." A week later, he scratched off the "no dogs."

The restaurant critic's wardrobe is not always determined by fashion. My purse may be oversized to accommodate the menu and the belt that has to come off by the second course, as well as a plastic bag for storing food that I have to make disappear from my plate.

And I can never wear silk to a restaurant. Napkins slide right off a silk skirt, but grease is attracted to it like a magnet. If someone is eating fried chicken wings in a bar two doors down the street, the grease will find you and attach itself to your sleeve.

Once I wore a silk jacket to a chic lunch with a fashion editor who was ablaze in Armani. After lunch, when we were walking down the street, I glanced down and noticed a grease spot on my lapel. "Dammit," I said, "never wear silk to a restaurant."

"Oh," she remarked, "you came with that."

Other occupational hazards include watching people talk with their mouths full. (In her book *Forever*

Fifty, writer Judith Viorst explains that the middle-aged who talk with their mouths full do so because they fear they will forget whatever it was they were going to say if they wait until they've finished chewing.) And you have to be prepared to be reviled when you tell people what you do for a living: the excesses of the profession are not well regarded at a time of world starvation. I've been given looks of blazing indignation usually reserved for people suspected of murdering kittens for their fur or promoting tobacco use among primary-school children. I have heard writers rationalize the paradox of being a food critic in the midst of global hunger, but, in fact, there can be no rationalization for the inequities of the world.

This may not be the saddest story you've heard this week, but have you ever thought how lonely is the life of a restaurant critic? No one will invite me for dinner. Worse, because I have a critic's fear of being criticized, I wouldn't dare to invite anyone back.

There is an axiom of entertaining that holds that the more nervous you are about the company, the less successful you are likely to be with the dish designed to impress them.

Calvin Trillin is known for his wit and range of writing, including the current best-seller, *Remembering Denny*. I have been attached to his food writing since *American Fried* and revere his observations: "If there is a god, and he is truly a merciful god, why is there so much cholesterol in Italian sausage?"

We met Trillin and his wife Alice one summer in Nova Scotia at a dinner party. We got into a conversation about an interesting dish called Dutch Mess, a concoction of salt cod, cream, scrunchions and onions.

303

And so it came to pass that an invitation to dinner was out of our mouths before we knew what we were saying.

The success of the dish depends on the proper soaking and resoaking of the cod to remove the excess saltiness. In my anxiety to perfect it, I undersoaked the fish, and that night produced a dish with enough saline to soak the moisture from the rain forest.

Trillin ate his share and politely asked for seconds. By the end of the evening, when no one had remarked on the Dutch Mess, I thought maybe I had been overly critical, holding to an unreasonably high standard.

Several weeks later, we answered a knock on the front door. Trillin was there. Without a word, he walked the length of the house, from hallway to kitchen, and stopped at the sink. He turned on the faucet, put his mouth to the tap and drank for a solid minute. Then he raised his head and said, "I'm still thirsty."

Now there's a critic.

I hope that the hardships of a seemingly enviable profession will discourage contenders for my job. It may not be the easiest job in the world, but a girl's gotta eat.

Afterword

I have dedicated this book in part to my father, Martin Berney, and I want to tell you why.

As one of his four children, I shared an obligation with my siblings to prove to him that there was finally enough to eat.

His own father had died when he was an infant and his mother was away from home, working as a domestic, leaving him on his own to beg food from people in his small village in Poland. He nearly starved as a child, and decades later, as he overfed his own children, he would tell poignant stories of achieving a few sips of soup, or how a frozen apple found by the side of the road became a three-course feast. The soup deprivation stayed with him and, to the end of his life, whenever he could, he finished each meal with a bowl of it.

He came to Canada at sixteen, and through the next two decades educated himself, established a business and, with my mother, founded a family to replace the one that was being annihilated in Europe. For him, an abundance—or should I say, an overabundance—of food was a metaphor for safety. He bought cookies by the case, canned soup by the gross, olives by the barrel. We had extra refrigerators, extra shelves and, always, walk-in storerooms for food. He welcomed any chance to use it. He would greet everyone—from the most casual guest to a new addition to the family—in the same way: "Another mouth to feed!" he would say, delighted that he could do it.

Once he prospered, he extended his bounty to more distant hungers. He was instrumental in the development of an extraordinary system of irrigation and food production in the Negev desert in Israel. The technology will help Third World countries to increase their food supplies, to make manna from dust. That way, he continues to help other children triumph over starvation, just as he did.

Cynthia Wine
July 1993
Toronto